How the Stock Markets Work

How the Stock Markets Work

Colin Chapman

RANDOM HOUSE

BUSINESS BOOKS

First published in 1994 by Century Limited.
Ninth Edition first published in 2006 by
Random House Business Books

Business Books
The Random House Group Limited
20 Vauxhall Bridge Road, London SW1V 2SA

Random House Australia (Pty) Limited
20 Alfred Street, Milsons Point, Sydney,
New South Wales 2061, Australia

Random House New Zealand Limited
18 Poland Road, Glenfield,
Auckland 10, New Zealand

Random House (Pty) Limited
Isle of Houghton, Corner of Boundary Road & Carse O'Gowrie,
Houghton 2198, South Africa

The Random House Group Limited Reg. No. 954009

www.randomhouse.co.uk

A CIP catalogue record for this book is available from the British Library

Papers used by Random House are natural, recyclable products made from wood
grown in sustainable forests. The manufacturing processes conform to the
environmental regulations of the country of origin

ISBN 9781905211050 (from January 2007)
ISBN 1905211058

Typeset by SX Composing DTP, Rayleigh, Essex
Printed and bound in Great Britain by
Mackays of Chatham plc, Chatham, Kent

For Simon, Laura, Ben and Max

Contents

Introduction and Acknowledgements

Although Britain loves tradition and enthusiastically preserves and protects many relics of the past, the stock market is not one of them. The London Stock Exchange – and with it the concept of share ownership – has seen many revolutionary changes since its early beginnings in the late 17th century, with the most radical of them taking place in the last 25 years.

There is no resemblance between the stock markets of today and the immediate post World War II era; indeed what happens on the markets today has little in common with the way things were just 19 years ago when the first edition of this book was published. Anyone thumbing through a copy in a second-hand bookshop might find it interesting, but certainly not relevant.

Whereas once insider trading was the way of life for people working in the stock markets, now it is a criminal offence. Whereas owning shares was once a privilege for the rich, now all but the unwashed and unemployed have a stake in what is happening to the 'footsie', the stock market index that covers Britain's largest corporations, even if many of them do not realise this is so.

Where once probity was governed by voluntary codes and the maxim, 'My Word is My Bond', now there are armies of bureaucrats waving thick books of complex rules designed to prevent cheating. And where once membership of the London Stock Exchange was the preserve of rich British individuals, now the markets and, indeed, the whole financial services industry is dominated by foreigners. As a young journalist arriving in Fleet Street I found that City editors all bought and sold the shares they wrote about; today this can be a sackable offence, and rightly so.

For all the changes that have taken place, the stock markets are enduring. Their collapse has never been a possibility, still less the near certainty predicted by Marx and Lenin. The markets have brushed off numerous predicted threats, some of which appear comical when considered in retrospect.

The chaotic damage that was predicted for computer systems at midnight on 31 December 1999 did not occur, and investors entered the twenty-first century without as much as a blip.

Yet many of those who took up share ownership in the nineties to ride the crest of the wave of one of the longest rising markets in history spent the first few years of the new millenium in fear and apprehension. Those who were seduced into believing that internet stocks could only surge to new heights ended up with paper certificates that were almost worthless. A new phrase was introduced into the lexicon: ninety per centers. They were those unfortunate enough to lose nine tenths of their original investment, and there have been plenty of them. Even those who made what they supposed to be a relatively safe investment by buying into unit trusts that track the main stock market index watched their savings wither. Those that kept their nerve can expect to reap their benefits. Those that sold out lost thousands. And those who used the most cautious of savings vehicles, bank deposits or gilt-edged securities, were able to hold on to their capital, but with poor returns because of the low interest rates.

Then came the worst act of terrorism in history, which struck at the heart of world capitalism in Wall Street, New York. Two commercial airliners, piloted by suicide pilots, were flown into the twin towers of the World Trade Center, the headquarters of leading stockbrokers and finance houses. About three thousand people died in the disaster, many of them courageous firefighters who ran into the crumbling tower blocks as those trapped inside tried to evacuate.

This calamity brought the American stock markets to a four-day standstill. Billions of dollars were written off the value of the world's major corporations.

Yet from the heroism of the New York firefighters, from the resilience of the stock markets in the face of economic uncertainty, the markets bounced back. There will always be rises and falls. That is the nature of the markets.

Many people have given me considerable help with this completely rewritten new edition of this book. Most of them are involved in the stock markets on a day-to-day basis. They are traders, analysts and salesmen. They are regulators at the new Financial Services Authority, and editors at Bloomberg, the *Financial Times* and the *Investors Chronicle*. They manage or work on the share markets in London, New York, Frankfurt, Sydney, Tokyo and Johannesburg. I would like to thank all of them for their readiness to spend time with me, and to talk freely about the way the markets work. I must add a special thank you to my publisher at Random House, Clare Smith.

And the book would have been much more difficult to complete had I not had the total support of Susan and our children.

Colin Chapman
September 2005

PART I

Past Glory, Future Uncertain

The London Stock Exchange was built in the heyday of the British Empire. But it did not die with it because it learnt to adapt to change. It is still learning.

1 What is a Share?

Finance is the art of passing money from hand to hand until it finally disappears.

Robert W. Sarnoff

What is a share? It is a simple enough question, but one which many find difficult to answer. Even the *Concise Oxford Dictionary* fumbles over it. 'A portion that a person receives from or gives to a common amount' is its best shot. The *American Heritage Dictionary* prefers the slightly more didactic 'part or portion belonging to, distributed to, contributed by, or owned by a person or group'.

It is as if these dictionaries were compiled by lawyers! Yet everyone has shares. The principle of sharing is part of life itself. We share toys, library books, meals and homes. We share aircraft flights by buying a seat from an airline. We share the cost of petrol on trips by car. As magazines become more expensive we share subscription costs and the use of the magazine. Some people even share jobs.

These share arrangements all have a value. If I share the use of a sailing boat with three others on an equal basis, I will pay one quarter of the costs, and perhaps have the use of it for one week in four. If one of my co-owners moves to Australia, then I might increase my share to 50 per cent by purchasing his share. Or the three remaining owners may collectively buy his stake so as to reduce the number of owners, with the result that each ends up with a third. Or a new partner could be found who might be expected to contribute more than the original amount paid for the one-quarter stake.

It could even get more complicated. It would not be unusual for the three remaining co-owners of the yacht to decide they want to reduce the time and money spent on sailing, so they may elect to bring in several more additional partners, creating ten shareholders rather than four. This would lead them to issue new shares at a price sufficiently high to ensure that although their holdings are diluted to one tenth each, they have still gained more than enough cash back to compensate for their shares being worth less. It would become more complicated still if there were restrictions on the newcomers' shares, preventing them from using the boat in the peak summer season, for example.

All of these situations are reflected in the world's stock markets, which first began through the same kind of sharing as in my sailing analogy. What happened, as I will describe in Chapter 2, is that adventurers planning a long sea voyage from Britain decided to find others to help them finance an expedition through the Arctic to see if they could discover a northern trade route to China. This voyage was somewhat more of a risk than a shared yacht moored in the Helford River, but the principle was the same.

The only difference between these kinds of shares and those held in a modern corporation is that, for the most part, a company's shares are of equal value. No one ordinary share in BP is worth more than any other BP share. Sometimes, but seldom, there are special shares, and some of these have differing values, but this is an exception I will explain later.

The price of a company's shares is determined by the same pressures that govern the price of anything else – a boat, a house, a car or an airline seat. That price is the point at which the amount the buyer is willing to pay matches the sum the seller is prepared to accept. And this point will move up or down according to supply and demand. If fresh cauliflowers are in plentiful supply at the vegetable market, the price will be lower than would be the case if drought had affected the crop. On the demand side, a television cooking series might have recommended a dish using cauliflowers, producing greater consumer interest and forcing prices up.

In precisely the same way, if there is a belief that there is over-production of silicon chips so that there are many more than enough to meet the needs of computer manufacturers, shares in Intel, the world's leading chip manufacturer, will fall. Note the word 'belief'. It is the market's perception of what will happen to the balance sheet of a business in the near future rather than the current facts that determines price movements. In the example mentioned, there will be more sellers than buyers until the price of Intel shares reaches a level that investors feel reflects their true value.

There is one important difference between the way a company's share price is determined and the other values discussed earlier. An airline seat is only of value until the flight for which it is booked takes off. Once the flight has closed, the seat cannot be sold, so it has no value, or liquidity. Shares in a big corporation like BP are traded very frequently, so there is high liquidity, and their price changes every few seconds. A market is at its most liquid when there are large numbers of buyers and sellers, and where this is the case the value of shares is most accurately defined.

Shares are one of the two essential planks of global capitalism. The other is debt, largely defined in bonds, which are equally important on stock markets.

So what is a bond? Again, this is a simple question that deserves a straightforward answer. There is one. A bond is an IOU. You are out of cash to pay the man who came to fix your broken car at the roadside, so you put your name and address on a piece of paper, write 'IOU £50' and sign it. He trusts you to honour the debt and send him a cheque or postal order. A bond comes finely printed on good paper and promises to pay its owner its value plus interest at a defined future date. If the date is in the distant future, then the IOU is known as a long bond. Hence the US Treasury long bond is an IOU from the United States Government which promises in fifteen years' time to pay you back the exact amount you have lent it. Do not be put off by the jargon; everyone can understand the bond markets.

As with shares, the value of bonds can change very rapidly. Some find this harder to understand; after all, a debt is a debt and has to be repaid by the person who has borrowed the money. But loans can be traded as easily as shares. Effectively the loan you have made at the agreed interest rate is handed over to someone else. If you have a standard savings account with a bank or building society you have the right to withdraw your money by presenting yourself and your pass book at the counter during opening hours. However, these accounts offer very poor rates of interest. If you agree to keep your money on deposit for a fixed term of two years, the interest rate will be higher, but still not matching the level offered by a bond. A bond will pay significantly more, but the interest rate is fixed until payback date. If general interest rates rise, your bond will earn you less than you would get elsewhere, so its value will fall. If you want to get rid of it you will have to sell it on the stock market at its market price, which will be different from the price you paid for it. If interest rates have gone down since you bought your bond, it will go up in value because of the better return it offers.

In today's world, anyone who has savings or the ability to save can own shares or bonds. Only the very poor are excluded from the stock markets, for the same reason that they do not own telephones and television sets, cars and washing machines, books and magazines, and all too often exist below the poverty line in totally inadequate housing, without health care, nutrition or education. The operations of the stock markets have not constricted wealth; they have spread it, albeit unevenly, and will continue to do so. The problems of the world's poor cannot be solved by a financial system, but only by concerted action from politicians brave enough to impose sacrifices on the power groups that elected them.

In a global economy a Briton can own shares in an Australian gold mine, an Asian hotel chain, or a German motor manufacturer. He can buy a stake in the world's biggest company, General Electric, where his greatest risk may be that the dollar may fall against the pound, or he can chance his money on one of London's smallest football clubs, Charlton Athletic, where relegation to a lower division could mean the loss of television income and financial disaster. If he doubts his own judgement he can put his trust in professional fund managers, and buy a share in a collective investment, which will give him a stake in a wide sweep of companies or countries, or both.

This freedom of ownership, of course, extends to billionaires and to large corporations, who are relatively free to move their money across national boundaries at a second's notice. Not all countries allow total freedom of capital movements, and some, most notably the United States, have restrictions on foreign ownership of certain assets. There is a widespread popular belief that America is the 'land of the free' so far as money movements are concerned, but this is not the case. Foreigners cannot take over an American airline, for example, though an American airline could buy a British one. Rupert Murdoch had to relinquish Australian citizenship and become American before he could acquire his US television empire. The Swiss were able to buy the British confectionary group Rowntree Mackintosh; Cadbury Schweppes would not be allowed to buy Nestlé.

Even so, this kind of protectionism, which successive rounds of talks under the aegis of the World Trade Organisation have failed to address, adds up to a fairly minor restriction on world share owner-ship, and it is still possible for both individuals and companies to hold minority stakes in restricted sectors or companies. That means that the only enterprises in the major industrial nations in which international share ownership is proscribed are the diminishing number of corporations owned by the state, or private, family-held companies. Many of these exist in Europe and Asia, but the trend is towards open ownership, and by the end of the first decade of the twenty-first century, most large businesses are likely to be listed on stock exchanges.

The last 20 years of the twentieth century will be remembered not just for the emergence of the internet, but also as the decade in which the world discovered financial markets. Since then the stock of financial assets has exploded. According to a detailed year-long study by McKinsey & Co. published in March 2005 the world's financial assets total more than $119 trillion, compared with only $13 trillion in 1980.[1] The value had doubled by the millennium, but then quadrupled again during the first five years of the new century. So much for those who grabbed headlines at the time of 9/11 predicting the collapse of capitalism. McKinsey thinks the figure will rise further to $200 trillion by 2010.

Whereas in 1980 the global financial stock was about the same size as world GDP, today it is about three times that size. How could that be? There are many reasons, but two stand out. The first is that much of the rise in financial assets is tradeable debt, money owed on bonds and other securities that can be bought and sold. In 1980 non-tradeable bank deposits accounted for 40 per cent of the global financial stock, whereas by 2005, they had dropped to just 30 per cent of the total. The second reflects my earlier point that the value of shares is calculated by perception, not by historic asset value, as will be explained later.

Of the $119 trillion, $33.1 trillion are shares in public companies, $31.5 are corporate debt securities such as corporate bonds, and $21.2 trillion in government bonds. The bond markets are where the growth has been, for share markets have fallen globally since the millennium, although they are 50 per cent larger than in 1996.

There are big variations across the world in the way this stock is composed, but in the United States, Britain, much of Asia and Australia, shares are about a third of the total. Only in the eurozone and in Japan does their share of the total fall much below this, because of the bigger role taken by banks. Even in communist China, the share market forms 27 per cent of the total capital market.

About half of the American population own shares, which is twice as many as in 1987, the year of the last big stock market crash. In Britain there are about 12 million private shareholders, three times as many as in 1987. In Germany, a country noted for cautious investors

---

[1] McKinsey Global Institute

preferring bank deposit accounts and bonds, one in five adults are now share owners.

The enthusiasm for shares has been driven by what has seemed to be an inexorable rise in values, greater even than the rising price of property in the major democracies. A detailed study conducted by Barclays Capital, a subsidiary of the British high street bank, found that provided shares are owned for a period of three years, historically they have produced better returns than high-interest deposits or bonds.[2] The study took a long view, looking at eighty years of performance since the end of World War I in 1918, and at both short and long periods within this epoch. Where investments were held for a decade or more, shares outperformed deposits in 97 per cent of ten-year spells, and did better than bonds for 94 per cent of the time. Even for short periods of only two years the incidence of shares performing better than either bonds or deposits was 70 per cent. One notable exception was after the 1987 global stock market crash, when it took six years for an investment in shares to outperform a high-interest deposit. One hundred pounds invested in the British stock market at the end of World War I in 1918 would now be worth almost £100,000. The same amount placed in a bank deposit would have grown to about £750.

This analysis may not have been much comfort to those investing in the stock markets at the turn of this century. In 2001 the total return on equities in Britain was a loss of 8.6 per cent, after adjusting for inflation. Equities underperformed bonds by 30.4 per cent in the year 2000, the widest margin of underperformance since the 1930s. The Great Depression years of 1930, 1931 and 1937 are the only times that have been as bad.

Still, optimists can have some faith in another study, available in much greater detail, which confirms that the longer the time interval, the greater the probability of a better performance from shares compared with bonds and bank deposits. The table below looks at the probability of equities outperforming bonds and cash.

Equity Performance since World War I

Probability of:	2 yrs	3-yrs	4-yrs	5-yrs	10-yrs
Shares Outperforming Cash	73	71	81	82	97
Shares Outperforming Gilts	69	79	84	81	96

source: Barclays Capital

---

[2] Barclays Capital Ltd, London.

This table shows how £100 invested in October 1979 in equities, gilts and cash has grown to £1180, £434 and £275 respectively

Over a ten-year period shares have outperformed gilts or bonds for 96 per cent of the time and cash for 97 per cent of the time. Even over short two-year periods the probability of equities outperforming cash has been 73 per cent and beating gilts by 69 per cent.

That does not mean that you can't lose money, especially if you invest only for the short term. Those who bought shares at the turn of this century found a year later that they had dropped an average of 8.6 per cent in value. Many private investors sold out – they could not know that within three years prices would rise to all-time highs.

The only studies that make sense – except to the speculator and frequent trader – are those that look at the long-term average, like the one by Barclays Capital. Another valuable source is the Global Investment Returns Yearbook, published by three London Business School professors in association with the Dutch bank ABN Amro.[3]

The professors gathered statistics for every year since 1900 from more than 30 countries with stock markets. These show that over the past 105 years British shares have produced an annual gain of 4.7 per cent. However if shareholders reinvested their annual dividends – rather like leaving interest on deposit accounts in the bank – their average annual return would have been 9.6 per cent. This compares

---

[3] Global Investment Returns Yearbook, 2005 by Professors Elroy Damson, Paul Marsh and Mike Staunton, London Business School

with annualised inflation in Britain over the same period of 4 per cent, returns from government bonds of 5.4 per cent, and cash on deposit in the bank of 5 per cent.

These studies are undoubtedly correct, but I would insert two notes of caution. Many long-term studies are based on the performance of indices like the *Financial Times* 100 index, and not on companies that were part of an index years ago but may now either be out of business, taken over by another corporation, or whose market capitalisation has slipped so much that it is no longer qualified to be in it. If you go back and look at the *FT* 100 share index in 1984 you will find that 72 companies that were listed then have since vanished.

The second caution is that shares can be volatile. Those who invested in Eurotunnel and Royal Mail privatisations have lost all or most of their money. Two of Britain's other big privatisation issues were trading in 2005 at substantially less than their value five years ago, and those who have these shares parked in government-sponsored savings schemes like personal equity plans have lost by holding on to them to 'save tax'. In many other instances investors can be caught out by bad timing. Ideally an investor sells out at the top of the market and buys in when shares are low, taking advantage of this volatility.

This illustrates another very important point, which is often overlooked by investors: you do need to keep your eyes on the markets. This does not mean being glued to a computer monitor for ten hours a day, but it does require a daily look at the numbers in the financial pages or on line. There are many techniques for spotting revived buyer interest. One of them is looking at the volume of trades as well as values.

So why did interest in shares not develop sooner? Shares used to be the preserve of the rich. Buying and selling them was expensive, and had to be carried out through a closed shop of stockbrokers, who preferred to deal with account holders of the same social class as themselves. Those who fared best on the stock markets were those in the know, or who had inside information. There was a clear pecking order for access to information. At the top of the list was the stockbroker himself and his preferred clients, either people who did him favours, such as supplying tickets for Royal Ascot or Wimbledon, or clients who traded often, thus providing him with high commission income. Next came people with connections, travelling companions in the first-class compartments of commuter trains to London from the 'stockbroker belt', and financial editors of major newspapers, who could be depended upon to write favourably about shares, thereby pushing the price up. Before the newspaper went to press, the financial editor would buy shares in companies in which he had good information. The third layer with access to information were the readers of the broadsheet newspapers, particularly *The Times*, the *Daily Telegraph*, the *Financial Times* and the *Wall Street Journal*. At the bottom of the pile came everyone else. With this as the scenario, it is hardly surprising the public felt excluded from the stock markets. The average family was no more likely to buy shares than to venture on to the Yorkshire grouse moors on 12 August, the start of the British shooting season.

I agree with Justin Urquhart Stewart, an investment manager, who argues that the process of dealing in shares needs to be demystified.

> It's depressing that people still think deposit accounts make better investments. The US is much more clued-up about share dealing than the UK, but it is hardly surprising given the poor level of financial education available in Britain. We learn about home economics, but practical financial education is not even on the school syllabus.

It is an irony that in the forties and fifties, while the punters were excluded from the stock markets, they were indirectly contributing to the growing wealth of the privileged few. Each week the 'man from the Pru', a sallow foot soldier from what was then Britain's largest life assurance company, would call on homes in the meaner streets of the country's towns and villages and collect a few pence towards a savings scheme. After the salesman's commission and other costs, the residue would be invested on the stock markets. The Prudential, and others who practised house-to-house selling, such as the Liverpool Victoria, Pearl Assurance and the United Friendly, were prime and favoured clients for the coterie of stockbrokers in the City of London. Each treated the other well.

Thus collective investments were born on the argument that small savers could more safely channel their meagre savings into the stock markets through giant institutions. The collective might of these organisations could wield the kind of power in trading that no individual could aspire to. Rather than risk investing in any one share, those holding collective investments could have their savings managed by experts who would achieve better results.

The theory made sound economic sense, and for a while it worked. But by the 1980s, as the financial services industry grew larger, and greedier, it began to sow the seeds for substantial public dis-satisfaction. Many, if not most, financial products designed for the mass markets were sold by commission agents, who preferred to use the term 'broker' or 'financial adviser'. Most of these were rewarded not with fees geared to the quality of their advice or the amount of time spent with their clients, but with a sizeable cut of the first eighteen months' contribution. Many so-called financial advisers sold families packages that were totally inappropriate, a practice that later became known as mis-selling, and was to cost the companies dearly in fines.

In parallel with this, the British Government, in common with many others, burdened the financial services industry with a complex set of regulations, which added greatly to costs. Some of the new rules were sensible and long overdue, such as a total ban on insider trading, which is now a criminal offence. Others were poorly drafted, hard to enforce and an encouragement to unnecessary bureaucracy.

It became hard to run collective investment schemes profitably, but the burden of regulation was not the only cost pressure. The greater force pushing prices upwards was that created by inflated salaries paid in financial centres like the City of London. It became commonplace for City fund managers and other executives to earn in excess of £400,000 a year, supplemented by an annual bonus of an equivalent amount. In Wall Street pay is much higher, sometimes four times higher. Mostly, these charges were passed on to the investor.

This development coincided with a revolution in technology. It became possible for the private individual to buy and sell shares, if not on equal terms with the professional traders, at least swiftly and efficiently, and at reasonable cost. At the same time it also became easy for the individual investor to obtain a great deal of relevant information free of charge.

The technologies that were the catalyst for change were not particularly new: the first was the telephone, and the second was the internet. What was new was the way in which one company, Charles Schwab, utilised these technologies for share trading by individuals, and then took the market by storm, transforming the industry as it did so.

Charles Schwab started his share trading business to serve cities and towns across America through bustling Main Street branch offices known as share shops. There, over a cup of coffee, a browse through the *Wall Street Journal*, and a look at the New York Stock Exchange prices running across a ticker, investors could buy and sell shares. Some sought advice from the Schwab staff on hand; others acted on their own.

By the early 1990s, the firm had become the largest out-of-town broker in the United States, but was hardly a threat to the titans of Wall Street, such as Merrill Lynch, known throughout the financial world as 'the thundering herd'.

Then Charles Schwab began to develop its telephone business, building call centres to accept buy or sell orders from customers, and executing trades immediately through its own team of traders based at the New York Stock Exchange. It also acquired the British company Sharelink, founded in Birmingham by the entrepreneur David Jones, to cash in on the interest in share trading created by the wave of privatisations in the years of Margaret Thatcher's Conservative government. Until Sharelink arrived, it had not been easy for ordinary Britons to trade shares, for the reasons mentioned earlier. Jones, helped by technologists from the University of Cambridge, created what was in effect a share trading factory on the first floor of an unpretentious building in a dreary quarter of Birmingham, a city mostly inhabited by insurance companies. Few people gave him much of a chance, and the London Stock Exchange, retreating only slowly from its old traditions of privilege and pretence, did its best to crush the business through a variety of legal manoeuvres. But Jones won through, built the business, and then sold it to Schwab, which built it up even farther and sold it on to Barclays Bank.

Charles Schwab's real breakthrough came with web trading, when its technology group created new software that allowed a server to take an order from a web browser on a personal computer, route it through the company's sophisticated back-end systems and mainframes, execute it, and send a confirmation back to the buyer's PC. It now processes more trades online than through traditional means. The numbers of people using the web site are little short of astonishing.

Schwab has not been without competition, but it has come from new companies rather than the financial services industry establishment. One of its major competitors is E-Trade, which had its beginnings at the Cambridge Science Park, and now operates in the United States, Britain, Australia and New Zealand.

Trading shares now could not be easier. Using one of the two major web browsers, Internet Explorer or Godzilla Firefox, you open the Barclayshare web site, select the market in which you wish to trade – for example, United Kingdom – and then log on using your account number and password. This will take you directly to the page containing the details of your account, including the latest prices of any shares you already own, and their value. If you wish to trade, you enter the name of the company whose shares you wish to buy or sell, and the number of shares to be traded. The next page to appear will provide you with the cost of the transaction, and ask you if you wish to proceed. If you accept the deal, the trade will be carried out and confirmed back to you.

It is as easy as purchasing an airline ticket, and a lot easier than booking a train journey. If you do not have computer access, buying and selling by phone is still available. All you need to know is what shares are, what makes them valuable one day and less valuable the next, how to pick and choose them and when to buy and sell. Now, a little history.

2   History

*The howling of the wolf, the grunting of the hog, the braying of
the ass, the nocturnal wooing of the cat, all these in unison
could not be more hideous than the noise which these beings
make in the Stock.*

Anonymous commentator
on the scene in Change Alley, London, 1695

*Stock-jobbing is knavish in its private practice, and
treason in its public.*

Daniel Defoe

Dictum meum pactum – My word is my bond.
Handbook of the London Stock Exchange

For most people the stock markets epitomise the concept of risk and
reward. With a modicum of risk, and the chance of achieving a good
reward, an investor can be on the road to riches. This has been true
throughout the three centuries of stock market activity.

Those who took a billion-pound risk in investing in satellite
television in Britain at the end of the twentieth century were opting for
the same choice as the few backers prepared to chance £3,200 apiece
on the Concepcion adventure in 1686. Then, a whiskery sea captain
from Boston called Phips sought investors for an expedition to the
north coast of Hispaniola to salvage a sunken galleon. Nine months
later the backers reaped their reward – £250,000 worth of fine silver.

Throughout history, one of the major threats to any investment
has been that people cheat. There are big cheats and little cheats, and
only a few of them have passed through the dock of the Old Bailey.
The excitement that greeted the trial in London of the Guinness Five
in 1990, or the humiliation of the president of the House of Nomura
a year later – or the imprisonment of Ivan Boesky and Michael
Milken in New York, Ronald Li in Hong Kong, Alan Bond in
Australia and Nick Leeson in Singapore – was only a latter-day
repeat of events in Britain in the late seventeenth century.

The collapse in 1995 of Barings, a famous London investment bank, set regulators searching for new solutions and tougher rules. It was much the same in 1697, when, following a wave of market rigging and insider trading, the British Government brought in an Act designed to 'restrain the number and ill-practice of brokers and stockjobbers'.

This followed a report from a Parliamentary Commission set up a year earlier which had discovered that:

> the pernicious art of stockjobbing hath, of late, so perverted the end design of Companies and Corporations, erected for the introducing or carrying on of manufactures, to the private profit of the first projectors, that the privileges granted to them have commonly been made no other use of – but to sell again, with advantage, to innocent men.[1]

As a result of the 1697 Act, all stockbrokers and stockjobbers had to be licensed before they plied their trade in the coffee shops, walks and alleys near the Royal Exchange in London. These licences were limited in number to a hundred and were granted by the Lord Mayor of London and the Court of Aldermen. They cost only £2, and entitled the licensee to wear a specially struck silver medal embossed with the Royal Arms, once he had taken an oath that he would 'truly and faithfully execute and perform the office and employment of a broker between party and party, without fraud or collusion'.

The rules of operation were strict. Brokers were not allowed to deal on their own behalf, but only for clients. They could not hold any options for more than three days without facing the certainty of permanent expulsion. Commission was limited to 5 per cent, or less. Anyone who tried to operate as a broker without a licence was, if caught, incarcerated for three days in the City pillory.

The Muscovy and East India Companies

The trade in shares began with City traders and merchants spreading the risk of two major entrepreneurial journeys: an attempt to investigate the prospects offered by the uncharted White Sea and Arctic Circle; and a voyage to India and the East Indies via the Cape of Good Hope.

---

[1] Archives of the Stock Exchange.

These ventures were to lead to the world's first two public companies: the Muscovy Company and the East India Company. Until then companies had been privately owned businesses, or partnerships between individuals. These companies were new and different. Their owners contributed money to what was called 'joint stock', and these contributions were verified through certificates which became known as shares. If later unwanted, these shares were freely transferable to anyone who would pay a price acceptable to both buyer and seller.

The Muscovy Company was created to finance a brave, risky and costly attempt by Sebastian Cabot in 1553 to find a north-east trade route from Britain to China and what was then known as the Orient. Cabot and his crew would face the physical hazards, but others were needed to share the financial risk. As one of the first shareholders explained at the time:

> Every man willing to bee of the societie, should disburse the portion of twentie and five pounds a piece: so that in a short time, by this means, the sum of six thousand pounds being gathered, three ships were brought.[2]

Two of the three ships that formed the expedition sank off Norway, and things looked bleak for the 250 merchants putting up £25 each. Fortunately, one of the leaders of the venture did make it to Moscow, where he persuaded Ivan the Terrible to sign a trade agreement. This yielded some returns, though not as good as would have been achieved had they been able to get through the Arctic icecap to Asia.

The East India Company was more successful, and was the first company to find shareholders prepared to put up money on a substantial scale. It needed modern, armed ships for the difficult and dangerous voyage to the Orient, and a home base of substantial docks in London. Although some ships sank on voyages, and the company hovered close to bankruptcy in its early days, it managed to raise more than £1.6 million over seventeen years. As the silk and spice trade developed, those who had invested in the original stock enjoyed returns of 40 per cent a year.

This quickly led enterprising developers to realise that raising capital through shares was a good way to fund less risky ventures which were still too costly for one person, however rich, to finance.

---

[2] Alan Jenkins, *The Stock Exchange Story*, Heinemann, London, 1973.

Why not create more joint stock companies for domestic projects? One of the earliest was established by Francis, Earl of Bedford, to fulfil his bold plan to drain the East Anglian Fens. The aim of this ambitious scheme was to create thousands of hectares of additional fertile agricultural land, and to provide London with its first supply of fresh water. Others were persuaded to add to his own £100,000 contribution, and in 1609 the 'Government and Company of the New River brought from Chadwell and Amwell to London' was founded. It become Britain's first water stock. Although the water company operations were bought out by the Metropolitan Water Board in 1904, the company still exists as the oldest to be quoted on the London Stock Exchange.

Coffee Shops

By the end of the seventeenth century there were a number of large joint stock companies, and substantial dealing in their shares. The historian W. R. Scott estimated that by 1695 there were 140 joint stock companies, with a total market capitalisation of £4.5 million. When people wanted to buy and sell shares in these companies, the place to do it was usually one of two coffee houses in the heart of the City of London. One was called Garraway's and the other Jonathan's, and both were near Change Alley, a haunt favoured by City merchants and traders. Change Alley is still to be found today in the narrow spit of land between Cornhill and Threadneedle Street, close to the Bank of England.

The patrons of the coffee establishments of the seventeenth century had style and colour. There were no grey suits to be seen; even the tinkers dressed up. The atmosphere was convivial, the talk was of adventure and new ideas. The British Empire was expanding, and there was money to be made, and shares to be bought and sold. Over coffee you could also run your eye down a sheet of paper containing the latest prices of most commodities, and of those shares traded. The title of this daily sheet was also an accurate description of it: *The Course of the Exchange and Other Things*. It was to be the precursor of greater publications to come – the *Stock Exchange Daily Official List*, the *Financial Times* and the *Wall Street Journal*.

A writer of the day set the scene:

The centre of the jobbing is in the Kingdom of Exchange Alley and its adjacencies: the limits are easily surrounded in about a Minute and a half stepping out of Jonathan's into the Alley, you turn your face full South, moving on a few paces, and then turning Due East, you advance to Garraway's; from there going out at the other Door, you go on still East into Birchin Lane and then halting a little at the Sword-Blade Bank to do much mischief in fervent Words, you immediately face to the North, enter Cornhill, visit two or three petty Provinces there in your way West; and thus having Boxed your Compass, and sail'd round the whole Stock Jobbing Globe, you turn into Jonathan's again; and so, as most of the great Follies of Life oblige us to do, you end just where you began.[3]

The South Sea Bubble

This coffee society was to thrive for more than fifty years, and by 1720 Change Alley and its coffee houses were thronged with brokers. It was the place to be. Throughout the day the narrow streets were impassable because of the throng of lords and ladies in their carriages. The Act regulating and restricting their access to the narrow streets lapsed by default, because nobody took any notice of it, and no one tried to enforce it. The scene is described in an eighteenth-century ballad:

> Then stars and garters did appear
> Among the meaner rabble
> To buy and sell, to see and hear
> The Jews and Gentiles squabble,
> The greatest ladies thither came
> And plied in chariots daily,
> Or pawned their jewels for a sum
> To venture in the Alley.[4]

The principal attraction was the excitement caused by the booming share price of the South Sea Company, which started to be sold at the beginning of 1720 at £128 each, and swiftly rose as euphoria about the company's prospects was spread both by brokers and by the

[3] E. V. Morgan and W. A. Thomas, *The London Stock Exchange*, St. Martin's Press, NY, 1969.
[4] Alan Jenkins, *The Stock Exchange Story*, Heinemann, London, 1973.

government. By March the price had risen to £330, by May it was £550, and by 24 June it had reached an insane £1,050. The South Sea Company had been set up nine years earlier by the British Government, ostensibly with the aim of opening up trade and markets for new commodities in South America. It also had another purpose, which, these days, has a familiar ring about it. By converting it to a public company, rather than a government department, it reduced the Treasury's public debt by £9 million.

For eight years the company was moribund and unprofitable. Its shares were dormant. It had only one contract of any size: to supply black slaves to Latin America. The Government then adopted the concept of privatisation of a state-owned concern, something much more audacious than the sales of British Telecom or British Gas over 250 years later. It offered shares in the South Sea Company to the public, hoping that it would raise enough money to wipe out the entire National Debt of some £31 million.

The Government was persuaded to do this by a wily operator, Sir John Blunt, who was a director of the company, and who effectively underwrote the issue. An underwriter in the financial markets guarantees that if there are not enough people willing to buy the shares on offer, he will do so at a discount. The issue was made on a 'partly paid' basis; which means an investor has only to find a small proportion at the time, but then pays for the full cost in instalments. The offer was heavily oversubscribed, and many people who had hoped to get South Sea shares missed out. There was considerable irritation when it was discovered that Blunt's acquaintances, and other people of influence, had been given an extra allocation, a circumstance that was to repeat itself in Britain during the Thatcher government's privatisations.

The Government realised it would be possible to raise even more money on the strength of the supposed bright future of the South Sea Company. To encourage wider share ownership, the company made loans to the public to buy its shares, with the loans secured on the shares themselves. Three centuries later the practice was to emerge again with the issue of junk bonds (see Chapter 11).

Sir John Blunt proved adept at adopting the techniques of public relations to push the share price up. There were hints of lavish dividends to come, prominent people offered thinly disguised bribes to buy shares and talk about it. Even the peace negotiations under way with Spain were frequently deployed for propaganda purposes, since the prospect of an end to conflict meant more trade with South America.

The astute reader will by now have guessed the inevitable outcome. The smart money, including that invested by the Prime Minister, Sir Robert Walpole, sold out at the peak of the boom. The Prince of Wales, the Duke of Argyll, the Chancellor of the Exchequer and many Members of Parliament made handsome profits. The bubble burst, and triggered off the first ever bear market. Within eight weeks of rising above the £1,000 mark, the share price plunged to £175. By December 1720 it had sunk to £124, bringing ruin to those who had seen the South Sea Company as the chance of a lifetime. There was an outcry, forcing the Government to introduce legislation in the shape of the Bubble Act, designed to prevent a rash of similar speculative ventures from springing up. There was the inevitable Parliamentary inquiry, which concluded that the accounts had been falsified and a government minister bribed. One of the few public figures to pay a penalty was the hapless Chancellor of the Exchequer, John Aislabie. Before he had a chance to enjoy his £800,000 capital gain, he was committed to the Tower of London upon being found guilty of the 'most notorious, dangerous and infamous corruption'.

It was – and remains – the most fabled episode in British financial history. It took a while for investors to recover their nerve, and it was a long time before the fledgling stock market got back into its stride. Indeed, it wasn't until the next century that another large crop of joint stock companies was formed, and this only came about because of an acute shortage of capital for major projects both at home and abroad.

Mines, Railways, Canals

By 1824, the end of the cyclical trade depression, there were 156 companies quoted on the London Stock Exchange, with a market capitalisation of £47.9 million. In the following twelve months, interest in investment increased sharply. Prospectuses were issued for no fewer than 624 companies, with capital requirements of £372 million. The largest group were general investment companies, mostly with extensive interests overseas, which raised £52 million. Canals and railways came next, raising £44 million, followed by mining companies with £38 million and insurance, a new industry, with £35 million.

The insurance industry was founded on the same concept as the stock market: the pooling of risk. As the City became more built up and more congested, there were considerable fears that there could be a repeat of the Great Fire of London of 1666 when most of the City had been wiped out. Companies were formed to offer protection against fire, and this protection included the promotion of safety measures and the provision of fire brigades. With the chances of a repeat inferno much reduced, the fire offices began to accept premiums in exchange for taking on the risk of fire at individual premises. They insured not only buildings, but also the financial loss suffered by a business if it was forced to close or move as a result of a fire. Soon this concept spread to public and individual liability, theft, loss and accidental damage, and to individuals' lives. Thus the third major plank of the financial services industry was born, and expanded rapidly worldwide.

Meanwhile the railways proved to be a great benefit for the promotion of investment, even if most of the investors lost their money. The Duke of Wellington had opposed the development of railways, arguing imperiously that 'railroads will only encourage the lower classes to move about needlessly'. His words proved to be prescient. Not only did people start to travel, but the upper classes living outside London were spurred into owning shares. A new word entered the financial vocabulary: stag, a person who applies for an allotment of shares with the clear intention of selling them to someone else before having to meet the cost of buying them.

The stags were out in force in 1836 when George Hudson, a bluff Yorkshireman, raised £300,000 for the York and North Midland Railway under the slogan 'Mak' all t'railways coom t'York'. The £50 shares were oversubscribed and quickly traded at a premium of £4 each. Within three years the line was opened, and the bells of York Minster pealed out in joyful celebration. Much of the joy was short-lived. So many railway lines spread out across the country that many rail companies could not pay the wages of the train drivers, let alone dividends for shareholders. Many companies were overcapitalised, but instead of returning the cash to shareholders, managements found other ways to use the surplus funds, much to the chagrin of investors.

Despite these setbacks, by 1842 there were sixty-six railway companies quoted on the London Stock Exchange, with a capital of almost £50 million. During the boom in railway issues, the *Economist* was moved to publish an editorial which, with a change of name and date, might well have fitted into the British Telecom era of 1985: 'Everybody is in the stocks now,' it purred. 'Needy clerks,

poor tradesmen's apprentices, discarding serving men and bankrupts
– all have entered the ranks of the great moneyed interest.'

Provincial stock markets were also established. Local investment
opportunities were featured in the advertisements for share auctions
which regularly appeared in a Liverpool newspaper after about 1827.
It was quite usual to use a property auction as the opportunity to
dispose of a parcel of shares. By the middle of 1845, regional stock
exchanges had been formed in twelve towns and cities, from Bristol
in the south to Newcastle in the north, with Yorkshire claiming the
greatest number. But only five of them were to survive the trading
slump of 1845 to become permanent institutions.

Government Debt

All through this period Government debt had been growing.
Compensation to slave-owners whose slaves had been freed, the cost
of the Crimean War and the purchase by the Government of the
national telegraph system combined to blow out the deficit.

Raising the cash to fund it provided the most lucrative and reliable
form of income for stockbrokers. By 1860, British Government funds
amounted to more than all the other quoted securities combined, and
created by far the widest market in the Exchange. Government
stocks, or bonds, were bought daily from the Treasury by the City
figure called the Government Broker, who then sold them on in the
marketplace. The idea was that these stocks, to become known much
later as gilt-edged securities, would be used to reduce or even
eradicate the National Debt. Of course issuing these bonds had the
opposite effect, because they added to the debt, but they quickly
became a way of funding unpopular measures. Had the Government
not been able to borrow money through these tradeable bonds, it
would have had to resort to taxation.

It was not long before local authorities also jumped on the
bandwagon. The City of Dublin was the first to raise money through
bonds, followed by Edinburgh, Glasgow and the Metropolitan Board
of Works.

The First Exchange

By this time the brokers and other money dealers had long since left
their colourful but damp pitches in Change Alley. The friendly coffee

houses had become too crowded for comfort, and everyone knew everyone else's business. The nature of the customers also changed, as Change Alley played host to people described by the established professionals as 'riff-raff'. When Jonathan's was finally burnt down after a series of major fires around 1748, the brokers sought refuge in New Jonathan's, rebuilt in Threadneedle Street, where they were charged a sixpence-a-day entrance fee, a sum sufficient to discourage tinkers, money-lenders and the other parasites who had frequented the previous premises. Soon afterwards a sign was erected over the door: The Stock Exchange.

The stock market continued to operate in this way, more or less as a private club, for thirty years, until its members decided something more formal was needed. On 7 February 1801 the Stock Exchange was shut down, to reopen one month later as the Stock Subscription Room. The per diem entry fee was stopped: instead, members had to be elected, pay a fee of ten guineas, and risk a fine of two guineas if they were found guilty of 'disorderly conduct', the penalty going to charity. There does not seem to be an accurate record of how many charities benefited from this provision, or how many fines were levied.

The Stock Subscription Room had a short life, for members quickly decided it was too small, and in the same year laid the foundation stone for a new building in Capel Court. This stone records that this was also the 'first year of the union between Great Britain and Ireland', and notes that the building was being 'erected by private subscription for transaction of the business in the public funds'.

Not all members of the public were impressed by this new monument. The old lady who sold cups of tea and sweet buns outside Capel Court moved away because, she said, 'the Stock Exchange is such a wicked place'. But with monuments come tablets, and it was not long before members were forced to draw up new rules of operation. Adopted in 1812, these were to survive, more or less intact, for the next 150 years. Neither members nor their wives could be engaged in any other business, failures had to be chalked up above the clock immediately so that there could be a fair distribution of assets to creditors, and members were informed that they had to give up 'rude and trifling practices which have long disgraced the Stock Exchange'.

The Capel Court building was to last a century and a half, and in the end it was not size but ancient communications that made it unworkable. The decision was taken to rebuild, and a 'state-of-the-art' twenty-six-storey concrete tower was established as the new London Stock Exchange in Throgmorton Street almost on the spot where New Jonathan's had once flourished. Opened by Queen Elizabeth in 1972, it stood as a seemingly unassailable bastion of capitalism in a climate where the City of London was often under political scrutiny and attack.

The early years in 'Throg Street' were good ones for the practitioners in the market. While heavy industry had crumbled – and much of manufacturing industry had vanished under international competition from Europe and south-east Asia – the banks and other financial institutions that provided a large part of Britain's invisible exports thrived and prospered. Britain was still merchant banker to the free world, and overseas governments, corporations and individual potentates entrusted their dollars, gold and silver to financial houses in the square mile of the City. In the early 1980s more than £50 million worth of foreign currency changed hands each day in London, yielding banks and other dealers large sums in commission and making London the dominant market in foreign exchange with one third of world business.

The City was a club, as cosy and impenetrable as any of the establishments two miles away in St James's which served diplomats and the officer and executive classes. Those invited to share its mysteries at generous lunches or livery dinners sniffed an uneasy air of narrow bonhomie and patrimony. Above all it was a closed shop.

The members of the London Stock Exchange were particularly well protected. No one could buy or sell shares except through one of their member firms, most of which had each been in the hands of a single family for decades. The closed shop meant investors had to pay twice for each transaction: a commission for the stockbroker and a mark-up for the stockjobber.

Commissions were fixed, in the manner of most professional fees at the time. For a broker to discount a commission, even to a friend, was as serious an offence as a doctor committing adultery with a patient or a farm worker poaching a landowner's pheasants. Stockbrokers brandished a pocket guide, published by Messrs Basil, Montgomery, Lloyd and Ward, which set out an elaborate sliding scale of charges. In 1975 the scale was generating average commissions of about 0.75 per cent, no matter how large the deal. Thus a £10,000 trade would cost £75 in commission; while the same trade today could be carried out for £12 or less. Ten years later in 1960 the commission rate went up to 1.25 per cent on small trades, penalising the small shareholder.

At these levels, and with the volume of business that was available to the limited number of stockbrokers, it was a profitable and relatively stress-free occupation. Advertising was banned, so clients were obtained through personal networking – usually over a substantial lunch, a game of cards in the first-class rail compartment on the way home, or a round of golf. The better broking firms used some of their profits to undertake detailed research into the activities of major companies, the results of which were made freely available to the investing institutions and moneyed private customers.

The stockbroker did not have to involve himself in direct financial bargaining with other brokers; indeed, until 1986 he was prohibited from doing so. Share trading was in the hands of stockjobbers, shrewd and resilient characters who stood or perched on stools at the elevated benches on the floor of the London Stock Exchange. Many of them had a demeanour more akin to a barrow-boy or bookmaker than to a City gent, and their daily work had many similarities. The jobbers made the market, deciding at what price they would buy or sell the shares on offer. Their profit was the difference between the buying and selling price, known as the 'jobbers' turn'.

Jobbers never dealt with the investing public, at any level. They traded only with dealers, usually junior employees of stockbroking firms, who were based on the floor of the Exchange, and who took their instructions by telephone or by sign language from colleagues standing nearby. Trading started at nine and finished at four thirty, with an hour's break for lunch, and at peak times provided a colourful spectacle to visitors peering down from the gallery above. Occasionally trading would be punctuated by the ringing of a bell, signifying an announcement to the Exchange, which would usually be followed by a roar of approval or derision, a quick revision by jobbers of their prices and another burst of trading.

Big Bang

October 1986 was the most momentous month in the long history of the London Stock Exchange – a combination of forces for change known as Big Bang. One force was the prime minister of the time, Margaret Thatcher. As part of her assault on trade unions' restrictive practices, she determined that fixed commissions charged by stockbrokers should be abolished, and that all major financial institutions should have free and open access to the capital markets. The principal barriers between banks, merchant banks, investment institutions and stockbrokers should be broken down: all should be able to set up as one-stop financial supermarkets if they wished. Why not allow one company to buy and sell shares for clients, raise capital for business, invest in new ventures and trade in international securities like eurobonds?

But by far the biggest force for change was technology: the combination of high-speed telecommunications and the microprocessor meant that international deals could be carried out anywhere. There was no need for any of the very large trades to pass through the Stock Exchange at all.

Immediately prior to Big Bang, 62 per cent of trading in one of Britain's largest companies, ICI, was being transacted off the London Exchange, mainly in New York. A large share of the buying and selling of other major British companies had also been taking place in the United States. This trading was by no means confined to American investors, for some of the big British institutions found that dealing across the Atlantic was a cheaper proposition. An official of Prudential Assurance explained to me at the time: 'When we have a significant buying programme on we check all available markets. We take the attitude that we deal wherever we can get the best price.'

Effectively the big traders had begun to bypass London, where the complicated system of brokers and jobbers was costing them much more in commission, government stamp duty and Value Added Tax.

For Sir Nicholas Goodison, then chairman of the Stock Exchange, sweeping reform was the only solution. If the Stock Exchange was to compete with the giant American broking houses, it had to change. There was no choice when competition was creaming off the top business, in both value and volume. Otherwise there would be nothing left for the old-fashioned Stock Exchange, and the jobbers would be left standing at their pitches.

Making the necessary changes took time and considerable resolution. It meant ending a way of life that had been a tradition for more than a hundred years. Even though its members could see that the system was under threat, the Stock Exchange Council had to be given a firm nudge by the Government in the direction of change. This happened almost by accident. The Office of Fair Trading had argued that stockbrokers should be treated no differently from other sectors of the community – solicitors, estate agents, motor traders, soap powder manufacturers – who had been barred from fixing prices amongst themselves, and were now bound to offer some semblance of competition in the marketplace. When the Stock Exchange demurred, the Government decided on legal action, using the weight of the Monopolies Commission to take apart the entire rulebook of the Exchange as a litany of restrictive practices. It was estimated that the proceedings would take five years to complete, and cost at least £5 million in legal fees. It was, of course, like using a sledgehammer to crack a nut and an absurd way of challenging an entire trading system. As Sir Nicholas Goodison was later to say:

> It was a foolish way to study the future of a great international market. It was a matter which needed long and close study, and preferably a public examination not constrained by the requirements of litigation or the strait-jacket of court procedure. Unfortunately the government turned down the suggestion of such an examination, and we were forced into a position of defence of rules, not all of which we would necessarily wish to keep. Thus open debate became impossible because anything said could, as it were, be taken down in evidence and used in court. The case pre-empted resources, effort and thought.[5]

It did, however, concentrate the minds of the members of the Stock Exchange. The Government was clearly in no mood to set up a Royal Commission to inquire into the Stock Exchange; ministers saw that as a waste of time. If the legal case went on, with each side producing volumes of written evidence, as well as witnesses for examination, cross-examination and re-examination, the Stock Exchange would end up in an unwinnable situation. There would also be unfavourable publicity. And even if the Exchange won the legal battle, its joy would be short-lived, for such was the resolve of the Thatcher government to curb the restrictive power of trade unions that it could hardly spare a notorious City club, and would feel obliged to legislate to change the law.

In July 1983, the Government offered a compromise. It offered to drop the case against the Stock Exchange if the Council would follow the example of New York in 1985 and abandon fixed commissions. It did so, and the die was cast for the biggest transformation since the days of the Change Alley coffee shops.

With the abolition of fixed commissions, which provided a steady and solid income, more or less indexed to the rate of inflation, many

---

[5] Interview with the author, 1985.

stockbrokers could not survive. Competition over commissions might be acceptable in a rising or bull market, but when the bears emerged in strength there would be trouble. 'Bull' is the name for the optimist who believes that prices are likely to go higher, and who charges into the market to buy; if there are enough bulls, their confidence is sufficient to push up prices, and commissions. A bear is the opposite market animal, who fears the worst, and expects a fall. When the bears run for cover, you have a bear market. For stock-brokers, a bear market generates fear, for although there are good commissions to be had when there is pronounced selling, the prices on which those commissions are based are lower, and interest dies.

From the perspective of the old-style broker, the future was grim. New technologies would force a change in the clubbish lifestyle. There would be fewer lunches at the club, and days out on the golf course. Those who wanted to survive would have to behave like Chicago futures dealers. Life would become unbearable – just like a job on the money or commodity markets, with young men and women arriving to a room full of telephones and computer terminals at 7.30 every morning, shouting at them and at each other for at least twelve hours, and leaving exhausted in the evening. This would be a world where the mid-life crisis could be expected at the age of twenty-six.

They also felt that competition would be so fierce there would probably be less profit. With no fixed commissions, firms would have neither the time nor the resources to undertake company or sector research, let alone visit a firm and enjoy a good lunch in a country hotel with the chairman and managing director. Instead they would spend their days peering at computer monitors, and yelling down the telephone.

As for open ownership, the senior partners would sell out, pocket their millions and go to live in Bermuda, whilst those left would not know who their bosses were, only that they worked for some large bank, almost certainly under foreign ownership. It was hard for brokers to imagine so great a change from the way things had been.

Despite their defeat over commissions, the old guard held out against other reforms. However, on 4 June 1985, the 4,495 members of the Stock Exchange were confronted with an historic choice: to face up to the future or face the consequences of living with the past.

Two resolutions were put to the members voting on the floor of the Exchange. For chairman Goodison, whose passion for old clocks belied his modern outlook, the issue was clear. It was about 'whether or not members want to keep the bulk of the securities business in this country and in the Stock Exchange', he wrote in a letter to all members of the exchange. 'It is about keeping and strengthening the Stock Exchange as the natural market in securities.'

After much angst, members voted by 3,246 votes to 681 to allow outsiders – banks, international finance houses, money brokers – to own up to 100 per cent of a member firm, instead of only 29.9 per cent.

The outcome meant the biggest financial groups in the world could join the club for only one share, negotiating the price not with old members, but with the Stock Exchange Council.

The World's First International Exchange

To complete the process of Big Bang, Goodison had next to win over the large group of securities houses trading international stocks who saw no good reason why they should be part of the new London Exchange.

These houses had formed themselves into ISRO, the International Securities Regulatory Organisation, which, despite its grandiose title, showed very little affection for regulation. Its members traded in the stocks of about four hundred of the world's major corporations for the benefit of about eighty institutions. It was an exclusive club for the big boys, who argued that since they all knew each other, not many rules were needed.

Prior to Big Bang, ISRO and the London Exchange were not the best of friends; indeed, they often traded insults. Since international equities were stocks which were traded beyond their own country boundaries, it was argued that they should not be subject to rigid domestic rules. And a new class of international equity was being spawned: issues by international corporations underwritten and distributed in overseas countries. The first really large issue of this kind was British Telecom; when it was floated off by the British Government, a large proportion of the stock was successfully offered to institutions in North America, Europe and Japan.

Such international equity issues were organised by investment banks and securities houses, who offered tranches of stock directly to favoured clients without dealing through the stock markets. Because of London's position at the centre of the world time zone, most of this business was conducted there. Goodison approached ISRO and suggested that sooner or later some form of ordered regulation for the conduct of global equity markets would be forced on it, if it did not form an international standard of its own; and since the London Stock Exchange offered the nearest thing to such a standard, why not merge with it?

For the Stock Exchange the attraction of a deal averted the possibility of the world's financial giants setting up a competing marketplace in London.

On 12 November 1986, members of the Stock Exchange voted for the merger, and the combined body became known as the International Stock Exchange of the United Kingdom and Northern Ireland. The old guard knew there was no choice – the new Exchange was going to be dominated by foreigners, but so what? The previous changes they had approved had already allowed foreign financial houses to take over two thirds of large British broking firms, and so domination by the likes of Citicorp, American Express, Deutsche Bank, Merrill Lynch, Nomura and the Swiss Banking Corporation was anyway inevitable. There was also a sweetener of £10,000 for each member when they retired or reached the age of sixty.

The New Conglomerates

The establishment of giant new conglomerates which accompanied Big Bang led to an undignified scramble as City and international broking firms, banks and finance houses rushed to jump into bed with each other. So unseemly was the haste that some parted company with new-found, if expensive, friends within days rather than weeks, in a kind of financial promiscuity which must have left old faithfuls gasping for breath. One major bank bought a firm of jobbers only to find that, by the time the ink was dry on the contract, the best people had all left en masse to join a rival. Since these people had been almost the firm's only asset, the acquisition was more or less worthless. The Deputy Governor of the Bank of England, George Blunden, put his finger on the problem:

> If key staff – and on occasions whole teams – can be offered inducements to move suddenly from one institution to another it becomes very difficult for any bank to rely on the commitment

individuals will give to implementing its plans, and adds a further dimension of risk to any bank which is building its strategy largely around a few individuals' skills.[6]

The banks and merchant banks were the predators, but they found even the very large broking firms only too willing to submit. Typical of the alliances formed was Barclays de Zoete Wedd, a merger between the investment banking side of Barclays Bank, the stock-brokers de Zoete and Bevan, and London's largest stockjobber in gilt-edged securities, Wedd, Durlacher & Mordaunt. Barclays became top dog, owning 75 per cent of the shares, but by the end of the decade had sold a big chunk of the business. Another group was Mercury Asset Management, formed by S.G. Warburg and Co. and three major broking and jobbing firms. Each of these two giants was able to issue securities, to place them with its large client base, and to buy and sell speculatively on its own account. MAM survived only one decade before being gobbled up by the world's largest securities business, Merrill Lynch.

All but one of Britain's top twenty broking and jobbing houses were absorbed into large new financial conglomerates. Among the leading firms, only Cazenove and Co. remained independent, a status it retained until 2005. The City's oldest broker, whose clients have included the Queen, ended 182 years of independence to merge with J.P. Morgan, the US bank.

The newly created megagroups were able to act as bankers to a corporation, raise long-term capital for it through debt or equity, make a market in its shares, retail them to investors, and buy them as managers of discretionary funds. The question at the time was how the public could be sure that those at the marketing end of the firm were not privy to insider information, and, if they were, how they could be prevented from acting upon it. Sensitive information does not, of course, have to be in written form in a report. A nudge and a wink over lunch is a more subtle and less detectable way of passing secrets. The official Stock Exchange answer to this problem was that 'Chinese Walls' had to be erected between the various parts of a financial services company, so that the interest of the public or investors would always be put first. Whether this has happened is still open to debate.

The arrival of the new monoliths badly upset the staid City career

---

[6] George Blunden, speech given at Mansion House.

structure. Salaries rocketed as a game of musical chairs for all but the most mundane jobs got under way. Staffs of merchant banks and broking firms, whose only regular bright spot had previously been the annual bonus payment, suddenly found, to their wonderment, that they had taken over from soccer professionals as the group in society most likely to be able to bid up earnings without lifting their game. 'The trick,' one twenty-six-year-old woman employed by a Swiss bank told me, 'is to always appear to be in demand. If they think you are about to leave, they will offer more without you having to ask for it.'

One might have expected the level of poaching to diminish over time. But more than ten years after Big Bang, generous offers were still being made to whole teams of analysts. One of those to suffer worst was Deutsche Morgan Grenfell, an institution formed out of an alliance between one of London's oldest firms and the powerful Deutsche Bank. In 1997 it lost its entire four-person emerging market bond team to the Japanese group Daiwa Europe. In the same month its deputy chairman, Peter Cadbury, responsible for some of Morgan Grenfell's most important relationships, left to become joint chairman of a large corporate finance institution.

Some of the individuals involved cut a very high profile, none more so than Nicola Horlick, mother-of-five from London, who made the headlines when she parted company with Deutsche Morgan Grenfell after being seen having lunch with senior officers from another company. It was alleged that she was planning to leave the company, for whom her team had quadrupled the value of the funds under management, a suggestion she strenuously denied. But within six months, after a series of tear-jerking stories in the tabloids about how as a woman in the City she had been 'picked on', she was leaving her £3 million home shortly after dawn each morning for a new job at DMG's deadly rivals, the French-owned Société Générale Asset Management. She was joined there by an old friend, John Richards, who had been on 'gardening leave', a euphemism for sitting at home doing nothing, after resigning as head of institutional investment management at another rival, Mercury Asset Management. Horlick's lifestyle, her £1 million plus a year income package and her huge responsibilities led to her being dubbed 'superwoman', a highly sexist remark because no one would ascribe the title 'superman' to a male with comparable responsibilities. On the other hand, few would agree with Nicola Horlick's own description of herself as 'an ordinary person doing an ordinary job'.

Another high-profile defection took place in 1999 when ABN Amro, the Dutch international banking group, lost its entire top-ranking banking research team to rival Morgan Stanley. For ABN Amro it was an unhappy year, for it had already seen the head of its oils team, and its entire pharmaceuticals team walk out. ABN Amro was philosophical. 'This is just part of the natural ebb and flow of analysts,' the company said.

Such is the new City: highly competitive, and with little loyalty.

Along with a move towards a superleague of financial conglomerates came another switch of attitudes – an obsession with short-term performance. It has become clear that fund managers – the men and women who manage the money in pension funds, life assurance companies and unit trusts – are no longer prepared to play safe by concentrating investments in large holdings in giant but dull corporations. The marketing men began to demand performance, as measured by league tables appearing regularly in the financial press. Fund managers' huge bonuses depended on achieving good returns. Not so long ago the average institutional investor shared his portfolio between government gilt-edged securities (interest-bearing bonds) and blue-chip equities (shares in well-known companies like Unilever, BP and ICI).

3   Shares, Bonds and Other Paper

It's paper anyway. It was paper when we started and it's paper now.

Sam Moore Walton, founder of Wal-Mart

When stocks go down, shoeshine goes down. It's rough.

Wall Street shoe cleaner

Risks are explicit, and well priced. The skills of the bookmaker have proved more reliable than those of the banker.

Anthony Harris, *The Times*

From time to time television newscasters tell us in their staccato, headline style that billions of pounds – or dollars, yen or euros – have been wiped off the value of shares. To most ordinary people, such stories are meaningless; since they are inclined to believe that shares are not for them and they do not take much interest. The minority of viewers who are financially literate may pause to ponder why BP or BT are worth millions of pounds more or less today than yesterday, but will then shift their attention elsewhere. The broadcasters, adopting their self-styled mission to explain, never let such stories pass without interpretation, sometimes plausible but often wrong. They frequently take the opinions of a young market analysts, rarely slow to offer opinions and once described contemptuously by a former Chancellor of the Exchequer, Nigel Lawson, as 'teenage scribblers'. So what are shares really worth?

Each share represents a tiny but equal percentage of a company. The actual value of a company whose stock is listed on an exchange will *always* be the price of each share at any given time multiplied by the number of shares in existence. A large company's value is not determined in the same way as the wealth of an individual. When an individual applies for a mortgage, the lender assesses his or her net worth by aggregating his assets and deducting from that sum his liabilities. Perform the same operation with a company, and you get its net asset value – or NAV. Divide that by the number of shares, and you get NAV per share. Neither figure is *real* value. Real value depends not on the assets-less-liabilities equation, but on the day-to-day perception of the market.

Often this real value seems illogical, especially when share prices appear to bear little relationship to the company's sales performance, or to the profit-and-loss account. Employees who see colleagues being made redundant at a time when share prices are at an all-time high are perplexed. This perplexity can turn to anger when they see their bosses reaping large bonuses when the share value is slumping.

But this lack of logic is what makes the stock markets fascinating. There are many reasons why shares move up and down, and here are some of them, starting with the obvious:

1. **The company is doing badly**. If a company has a poor year, as did Sainsbury's recently in the period prior to the departure of Sir Peter Davis, then the share price will fall. But remember that share price always reflects perception, or at least the investors' collective view as to where the company is going. If the market thinks a new chief will get it right, prices will rise. The market looks ahead. Much the same happened to Marks and Spencer in the same year. M&S was once a favourite share in many people's portfolios, but fell from grace when the perception of the company changed to the view that its fashions were stale, its goods too pricey and its buyers out of touch with the market.

2. **The company may be doing fine, but there is unease about the general direction of the economy and interest rates**. Frequently the market as a whole is unnerved by the prospects ahead. This could be because interest rates are believed to be on the rise, or because of a variety of global and regional economic factors which affect investor sentiment. Few shares move against a very significant downward trend in global markets, such as the world stock market crash of 1987, the Asian crash of 1998 or the bear market of 2001.

3. **The company has bold and strong leadership, which seems to know where it is going**. This has certainly been the case with many well-led large American companies, such as General Electric, headed until 2001 by the redoubtable Jack Welch; Apple, controlled by Steve Jobs; Michael Dell's Dell Computer, and Intel, inspired by Andy Grove. These high-profile personalities add an extra dimension to their corporations, and investors have faith in their leadership skills

and management philosophies. Welch, for example, held the belief that GE should be either number one or number two in each sector in which it operated, or out of it altogether. Conversely, a company which appears to have weak leaders who lack strategic direction will lose investor support, and shares will fall. Such was the case with BT and Marconi in 2001.

4. The government may interfere with the company. Gone are the days when many large companies were in danger of being compulsorily acquired by the state. The march of privatisation has meant that governments have been busy divesting themselves of businesses. But governments love to interfere, and often pass legislation which will disadvantage some companies. Or government-appointed regulators tighten controls – and limit profits – of near-monopolies like British Telecom and British Gas. In Britain in 2000, strong government intervention in the affairs of Railtrack after two serious railway accidents depressed share prices and finally led to its collapse.

5. The shares are in a sector that is trendy. Once a sector has caught on as fashionable, sometimes the whole sector picks up investor enthusiasm, whatever the fundamentals may say. This happened with internet stocks in the mid to late 1990s, when many companies that had never turned a profit suddenly built market capitalisations running into billions of dollars or pounds. Even though the companies' backers produced statements making it clear that profits could be some years away, investors, both large and small, piled in, creating vastly inflated values. Perhaps the best example was the on-line bookseller amazon.com, formed to sell books and other goods at a modest discount to shop prices, with one attraction being that it could almost always deliver the book you wanted within a few days. At one point during the dotcom hysteria its market value rose to more than $1.5 billion, making it apparently worth more than some long-established successful corporations like Ford or Proctor & Gamble. On the eastern side of the Atlantic there was Freeserve, an internet service provider set up by Dixons, the high street retailer. Freeserve's product was far from exceptional in terms of both technology and service, yet when it was floated off by Dixons at a well-chosen moment, its share price outstripped that of its parent.

All these internet 'stars' were hyped in the media, none more so than lastminute.com, whose co-founder Martha Lane Fox developed a star quality of her own. The idea behind the company was a good one: it would provide anything anyone needed at the last minute – a holiday, an airline seat, a theatre ticket. Yet like many other internet stocks, lastminute.com became a 'ninety per center', before starting a long and slow recovery. When sanity returned to the markets and analysts started applying the normal rules of accountancy to valuations, there was a huge drop in prices, and many companies vanished from the scene as quickly as they had risen.

6. **Investment gurus like certain companies.** There are a number of well-known investment gurus whose investment and speculative skills have helped them to become multi-millionaires. These men include Warren Buffett, Henry Kaufmann, George Soros, Peter Lynch and Ron Brierley. All have a strong following, and when they act in the market, it sets a trend.

7. **Competition may be so tough that profits are hard to foresee.** There is such fierce price competition in some sectors that the companies' margins are always under threat. In Britain this is true of the food supermarket sector, where well-run companies like Tesco offer safe rather than spectacular share price growth, and therefore can be unappealing to the investor looking for above average returns. Worldwide airlines fall into the same category. There is so much capacity – seats in search of a bottom on them – that air fares are too low to produce good yields.

8. **The company makes a major miscalculation.** Anyone can make mistakes, but sometimes the biggest blunders can be made by highly paid managements, often advised by well-rewarded management consultants. Usually the errors are as a result of strategic decisions. The former BBC Director-General, Greg Dyke, used to say to his team: 'Don't tell me you want to do something for strategic reasons, because I know then it will lose money.' It was for strategic reasons that BT, Vodacom and other companies overbid for third-generation telecoms licences, which loaded them with crippling debt and led, in one case, to the company being broken up. Marks and Spencer, mentioned earlier, adopted a new strategy designed to appeal to younger buyers, but ended up upsetting their traditional customers while failing to attract new ones.

9. **The company has been talked up in public relations campaigns.** Many companies employ investor relations managers or public

relations consultants to put a favourable spin on their activities in order to keep share prices high. A high share price – with the resultant high market capitalisation – makes a company less vulnerable to takeover, and therefore leaves the executives in charge feeling more secure. It also boosts the value of their own stock options. Watch for profiles of chairmen and chief executives that are 'placed' in newspaper feature pages to enable them to talk up the company.

10. **The company may be under family control**. Families sometimes have motives which go beyond profit. A company may be a way of life. The Dow Jones Company, which publishes the excellent *Wall Street Journal*, has been criticised by shareholders for paying more attention to style than earnings. Family ownership tends to cause particularly severe problems in media corporations, where wilful and strange decisions are often taken. A power-hungry media mogul may overpay to acquire another prestigious title, for reasons of ego as much as anything else. When Rupert Murdoch bought the *New York Post* from Dorothy Schiff it lost money, and has been leaking dollars ever since. But it was the only New York daily available, and Murdoch enjoyed owning it, even if it benefited the shareholders little. Much the same could be said of his acquisition of *The Times* in London. News Corporation is also not renowned for paying generous dividends; the Murdoch family don't need the money, which would be taxable, and prefer to continue to risk it in the business. In Australia a scion of the Fairfax family seriously mismanaged the *Sydney Morning Herald*, until new shareholders provided new management. There are also problems of succession to consider in companies where a family is the principal shareholder. Many companies survive one or two generations, but not many go beyond three, for there are usually too many grandchildren to fight over the spoils or the jobs.

DERIVATIVES

You will not hear about them on the television news, read about them in the tabloids, or learn about them in the classroom, but derivatives are now a major and growing part of the British and global stock markets. They are what their name suggests – securities that derive their value from other investments, which may be something tangible like a share or a bond, or something much more complex, like the global considered view of where British or American interest rates will be in six months time.

While derivatives are mostly traded by professionals, there is nothing to stop individuals buying and selling them, and most of us do it indirectly as they are widely used by investment management groups that manage our pooled savings.

There are many types of derivative, and at this point we will consider the most significant; a detailed study would require a 1,000 page manual.

Gilts or Bonds

Gilts is short for gilt-edged securities, better known outside the UK as Bonds. These are units of a loan tranche issued by the government to fund its spending. Gilts are issued for a fixed term at a fixed rate of interest, though no one is obligated to hold them for the whole period. But, like all fixed interest securities they offer the holder the security of regular interest payments, as well as repayment at maturity of the amount borrowed.

There are three types of gilts traded. Those with five years or less to run until redemption are known as shorts; those with a redemption period of between five and fifteen years are mediums, while longs are those stocks with a redemption date of more than fifteen years.

In the United States the equivalent bonds are known as Treasuries – because they are issued by the United States Treasury. Treasuries, particularly long bonds, have been popular over the years with Japanese investors, who have taken the risk that the rate of return in dollars will be greater than the decline of the dollar against the yen.

Corporate Bonds

Corporate bonds are very similar. They are generally issued by very large companies, and are IOUs which promise to pay those who hold them an annual rate of interest during the life of the bond, and then to repay the money in full at the end of the fixed term specified in the bond. Like gilts or government bonds, the interest stays the same throughout the term, but since general interest rates move up and down, the actual value of the bond will do the same. If general interest rates rise, making the rate on the corporate bond less attractive, then its value will fall, and vice versa.

Let me explain this further with a simple example. A company sells an issue of 8 per cent bonds at £100 each. That means holders will get £8 every year for each bond they own, so the yield is 8 per cent. Interest rates go up, and the price of the bond on the stock market falls to £93, reflecting the fact that its return is less attractive to the investor. If the original holder wants to switch investments and get out, he will only get £93 for each £100 bond he holds. On the other hand, someone buying the bonds at £93 each will still get the £8 per unit interest, and that means the yield is 8.6 per cent. If the purchaser holds on until the bond matures, he will also get the original value of £100 per bond, which means he will make a £7 profit on each unit.

Corporate bonds are less safe than gilts because they do not have the guarantee of a government. But they are much safer than equities. The company issuing the bonds must pay the yearly interest on them in good times and bad, and before it pays a penny in dividends to shareholders. Even if a company goes into receivership, bond holders will get their money before anything is paid to shareholders.

Corporate bond prices are also more affected by general interest rate rises than they are by the performance of the company. If a company's share price plunges, it does not mean that the corporate bond value will change, even if its equity falls. Only if the company looks like becoming insolvent, and being forced to default on its debt, would this become a problem. That means there are degrees of risk, which became only too clear after the terrorist attack on the World Trade Center on 11 September 2001. A food company like Unilever or a retailer like Tesco saw shares slip, but were still financially sound. On the other hand many airlines, including British Airways, lost a large percentage of their business and, burdened with debt to pay for aircraft, were financially compromised.

Although it is possible to buy some bonds on the stock markets, most traders are big institutions, because the minimum dealing level tends to be high. Many minimum lot sizes are as high as 10,000, which would mean that a purchase could not, for example, be put in an ISA (Individual Savings Account). This is unfortunate, and another example of market discrimination against small investors. Therefore it is usually wisest to get into corporate bonds by subscribing to a corporate bond unit trust or investment trust. That is because the fund manager can afford to buy in volume, and also to spread bond exposure among those who are due to be repaid soon and those who still have many years ahead. This reduces the sensitivity of the fund to interest rate changes.

Details of corporate bond funds can be found on the web site of the Investment Management Association (www.investmentuk.org) and performance tables are published in some of the better investor magazines, such as *Financial Advisor* and *Bloomberg Money*. Details of individual bonds on offer are less easy to find and are readily available only to institutions.

Options

Options are as old as history itself, and mean exactly what the name implies. Phoenician merchants bidding for the opportunity to buy the cargoes of the first ships to arrive in port used to purchase an option to acquire a vessel's contents – in other words, the right to be first in the queue. If the cargo turned out to contain little of any interest or value, the merchant would not exercise the option. Today, a family interested in a new house being built but unable to sell their own property might advance a small sum of money as a three-month option to buy at an agreed value. This would both prevent the developer from selling to anyone else during that period, and also assure the price. But if the option was not exercised, the purchaser would lose the cost of the option.

Options are now highly developed on global stock markets, and for those prepared to risk a little money on speculation, they offer an attractive prospect. Many people have been heard to say: 'I would like to be able to buy shares in BP, ICI, or Microsoft, but their prices are so high I could not possibly afford them.' Leaving aside the loose logic of that statement – for an individual can always buy fifty or even twenty-five shares if he wishes – it is true that the chances of a major capital gain on one of the large and better-known shares are slim.

Options increase opportunity, at a known cost and defined risk. For example, let us say that just before Christmas an individual thinks that a retail group is going to achieve record sales over the holiday, and that the margins on this extra volume will be such as to generate handsome profits for the full year. He fancies risking £5,000 on his theory that the shares will rise. But at 642 pence each his

£5,000 will only buy him 778 shares. Even if the shares rise by £1 to 742 pence, he will only have made a profit of £778, less the broker's commission on both the sale and the purchase, which would bring the profit down to about £650.

By using his £5,000 to buy options he would have done much better. At a cost of 30 pence each, his £5,000 would have bought him 16,666 three month call options – giving him the right to buy the shares at any time during the next three months for the original 642 pence price. If the shares do not go up he does not exercise the option – and loses his £5,000. That's the risk. But if they do in fact rise by £1, as in the previous scenario, he will have made a capital gain of £11,666, (£16,666 less the £5,000 spent for the options).

If the stock is one in which the Stock Exchange runs a traded options market, then the investor has another possibility open to him, and that is to sell the option to another investor. The price of a traded option is decided by two factors: the underlying price of the share itself, and the market's expectations as to which way it will move in the weeks or months ahead. Obviously those operating in the traded options market expect to make a profit, so there is a premium to be paid for selling the unexpired portion of an option rather than sitting it out. But where an investor fears he has made a major misjudgement he can, to some extent, cover a big position by using the traded options market.

Another form of option is the put option, which is the opposite of a call option. A put option is taken out in anticipation of a fall in the value of the relevant share, and gives the owner the option to sell a quantity of shares at a given price. A put option can act as insurance against an investment in ordinary shares falling in value. The profit on a put option could offset any loss in the value of the underlying share.

Information about the prices at which you can buy or sell both call and put options is readily available in the daily newspapers that take investment seriously, such as the *Daily Telegraph* or the *Financial Times* in Britain, or the *Wall Street Journal*. Reproduced below is part of a table from the *Financial Times*. The column on the left lists some of the better known securities in which options are traded. The first numbers column shows the price at which the holder of the option can buy or sell the underlying share at the given dates, listed at the top of the remaining columns. The prices in these columns are the amount that has to be paid per share to obtain the options.

A Typical Option Price Selection from the *Financial Times*

Option		CALLS			PUTS		
		Oct 99	Jan 00	Apr 00	Oct 99	Jan 00	Apr 00
Abbey National	1100	34½	107½	139	19½	77	116½
(*1114)	1150	13	82½	111	48	101½	139
Allied Domecq	550	33	58	74½	1½	19½	29½
(*581)	600	4	31	49	22½	43	53½
Ald Dom ex	330	16	35	47	3½	18	25½
(*342)	360	2½	21½	32½	20	34	41½
Allied Zurich	700	22	60	83	4½	40	51½
(*711½)	750	3½	36½	57½	38½	65½	76½
Astra Zeneca	2800	61½	206	275	32	142	193
(*2827)	2900	18½	156	224	89½	192	241½
BAA	420	34	48	60	½	14½	21½
(*453)	460	6	26	39	12½	33	40
BAT Industries	460	17	45	57½	4½	27	43
(*472)	500	1½	27	39½	29½	49	66½
Barclays	1800	73½	186½	236½	19½	111½	164
(*1851)	1900	23	134	188	69	159	214
Bass	700	30	57½	75½	5	40½	53½
(*724)	750	5½	34	53	31	69	81½
Boots	600	40½	61	80½	1	21	33
(*639)	650	7	34	54½	17½	44½	56
British Airways	300	17½	31	41½	1	16	22
(*316)	530	2	17	27½	15½	32½	37½
BP Amoco	550	20	50	68	5½	30½	46½
(*563)	575	7	37	55	18	42	58½

*Price on date of publication of table

Taking the example of British Airways, the table shows that a call option to buy 1,000 shares at 300 pence in the airline any time between 14 October 1999 and January 2000 may be bought for 31 pence per share. If a longer call option period were required to buy BA at the same price, the option cost per share would be 41.5 pence. A put option for the same dates would, however, cost less – 1 pence and 16 pence per share respectively. These figures indicate that those writing the option – in other words taking the risk – expect BA shares to rise marginally rather than fall.

Writing an option contract – as distinct from buying traded options – is a job for a professional. It reverses the risk of buying and selling an option. Essentially the option writer is taking a gamble that the option will expire worthless, and that he will garner his profit from receiving the put or call money for taking the risk. The job is not unlike that of an insurance underwriter, who charges a premium in the hope that you never make a claim, or not one that is anywhere near the value of the premiums. Just like a risk underwriter, those offering options need a thorough knowledge of the markets and companies concerned. Those who do write options have to deposit cash, called margin money, with their broker as security for the performance of their obligations.

In Britain the concept of investing in options has been slow to catch on among general investors, although it plays a major part in the lives of the professionals. There is no reason for this, other than lack of education about the markets. In the United States, where attitudes are very different, options are booming.

The Chicago Board Options Exchange is the third largest securities market in the United States, after the New York Stock Exchange and NASDAQ, and more than two thirds of those who use it are private investors. It is helped by the attitude of the US regulatory authorities, who are strong supporters of options trading, with the Securities and Exchange Commission arguing that it significantly enhances liquidity and makes for better and more accurate markets.

Europe is catching up. In 1978 there were only two equity options markets in Europe, one in Britain and the other in Holland. Today they are either established or being set up in every advanced country.

In Britain, futures and options are traded on LIFFE, the London International Financial Futures and Options Exchange. Until a few years ago, LIFFE's dealing room underneath the platform of Cannon Street railway station was one of the City's most interesting spectacles, as young men and women dressed in brightly coloured blazers in the livery of their firm traded by shouting and yelling under an auction system. Alas, like the London Stock Exchange, the trading floor is no more, and LIFFE operates through a state-of-the-art electronic dealing platform called LIFFE Connect, accessible from anywhere in the world.

In equities, LIFFE offers option contracts on about one hundred British companies, as well as a number of indices.

If you imagine that by buying options you are sure to win a fortune, be warned by the following remark from Stephen

Figlewski, the Associate Professor of Finance at New York University: 'Small investors lose because they believe their information is better than it really is. They take positions that aren't any better than their beliefs, and their beliefs aren't any better than throwing darts.'

As with other risky investments, it is as well to experiment with notional or paper money before taking the plunge and opening an account with a broker. Another way of trying your hand without getting burnt is to use the trading simulation game thoughtfully provided by LIFFE on its web site (www.liffe.com/usf). This enables you to practise trading in real time, exposing yourself only to embarrassment rather than real financial loss.

A more frequent use for options is as insurance. An investor may believe that a share will rise, but wants to protect himself against a potential fall, so cushions this risk with an option. Or you may have a large bundle of shares that you do not want to unload because of liability to capital gains tax, but fear that they will fall. So you buy options as an insurance against this happening, using a put spread.

There are other forms of share options that are much more familiar to members of the public, those that are available to employees of public companies. These are often, though not exclusively, reserved for executives, and usually allow the employee the right to buy a limited number of shares in the company for which he works once he has completed five years' service. These options are available for nothing, and the price is normally set at a discount of the actual share price at the start of the option period.

Another options scheme involves employees putting their own money into the company they work for through savings for shares. Some far-sighted employers in Britain encourage all employees to join a government-backed scheme that gives tax incentives to companies who promote a long-term saving plan with a building society or bank where the final amount saved is used to buy shares at a low-cost pre-set option price. Unless you work for a company that is on the slide, these are the best form of savings plan available, combining the benefit of regular commitments via a building society with the chance of cashing in on long-term capital appreciation. It is perhaps the only risk-free route to the stock markets. Unfortunately many companies fail to explain these schemes adequately to their workforces; if they did, there would be a much higher percentage of the workforce owning shares.

Futures

If trading in options sounds a little like a casino, it is dull by comparison with the activities on the futures markets. There are futures in everything – commodities like cocoa, coffee, wheat, lead, zinc and gold; meats like beef and pork; currencies like the dollar, the yen, the euro and the pound; and, of course, shares.

Buying futures is speculation, and some people make and lose millions doing it. It requires knowledge of changing circumstances, as well as intuition as to the way events will turn out. If you think that there will be a severe frost in Brazil – or are prepared to bet that this will be so – you may buy six-month coffee futures, in the belief that by the time your coffee is delivered at the end of the period, it will be worth a lot more. Of course you have no intention of taking delivery of the coffee for you would not know where to put it; if the frost comes, the price of your futures contract will rise sharply, and you will sell, and make a profit. If the price falls, you will still sell the coffee delivery to someone who needs it, but at a lower price.

There are, of course, good reasons for buying futures other than speculation. If you are a coffee wholesaler and you fear a cold snap in Brazil, you will buy futures to protect yourself, regarding the extra cost of the contract as an insurance premium. The same is true of the manufacturing industry. If you have ordered an expensive set of machine tools from Germany, due to be delivered in six months' time, you will not want to pay for them until delivery. But supposing the pound falls against the euro in the mean time? You cover yourself by buying the required amount of euro futures. This process is called 'hedging'.

There are futures markets in all the major financial centres, while Chicago has assumed pre-eminence in the trading of commodities.

There has been considerable growth in bond futures, for the increase in the number of gilt-edged market makers has placed a premium on hedging contracts. For instance, a fund manager may know that in three months he will receive cash for investment in gilts, and he has picked long gilts – those maturing in fifteen years' time. Rather than waiting to see what the interest rate will be at that time, he can lock into today's rate by buying LIFFE's long gilts futures contracts for delivery in three months' time. If gilt yields then decline, the investor will have to pay a higher price, but the price of the long gilts futures contracts will have risen, and the fund manager's profits will reduce the effective cost of buying the stock.

There are also futures contracts on most stock market indices. The FTSE 100 futures contract is priced by taking one tenth of the value of the FTSE 100 Share Index published throughout each business day. It may be used by an investment manager concerned that the market will rise before he can place funds becoming available to him.

Dabbling in futures carries a greater risk for private investors than do options. This is because of the greater leverage involved. Investing in commodity futures, in particular, has proved a fatal attraction for many speculators who have wrongly assumed that they can pit their wits against the experts: I do not recommend it. Let me give you an example of how a commodity futures contract works. Suppose coffee for delivery three months from now is trading in London at $900 per tonne. A speculator buying ten tonnes will have coffee worth $9,000, but will have to pay only a 10 per cent deposit for a contract providing for delivery at the end of the quarter. The speculator does not, of course, take delivery. If the price goes up to $1,000 a tonne, he sells the contract and takes a handsome profit of $1,000. Although the coffee price has gone up only a little over 10 per cent, his return on capital is well over 100 per cent. But if coffee goes down to $810, he will be obliged to buy the coffee at the agreed price of $900, and then sell it again before delivery at its lower market rate. The loss would probably more than wipe out his deposit; in other words, he would have lost his bet.

Many people imagine that they can follow stories in newspapers and on the wires and second-guess what tropical storms or frost will do to coffee prices. They are much mistaken. The professional buyers, working for companies like Nestlé, Costa and Starbucks, have agents on the plantations and know exactly what the crop will be. My guess is that anyone seriously interested in trading futures will probably not be reading this book.

Warrants

When you buy a warrant you acquire a piece of paper or security – which usually you never see as it is held electronically like an airline E-ticket – which gives you the right to buy or sell a related security at some later date. A warrant only has a limited life, and when that time expires it has no value whatsoever. It is like an option, but issued for a longer period and by a business authorised to issue them.

At its most simple you could, for example, buy a warrant to allow you to buy 1,000 shares in company A at a specified future date, or perhaps at any time prior to that date, for a specified price. If the share price of the company rises well above the exercise price of the warrant, a substantial capital gain may be made, or the shares may be held, having effectively been bought at a discount.

Take the example of a share priced at £20, with a warrant available to buy the share at this price two years hence. Buying 1,000 shares would cost £20,000, but the warrant might be available for £3, so you would outlay only £3,000. If, on the expiry date two years later, the share price has risen to £30 you would have to pay £30,000 plus commission on the open market for 1,000 shares, but by exercising the warrant the total outlay would only be £23,000 (£3,000 for the warrants plus a notional £20,000, which would not have to be paid in cash if you sold the shares immediately). So for an expenditure of £3,000 you would have paid a capital gain of £5,000, a 166 per cent return. Had you bought the actual shares you would have made the same gain, but only after outlaying £20,000, with a loss of the use of the money or interest. The gain would only be 25 per cent. Of course had the price of the underlying share fallen over the two-year period, the warrant would have been worthless at the exercise date: that represents the risk factor.

It sounds like a gamble, and if you are taking a bet that the underlying share will rise that is exactly what it is. But warrants can be bought giving the holder the right to buy shares at a *lower* price than at the time of issue. Thus someone with a portfolio of BP shares held in the belief they will rise over a two-year period might hedge his bets by buying warrants for the lower price to minimise risk if the shares do not go up.

The securities to which warrants are related do not have to be shares or bonds. They can be groups of shares, such as all those in the FT-100 index, known as FT-100 warrants. These index warrants have an exercise level (the level of the index nominated for the exercise date) and an index point, which is the amount paid out if the index is higher than this level in the case of a call warrant. So if the index multiple is five pence, then that is the amount paid on each warrant for each point the index has risen above the exercise level.

There are what is known as call or put warrants. Call warrants benefit from an upward movement in the underlying instrument; put warrants benefit from a downward trend.

4   Collective Investments

There are many people who do not own a single share, but who have a significant stake in the stock markets, though some of them do not realise it. This is because they have their savings in what are known as collective investments, which include pension funds, unit trusts, life assurance and endowment policies, and a string of 'tax-efficient' investment vehicles such as Individual Savings Accounts and Personal Equity Plans that have been introduced by governments as a way of encouraging people to save more for the future.

The money contributed to these and other forms of collective investments is managed by companies set up solely for this purpose, although some are subsidiaries or associates of large banks and insurers. Together they form the huge fund management industry, whose members are the main players on the world's stock markets. In Britain alone, investment funds under management at the end of 2004 totalled £275 billion. Having control of such a large sum gives fund managers enormous power and huge responsibility.

They can make or break the managements of companies by buying or selling their shares. Equally, bad decisions by fund managers can lead to a reduction in the value of an individual's pensions. There is an increasing bank of rules to prevent reckless or feckless actions, and this issue will be developed later in the book. For now I will review the most common forms of collective investments available to individuals and through which they own shares or bonds, often in blissful ignorance of what takes place in the fund management industry.

Life Assurance

The concept of life assurance is making provision for your dependents after your death. The idea has been refined to provide a method of savings, whereby for premiums over a fixed term a life assurance company will invest your money and return it to you with bonuses at the end of the term, or upon death, if that happens sooner.

These are known as with profits endowment policies, and in the 1950s and 1960s many people were persuaded to take them as part of a mortgage arrangement.

Today more than £300 billion of our savings is tied up in endowments. They are part life assurance and part savings, and were a favourite among financial advisers and insurance brokers because of the high rates of commission – usually 7 per cent – they were able to earn. Rather than taking a simple replacement mortgage, whereby the interest reduces as the capital is repaid, the endowment holder pays interest only, with the whole of the capital repayable from the sum assured when the policy matures.

Money contributed to with-profits policies is invested in bonds, shares and property, but the policy holders do not get to know the details as life assurance companies tend to be secretive. Unlike share holders, who are free to sell their holdings at any time at the market price, an endowment policy holder has little choice but to stay the course, which could be twenty years or more. Policies can be surrendered, but the surrender value is likely to be less than the amount spent. Despite this, one in five savers give the policies up within the first five years. Brokers specialising in used policies will pay a little more than the official surrender value, but they expect to make high margins, not least because endowments are out of fashion and unpopular.

The attraction of endowments to investors took a heavy blow after the mis-selling scandals of the late nineties, when household name life assurance companies were fined heavily for foisting these products on those who could not afford them. Up to three million home-owners found that the policies would not produce enough money to pay off the mortgage – leaving them with a shortfall. What little favour they had was knocked again with the scandal surrounding Equitable Life, which was forced to close its doors to new business, downgrade bonuses and impose exit penalties after a series of decisions which exposed the incompetence of its management. There is not space here to go into the whole sorry Equitable Life saga which has left a stain on the City. Suffice it to say that before anyone entertains a call from a life assurance salesman, they should spend a couple of hours on the internet reading up about it. Better still, just tell the salesman to go away!

It is regrettable that life assurance companies, which, after all, are a core part of the City establishment, have behaved so badly, because the basic principle behind endowment policies is not a bad one. They offer a way of getting returns from the stock market without nail-biting direct exposure to daily fluctuations. They do this through bonuses, which are paid annually based on the performance of the life fund, and of the life company itself. In good years the bonuses are not as high as they could be because money is held in reserve for poor years, when at least a modest bonus is paid. The bonuses are added to the value of the policy, and cannot be taken away. At the end of the policy's term a final or 'terminal' bonus is paid, at the company's discretion. In other words, policy holders are not told why the final bonus is the amount it is, or how the figure is made up.

In 2001 the Treasury commissioned Ron Sandler to look into the savings industry, with a particular focus on with-profits policies. His report, though couched in polite language, was damning. In his introduction he wrote:

> The savings marketplace is generally daunting for the consumer, with much jargon and a vast range of subtly differentiated products. Information on underlying costs and performance is often opaque – or even, in the case of many with-profits products, entirely absent. Consumers rely heavily on advice from inter-mediaries, although they have almost no understanding of the costs of obtaining this, and are unable to gauge its quality. Moreover, the advice itself is often compromised by the incentive effects of commission paid by product providers.

The Chancellor, Gordon Brown, and the chairman of the FSA, Howard Davies, both welcomed the Sandler report, but nothing much has changed for the better.

Unit Trusts

Unit trusts have become an important part of personal investment in Britain. They allow savers to buy into the world's equity markets without staking their money in an individual company. The risk is spread across a wide range of shares, categorised by sector, region, or degree of risk. Putting it another way, they allow individuals to pool their money with others to share the risk. There is a unit trust for everybody, as a scan of the weekend newspapers will show. There are trusts that offer the prospect of capital gain; those that offer income; some that invest only in low-risk government bonds or those of blue-chip companies; those that specialise in technology stocks; and others that back high-risk stocks, often referred to by the euphemism 'recovery' or 'special situations'.

There are trusts for those who will only invest in so called 'ethical' propositions. These eschew stakes in arms and tobacco companies, for example. Companies that conduct animal testing are often considered unethical, but this is a problem because only a small part of a very large corporation may conduct these tests.

There are about 1,970 unit trusts in Britain alone, managed by over 150 separate groups for more than seven million unit holders.[1] Some of the groups are very large. Almost all unit trust management companies, many of them owned by banks or other huge financial groups, operate worldwide, and have special country funds. The most popular are those with portfolios in the United States, Europe and Australia, or the more stable countries of Asia.

A good idea of the range available can be found by looking at the pricing tables in the Saturday editions of *The Times*, the *Daily Telegraph* or the *Financial Times*. The biggest group is Fidelity Investments, which is a subsidiary of the eponymous group head-quartered in Boston, United States. Worldwide it has 20 million investors, with £640 billion under management. In Britain it lists more than 40 unit trusts. Some of these funds have very specific investment goals, such as those that invest in growth in Europe, Japan, the ASEAN region, South East Asia and the United States. There are higher-risk funds, such as American Special Situations, Japan Special Situations, European Opportunities, and one intriguingly named as the UK Aggressive Fund.

Many people still buy unit trusts through brokers, who take a commission, but the industry has stepped up direct marketing through mail shots and the internet. They are taking advantage of government savings schemes, known as ISAs, which allow individuals to save up to £7,000 a year in an approved scheme, and avoid both income tax on dividends and capital gains tax on profits. Some big unit trust groups run what amount to financial supermarkets, offering units in a range of competitors' products as well as their own. Henderson Global Investments, for instance, has a web site called www.ample.com which offers investments from Fidelity, Gartmore, Schroders, M & G and Invesco Perpetual as well as its own.

---

[1] Association of Unit Trusts and Investment Funds, July 2001.

Investment Trusts

Often confused with unit trusts, but different in concept, are investment trusts. Like unit trusts, investment trusts allow the smaller private investor to benefit from having a stake in a large portfolio of widely spread shares. But there the similarity ends. Investment trusts are public companies like any other and their shares are traded on the stock markets.

Instead of making motor cars, running hotels or operating department stores, an investment trust company exists purely and simply to buy and sell shares in other companies, for both short-term speculative gain and long-term capital growth. Those who manage investment trusts are full-time executives responsible to a board of directors, and they buy and sell shares on the world's stock exchanges, exercising their judgement as to what will be a profitable investment. Just like any other public company, they make profits and incur losses, and pay dividends to shareholders. Investment trust executives can borrow against the assets of their companies, and are able to take both a long- and a short-term view of the money entrusted to them. Capital gains on share trading are not distributed in cash but are used to build up portfolios and, through the generosity of the Treasury, escape taxation. This means that the fund manager can realise the profits on the trust's investment at the most opportune time. Trusts can also offset their management charges against tax.

Investment trusts are cheaper to invest in than unit trusts. Every £1,000 invested in unit trusts costs around £50 in an initial management charge. The same amount used to purchase shares in an investment trust would incur less than £30 in stockbroker's commission and government stamp duty. Unit trust managers also charge an annual fee of between 0.75 and 1 per cent for looking after their trusts; investment trust management charges are much lower.

Unlike individual investors, investment trust portfolio managers can take profits without paying tax, and move in and out of companies paying only dealing charges. There is also a very wide choice of funds across many markets and sectors.

So why do average investors not flock to investment trusts? The answer is that unit trusts are well marketed, and designed to appeal to modest investors. Unit trusts are prolific advertisers in the financial press, and therefore get much more than their fair share of space in the editorial columns. By contrast, investment trusts get comparatively little press attention. Newspapers provide free space to unit trusts to publicise their prices, acknowledging it is a public service to do so, but provide only limited price information on investment trusts.

The investment trusts themselves have initiated advertising campaigns, but some of these have been less than impressive, and have not hit home. As one head of an investment trust company put it:

> Investment trusts have been their own worst enemies: the people who run them and the investors who own them realise the large advantage they have over most other forms of savings, but they have been remarkably coy in spreading the good news to a wider audience.[2]

Moreover, unit trusts are, like most life assurance products, sold by middlemen – insurance brokers, financial advisers, even accountants and solicitors – who receive a handsome commission from this form of activity, most of it upfront. With the exception of investment trust savings schemes, there is no commission for intermediaries on investment trusts, who, for the most part, do not recommend them. The 350 or so investment trusts in Britain deserve a place in everyone's savings portfolio, and, in many cases, offer a better return than the average with-profits policy.

Another important difference, seldom understood, between investment trusts and unit trusts is that while the latter tend to be priced according to their net asset value (NAV), investment trusts, like other equities, are valued according to what the market thinks they are worth, which is more often than not below the value of their underlying assets. The assets, of course, are the shares the trusts hold, which can be valued on a daily basis, thereby allowing their NAV to be calculated with the same frequency. Some investment trusts, particularly those with a strong following, trade at a premium. Buying at a discount does not always mean you are getting a bargain, although once the discount is more than 15 per cent, that probably is the case.

Within the investment trust sector are split capital trusts. These trusts, which have a limited life, contain two or more classes of share within them, each with different entitlements for shareholders on wind-up day. The types of shares common within split trusts are:

---

[2] Jeremy Tigue, head of investment trusts at Home and Colonial, on *Bloomberg Money*, April 2001.

- Zero-dividend preference shares. There are no dividends from these securities but a fixed capital return at the end. Their price will be affected by changes in interest rates and bond yields, but they can generally be considered as safe as quality corporate bonds or gilt-edged securities. In effect a zero shareholder gives up the right to any income on his holding in return for a future capital sum.
- Income shares. These are shares of companies that would be in a good high-income unit trust or investment trust.
- Growth shares. These are used to lift the value of the fund on wind-up.

In summary, splits allow investors to mix caution with risk. Zero-dividend shares will protect capital and generate a final income, while warrants will offer the chance of a big gain.

Tracker Funds

Tracker funds operate under both the unit trust and investment trust umbrellas. They enjoyed a surge in popularity during the bull market in the nineties when the stock market indices they track all rose. They mirror the performance of the index they track, and most indices are managed by more than the average managed unit trust, especially when management costs were taken into account. During the first two years of the twenty-first century, however, the story was rather different: indices tumbled by more than the better-managed defensive funds, and those who bought into trackers at the top of the market have lost value.

Managing a fund to follow precisely the path of an index is more a matter of mathematics than judgement, so costs should be less, but not all tracker funds are run in the same way. Some of the funds that track the FTSE 100, for example, hold all of the stocks that make up this index, in proportion to their strength in the index. This is called full replication, and should provide a line graph which is exactly the same as that on the FTSE. Others work more like an opinion poll, taking a representative sample in the hope that it will mimic the index.

There is another complication. Investors are happy when a tracker fund follows an index sharply up, but in a falling market would prefer that it falls less steeply. Some tracker funds use judgemental and technical skills to avoid the drop, for example selling stocks that look likely to be serious casualties of a recession. An example of the use of a technical tool would be identifying stocks which, because of their steadily falling market capitalisation, are likely to drop out of an index like the FTSE 100. Once gone, their prices tend to fall, if only because all the funds using the full replication technique will sell, so the astute manager will anticipate their departure and offload them. Conversely, stocks likely to replace them in the FTSE could be bought ahead of their entry.

Anyone considering a tracker should enquire about the tracking methods used, and, above all, consider the charges, which vary from a low of 0.3 per cent annually to a high of just under 1.5 per cent, which is extortionate for the amount of work involved.

Fund of Funds

Another concept is the fund of funds, designed to minimise risk for the small investor and to remove him one stage further from direct purchases of shares. Instead of having to pick and choose between many hundreds of unit trusts, the investor can buy units in a master fund, which in turn will buy units in one or more of its subsidiary funds. From the point of view of someone with a small amount of capital to invest – but no clear idea if and when to move out of a British equity trust and into a Japanese, German or American one – the fund of funds seems no bad idea. Let someone else do the worrying and save yourself the expense of having a stockbroker to manage a portfolio of unit trusts.

Like most bright ideas, the notion is not a new one, and has had to live down a bad reputation. Funds of funds first obtained notoriety as a result of the exposure back in 1962 of the international investment swindler Bernie Cornfeld, whose misdeeds are well spelt out in a brilliant book, *Do You Sincerely Want To Be Rich?*, by Charles Raw, Bruce Page and Godfrey Hodgson. This cautionary tale should be required reading for both investors and all those involved in the financial services industry. As the authors said:

> The salesman's rationale for the Fund of Funds was an unusually owlish piece of nonsense – one of those things that sounds impressive until you really think it through. Mutual funds, and all investment concerns, are sold on the proposition that the ordinary man needs investment advisers to make choices for him.

The Fund of Funds went further and suggested that the ordinary
man now needed professionals to choose the professionals who
would make the choices. The Fund of Funds would take your
money, and invest it in other mutual funds – but only in those
whose values were rising most rapidly.

A lawyer from the US Securities and Exchange Commission
exploded the fund of funds argument succinctly: 'If funds of funds
are permitted to proliferate, how would an investor decide among the
many companies seeking his investment dollar? Would he not need a
fund of funds of funds to make this decision?'

Cornfeld's Fund of Funds, run by his Investors Overseas Services
and given the hard sell by thousands of salesmen calling themselves
'financial counsellors', gathered in $100 million of people's savings
within two years of its launch. The customer's money was transferred
immediately into separate proprietary funds, for a brokerage fee
which was pocketed by IOS. For the privilege of investing at all, the
customer had to pay what has become known as a 'front-end load',
much of which went in commission to the salesman who had
persuaded him to part with his money in the first place. For every
$3,000 invested in Cornfeld's Fund of Funds, $540 vanished
immediately in fees. A further 10 per cent of any income generated
also went in fees, as did 10 per cent of any capital gain. According to
Raw, Page and Hodgson, an investor had to wait six years before he
could even get his money out without loss. An investigation found
that money which was supposed to be held on trust for customers
was being used for the benefit of IOS itself, its directors, employees
and friends; and that the IOS sales force was engaging in illegal
currency transactions on a major scale, and constantly misrepre-
senting the investment performance of its largest fund.

The shock waves that surrounded the fall of IOS were such that the
British government introduced strict new rules. An approved fund of
funds is restricted in its investments to its manager's own unit trusts,
in total contrast with the United States, where master funds may
invest in anything but their own in-house trusts. A new fund of funds
must also be in a group holding at least four subsidiary trusts, and
not more than 50 per cent of assets can be invested in any one of
them.

These restrictions have narrowed the options, but one area where
the fund of funds concept has continued to flourish is in investment
trusts. There are several investment trusts whose *raison d'être* is to

take shareholdings in other investment trusts. Instead of having to pick stocks for income or performance, a fund of funds unit or investment trust can pick off the best-performing and cheapest trusts, and buy and sell at discount prices.

In recent years the more reputable fund management groups have turned the argument against these vehicles on its head by giving investors a free hand to decide for themselves when they wish to switch from one type of inner fund to another. For instance, someone approaching retirement may decide to switch out of a growth fund and into one offering higher income. Here advantages come into play, because if the investor switching funds was not in a fund of funds he or she would have to realise gains from one fund, pay capital gains tax of up to 40 per cent, and buy into another, paying stamp duty along the way. Though a sensible move in investment terms, it would decimate his savings. With a fund of funds the transfer could be carried out for only the charge made by the fund management company. These charges, which can be as much as 2.5 per cent of the value of the fund of funds, are not modest, but they do work out a lot cheaper than paying the taxes.

One problem that may arise is that not all funds within any one group have top-rate managers. A group may have an excellent European income fund manager, but a poor record in Americans. Once you are locked into one group, you cannot do much about that, other than assess the fund managers' overall performance.

Hedge Funds

Hedge funds are the newest and most exciting trend on the stock markets, and operate at the cutting edge of global markets. Because of the complex nature of today's market, many sophisticated investors are turning to hedge funds, which do not depend on the ups and downs of the market for success. There are more than 6,000 hedge funds in the world today managing about $600 billion of assets. These funds are just as likely to make money if the share and bond markets fall; their managers set profit targets and devise techniques to achieve them.

Managers of hedge funds are not as tightly regulated as other stock market based investments, and they have a lot of latitude in managing money under their control. Most of them make extensive use of derivatives like futures and options to get greater leverage, and this leverage is often increased by a significant percentage through heavy borrowings, with the derivatives held used as securities. This means that they have a much greater degree of risk.

One of their most commonly used techniques is short selling, a practice denied to most small shareholders. In a falling market, they sell shares they do not own, buying them back if they can at a lower price, in order to make a profit.

Many people find it hard to understand short selling, so I shall strive to explain it, and apologise to those who find the explanation simplistic. Let us suppose you believe that BP shares, standing at a price of £5.60, are likely to fall. You do not own any BP shares, but nonetheless you place an order to sell 1,000 at 560 pence plus commission. (For the purpose of this calculation I will leave out commission.) This sale realises £5,600, or would do if you had the shares. You have three days to prove that you have the shares; effectively to hand them over to whoever has bought them. You can't. So sometime in the three days you must buy 1,000 BP shares. If the share price has fallen by, say, 30 pence to 530 pence, this will cost you £5,300. But you have sold them for £5,600, so you have made £300 without putting up any money, other than commission. Of course if your prediction was wrong and BP shares rise in the three days to settlement, you will have to pay more, and therefore lose money.

No one would short-sell on such a small trade, but if you are trading in tens of thousands in a falling market there are huge sums to be made. Bloomberg Television has banned its presenters from talking of a bad day on the markets when shares fall, because for hedge funds that have been active in short selling it could be a very good day indeed. Hedge funds borrow money from banks and elsewhere in order to trade in greater volumes – a practice known as leveraging. Your bank manager and mine would not lend us money to do this with stocks, but those of us with mortgages on their homes are in fact adopting a similar technique. Take a 95 per cent mortgage and if the value of the house goes up 10 per cent, you have made a 100 per cent profit on your five per cent investment. Of course if the house falls in value by more than five per cent, you have lost your entire investment, at least in cash terms. Successful leveraging of stock market investment can earn big returns at a considerable risk.

By using borrowed funds and by leveraging the market through derivatives, hedge funds can muster huge funds, known in the trade as a 'wall of money'. When they do this, their activities can be self-fulfilling; if they decide to put a particular stock under pressure – they call it testing the market – there need to be some fairly determined buyers around to stem a fall. This kind of power has made both markets and their regulators uneasy. If their actions create a tsunami effect on the shares of companies that are vulnerable to takeover, the reduction in prices can make them immediately vulnerable to takeover.

But hedge funds are growing ever more popular, and are here to stay, though as yet few people understand their complexities.

PART II

The Players and their Markets

Each day, across the world, the markets link thousands of buyers, sellers and traders. All of them have a single goal – to make money. Unfortunately, it does not quite work like that.

5   The Big Institutions

Save a little money each month, and at the end of the year you'll be surprised at how little you have.

Ernest Haskins

If all the rich people in the world divided up their money among themselves, they would not have enough to go round.

Christina Stead

However strong the rise of share ownership in the past 25 years, the share buyers with the most clout are the big institutions that operate and control the fund management industry. These groups, many of them multinational monoliths, operate from the financial capitals of the world – New York, London, Frankfurt and Tokyo – and from agreeable cities where there has been a long tradition of fund management, such as Boston, Edinburgh and Sydney.

In Britain this tradition grew out of the life assurance industry, where the millions of pounds garnered in premiums had to be invested prudently against the day when claims had to be paid out.

To assess their power in Britain, you have only to look at who owns the shares in the top 100 companies, which account for over four-fifths of the total value of the United Kingdom stock market. Just under 18 per cent of the shares are held by insurance companies and 16.5 per cent by pension funds. Together they have the most clout.

A detailed study of share ownership in British companies in 2003 showed that just under half (48.7 per cent) with a value of £664 billion was in the hands of institutional investors, compared with only 14.9 per cent worth £203.9 billion owned by individuals.[1] The rest – just over a third – are owned by overseas shareholders. Of the institutional investors, those with the most clout are insurance companies (17.3 per cent), closely followed by pension funds (16.1 per cent). By comparison unit trusts and investment trusts have only small stakes, at just over two per cent each.

---

[1] Office of National Statistics 2004.

In the United States, the proportion of the market controlled by institutions is much the same as in Britain, and the total amount under their control is measured in billions. The top money managers in America manage over $5 trillion for third parties, with pension funds and mutual funds representing the greatest slice.[1]

Some of the pension funds are huge. The largest in Britain is that of BT, with assets of £27 billion, which makes it bigger than the company itself, and all of those in the top ten are valued at more than £10 billion apiece.[2] One of the biggest is the Universities Superannuation Scheme, with £22 billion. Almost all of these and other major pension funds do not manage their own schemes, but contract out to professional fund managers.

Most pension funds are organised as trusts – legal vehicles which are independent of the company whose pensions they manage. Trustees are part-timers and often have no experience whatever of investment matters; therefore they are not usually competent to make a judgement on the quality of the fund managers they have contracted. In 2001 Paul Myners completed a study into the way institutional investors work, particularly their decision-making process. He was asked by Gordon Brown, the Chancellor of the Exchequer, specifically to address the Government's concern that the big institutions may have an overwhelming focus on quoted equities and bonds, and avoid investing in small and medium-size businesses. The results of the study are outlined in the Myners Report which is well worth reading, as it points out many flaws in the savings industry. As Myners said when delivering the report:

> In the world we now face, an ever-higher premium is likely to be placed on efficiency and flexibility. The review's conclusion is that our present structures fall short on both counts.[3]

A survey conducted for the Myners inquiry came up with these worrying conclusions:

> Many trustees currently bring very limited time and expertise to their investment responsibilities. 62 per cent of those surveyed had no investment qualifications; 26 per cent received less than one day's training when they first became trustees, and 69 per

---

[1] New York Stock Exchange Factbook, 2004.
[2] National Association of Pension Funds Yearbook, 2001.
[3] Letter from Paul Myners to Chancellor of the Exchequer, 6 March 2001.

cent received two days or less. 54 per cent said they had no investment committee or in-house professionals to help them in investment matters; and 49 per cent of trustees spend three hours or less preparing for pension investment matters before a trustee meeting.

The results also suggest that most trustees do not have extensive knowledge of investment issues, and in particular do not have detailed knowledge of issues relating to their own funds. Of funds with a scheme-specific benchmark, 23 per cent of trustees said they did not know what their benchmark was.[4]

In other words, the people who are charged with looking after the future incomes of tens of thousands of British people do not have much of a clue as to what they are doing! Amateurism appears in various guises in British life, but when so many people's future incomes are dependent on their pensions, it is surprising that the Myners report did not produce a great outcry.

Insurance companies and pensions funds have interesting characteristics, for a number of them are not themselves publicly quoted corporations seeking to make profits for their shareholders, but mutual societies, owned and apparently operated for the benefit of policy holders; in other words, the customers. An even greater number used to be mutuals, but have opted to change their status in recent years: examples include Norwich Union, now Aviva; Standard Life; Clerical Medical; and Legal and General, now owned by Lloyds TSB.

Pension funds have the paramount objective of providing a retirement income in old age to those who have contributed either through their own payments or through payments made by employers. Risky investments must be avoided, or limited to a small proportion of the funds under management.

Generally there are two types of pension scheme – those that offer a pension amounting to a proportion of final salary based on years of service, and those that build up a money fund which is reinvested at retirement time to provide income. In the event of the first type of pension fund failing to provide the percentages of income pledged by employers, the employer has to make up the difference, so will obviously look for a pensions provider that can perform well and therefore avoid this unhappy eventuality. In recent years a great many big companies have abandoned these final salary schemes because of the costs involved.

---

[4] Report to the Treasury by Paul Myners, 2001.

With money-based funds, it is the contributor, or future pensioner, who bears the risk of poor performance, and his or her plight is made much worse by outmoded rules which usually require that the greater proportion of the fund be invested in an annuity upon retirement. With an annuity the value of a fund is handed over to a life assurance company, which pockets it and pays out a taxable annual income until death, at which point the capital becomes the property of the assurer, not the family of the deceased. Annuities tend to be very poor investments.

In the last two decades, there has been a shift to money-based schemes, even though they are less advantageous to employees likely to stick with one company. The argument for money-based schemes is that they are more portable, and in an age when lifetime employment in one company has become improbable, it is not surprising that employers prefer a system which for them provides a much lower-cost alternative.

Because of the need for prudence, most pension funds, including those run purely for the benefit of trades unions, buy stocks and bonds across a broad spectrum, preferring a diversified portfolio to excessive concentration in one or two stocks, or venturing into speculative projects or companies based in countries with weak or unsuccessful economies. Almost all portfolios include investments in the United States, Europe and the Asia-Pacific region.

Life assurance companies have a similar outlook. Their principal concern is to see that the premium incomes received are invested adequately to meet the eventual pay-out upon death or the end of a term. It is necessary for these huge investors to match their known obligations, calculated through actuarial tables, with investments maturing at the same time. For this reason assurance companies invest heavily in long-dated gilt-edged securities or bonds. Some governments actually insist that institutions like life assurance companies and pension funds, which so often are the beneficiaries of generous tax treatment, allocate a substantial proportion of their investments to government bonds. There is, however, a trend away from such rules. Australia, for instance, has abolished what was known as the 20/30 rule whereby for every $30 invested elsewhere, $20 had to be invested in government bonds. Japan, whose pension funds have colossal clout, has gradually been easing the restrictions which made it difficult for large sums of money to be invested in anything other than Japanese industry.

Life assurance companies have their own professionals running their funds, and also use fund management companies, described later.

Unit Trusts and Investment Trusts

Also under the heading of institutional investors are mutual funds (known in Britain as unit trusts), investment trusts and other managed funds. The products they sell were described earlier. In Britain there are more than 150 separate unit trust groups, but despite this and their high visibility through advertising and editorial exposure in the financial press, they account for only 2.0 per cent of total market capitalisation. Investment trusts have a slightly larger slice, at 2.3 per cent, but the big institutions account for two thirds of their activity.[5]

The Fund Managers

The people who actually decide which shares or bonds should be bought by institutions are fund managers. Many of them work directly for institutions, but, increasingly, a large body of professional fund managers are employed in specialist fund management companies, to whom the work is either contracted out or who work as a sounding board, often making recommendations but not carrying out the purchases or sales.

There are also highly specialist fund management companies, also known as 'boutiques', who concentrate in subject areas such as high-risk stocks, or in geographical areas, such as South Korea or Brazil.

An institution like an insurance company or pension fund will decide on its policy, and may carry out the more routine activities itself, like buying and selling bonds and shares in blue-chip companies. It may wish only to invest a small proportion of its assets outside Britain, or in riskier growth stocks, and because the choice of shares, bonds and funds is so vast it will call on experts, much as a solicitor will use a specialist lawyer for complex work. It would be uneconomical to run everything in-house.

Another reason is an increased emphasis on performance. As the Myners report put it, it was not 'simply about finding a safe pair of

---

[5] Office of National Statistics 2004.

hands to look after pension contributions: institutions focused increasingly on the ability of managers to "beat the market".[6]

The greatest centre for fund management is New York. Britain comes second, with by far the largest asset management industry in Europe, controlling funds of £200 billion. Switzerland is about half this size, and the total of the rest of Europe's fund management is less than that run in Britain. Within the industry there is considerable globalisation. For example, one of Britain's most controversial fund managers, Mercury Asset Management, was sold by S.G. Warburg to Swiss Bank Corporation, who passed it on to the American giant Merrill Lynch, where it has been absorbed into Merrill Lynch Investment Managers. Deutsche Bank owns the UK company Morgan Grenfell. Gartmore has been bought by Nationwide Mutual of the United States, but has kept its grand name.

The industry employs over 25,000 people in Britain alone.[7] Fund management has become one of the country's more important industries, and is a big export earner. The largest groups are in the table below.

Total Funds Under Management Value
Ranked by Value

1	Fidelity Investments	£25,667,364,000
2	Invesco Perpetual	£14,286,132,241
3	Threadneedle Investments	£13,742,545,798
4	Scottish Widows Unit Trusts Managers	£12,986,339,888
5	Legal & General Unit Trust Managers Ltd	£12,342,720,401
6	Schroder Investments Ltd	£10,423,813,955
7	Halifax Investment Fund Managers Ltd	£10,367,752,161
8	M&G Group	£10,147,730,972
9	Henderson Global Investors	£9,541,271,679
10	Mellon Fund Managers	£7,534,788,833
11	Jupiter Unit Trusts Ltd	£7,123,927,532
12	Gartmore Investment Management Plc	£6,735,271,191
13	HSBC Investment Funds (UK) Ltd	£6,059,578,409
14	F & C Fund Management Ltd	£6,052,976,709
15	Morley Investment Services Ltd	£5,873,516,285
16	New Star Asset Management Ltd	£5,800,095,073

---

[6] Report to the Treasury by Paul Myners, 2001.
[7] British Invisibles, Fund Management.

17	Capita Financial Managers Ltd	£5,742,039,186
18	SLTM	£5,648,322,828
19	Prudential Unit Trusts Ltd	£5,305,996,954
20	JP Morgan Fleming Asset Management	£4,979,222,389

Yet there is cause for considerable concern about the future of fund management. Although there are some outstanding fund managers with immense reputations, many of those in the trade are not all that good. This is an industry where success is measured by performance. Another concern is that fund management is becoming significantly more expensive, with the inevitable result that those at the retail end of the business have to charge more for financial products, making them less attractive. The main reason for the higher costs is the very high salaries paid to fund managers, often out of all proportion both to the value they bring and also to those with similar skills working elsewhere. The Myners report found that 'rewards for fund managers have risen at a rate well ahead of that for many other professions, even though profit margins have remained flat'. Other reasons for higher costs include the burden of additional regulation, and better corporate governance.[8]

A combination of these higher costs and less than brilliant performance has led many pensions trustees and other institutional investors to opt for what is called passive management, broadly meaning that computers do many of the jobs of the fund manager. Instead of picking stocks and exercising judgement on when to sell them, passive managers set a goal – for example, tracking the FTSE 100 index or the Dow Jones Industrial Average. They do this by buying every share in the index they are tracking, weighted exactly to each share's position. This is done through software solutions, so the computer takes over, and since there is no need for chartists, analysts or other highly paid specialists, costs are much lower. This style of investment management has become popular, accounting for just under one in four institutional funds. As the Myners report noted:

> Although there is a substantive question as to what index a manager tracks for a given market – and increasingly complex methods of execution have been developed – passive investing is essentially a commodity. Its most significant impact on the market for active investment management has been on fees,

---

[8] PricewaterhouseCoopers, Fire on the Horizon, 2000.

because active managers have had to compete against the availability of the cheap passive product.[9]

But are not the movements in these indices themselves largely the result of the decisions of the active fund managers? Myners agrees there is a concern here.

> As an investment strategy passive investing seeks to free-ride off the more or less efficient capital allocation of active fund managers. As such, it could in principle lead to odd pricing effects. However it would not be legitimate to argue on that basis that institutions should not use it. Their concern is not with the efficiency of the capital markets as a whole, except in so far as this may affect the interests of their beneficiaries. Passive investing is a legitimate strategy for an investor who values its tangible cost advantages over the possibility of achieving additional return through superior stock selection.[10]

Tracker funds built on passive management lost some of their appeal in the bear market that developed at the turn of the millennium, although, of course, for those not invested in them the lower value of the major indices could be seen as a tremendous buying opportunity. Fund management charges are likely to fall towards those levied by passive investment groups, probably to be replaced by a system of basic fees plus sizeable bonuses based on performance. However, experience in the United States, where high fees for outperformance have been tried, has not been wholly successful.

The issue that has to be confronted in Britain is the period of time over which performance is measured. While it is right that the management of a company should receive rewards based on their company's profits, it does not follow that this should be applied to fund managers. If the fund's objective is ten-year growth, then any reward should come when and if this aim is achieved, not if the first year proves to be a good one. Short-term success, while the prevailing paradigm of the City of London, should not enter into it. Unfortunately, many financial institutions treat their fund managers in exactly the same way as Britain's soccer club owners behave towards their team managers: sacking them at an early stage for poor performance.

---

[9] Report to the Treasury by Paul Myners, 2001.
[10] Ibid.

Significant and important though these issues are, they pale beside the question that surrounds the role institutional investors and their fund managers can and should play in the operation of the companies into which they have channelled investments.

Most fund managers or their institutional investor masters have never worked in manufacturing industry, managed a company, hustled for business in an overseas market or designed a robot, a machine tool or a new building. Whether based in London, New York, Tokyo or a handful of other financial centres, they wear grey suits and the introverted look of those who have spent too long staring at spreadsheets and annual reports. They take themselves, and their jobs, seriously. Hardly a working day passes when they are not meeting with directors or managers of companies in which they have invested. Although they deny that they have a day-to-day influence on managers, they do sometimes step in and wield their power when things go wrong.

Because their institutions can sack boards, determine the outcome of takeover bids and make or break corporations, they have to exercise this power judiciously. They are courted assiduously by corporations anxious for them to maintain or increase their holdings. When Granada mounted a hostile takeover bid for the Trusthouse Forte hotel group in the mid-nineties, Rocco Forte, son of the founder of the group, Lord Forte, ran a huge campaign to attempt to persuade the institutions not to accept the Granada offer. Simultaneously, Granada's Gerry Robinson and his team conducted their own battle for the hearts and minds of the same groups. At the end of the day the vote was close, with one key institution, Mercury Asset Management (now Merrill Lynch), holding sufficient shares to have the casting vote. MAM's fund manager, Carol Galley, cast it in favour of Robinson, sealing the fate of a great family business and ensuring that famous hotels like London's Grosvenor House and the King George V in Paris would lose the individual Forte touch. The unfortunate Rocco gained plenty of cash but lost his business, and had to start from scratch again. Galley was to favour Robinson again when she ended Greg Dyke's career at London Weekend Television by voting in favour of the company's takeover by Granada.

Questions have repeatedly been asked as to whether hard-headed individuals like Galley should have this kind of power, but it is difficult to see an alternative that would work. And there are many who believe that the investment institutions ought to be more interventionist, as discussed in a later chapter on corporate governance.

When it was revealed that some of the management of British Airways had been involved in a shoddy dirty-tricks operation against competitor Virgin Atlantic, some fund management groups complained to the airline's directors. But none of BA's institutional investors went so far as to call for changes in top management, even though there were demands in the media that senior directors should resign.

But this begs the question of who runs companies, and for whose benefit? The British Government of Tony Blair has suggested that business should be run for the benefit of stakeholders. This definition includes shareholders, but also customers and employees. This in itself has raised considerable debate, but also begs the question of who runs businesses – the management or the owners? And if it is ultimately the latter, how well equipped are institutional investors to throw their weight around? This will be discussed later.

6   Private Shareholders

The power to make money is a gift of God.

John D Rockefeller

The world has enough for everyone's needs, but not for everyone's greed.

Mahatma Gandhi

The British people are less keen on owning shares than was the case just before the turn of the century.There are many reasons for this, some more obvious than others. Despite the self-congratulatory nature of the Blair government, Gordon Brown's tenure as Chancellor of the Exchequer has not helped private shareholders, who are taxed when they buy stock and again if and when they sell at a profit. Paying Brown's 'stealth' taxes is bad enough, but almost worse is the amount of time spent keeping records for the Inland Revenue. Both are disincentives to share-ownership, which have taken their toll since the arrival of 'new' Labour.

But taxes and a left-of-centre government are not wholly responsible for the decline. Across the Atlantic in the United States there has also been less activity from small investors. Commissions from share trading on Wall Street fell 64 per cent between 2001 and 2004, leading one analyst to conclude colourfully that trading by private investors was 'in the commode'.

Both in America and Britain the financial services industry has to take some responsibility for the alienation of small investors, by providing poor service at higher cost. Although commissions on share trading have come down, many stockbrokers levy other fees and charges, and investors are penalised for small deals. The first two years of the twenty-first century also saw significant falls in market prices, and some investors did not wait for equities to regain an upward path. They sold out, never to return.

Disillusionment is not confined to people who buy shares directly, for many investors have lost faith in unit trusts and other managed investors, partly because of the high costs, but also because of dreadful performances. Recent studies by the *Investors Chronicle* have shown that private investors who stick to blue chips or bonds and fixed-interest deposits often outperform the City experts.

Internet and telephone brokerages have, as outlined later, made the markets more accessible to private investors, but it has turned them into second-class citizens as a result. By forcing members to use nominee accounts, in which an individual's shares are held by the broker, the private share owner is denied many rights – such as the right to attend and vote at annual meetings, automatic copies of annual reports and access to shareholders' perks as and when they are given.

This is unfair, especially as it is estimated that more than four out of five private shareholders hold their stock in one of these nominee accounts. Being able to check out how their portfolio is doing by going online to the broker's web site is poor compensation for not being treated as a proper shareholder, although some firms will send out an annual report if you ask them, and you can get reports of most companies through a free service provided by the *Financial Times*.

It is bad enough when brokers treat private shareholders as second-class citizens; it is unacceptable when companies do so. A particularly disgraceful episode occurred in early 2005 when a mobile phone company which decided that its nominee shareholders would not be allowed to take the cash option when the company rebranded itself O_2 and offered them the choice between a straight share swap or a five pence premium on the share price. David Blundell, chairman of the UK Shareholders' Association, said the company had forgotten that investors 'are the legal owners, and nominee investors should have the same rights as those with certificates'.

This is another example where UK private shareholders are at a disadvantage compared with their counterparts in the United States – and almost everywhere else. In America nominee shareholders have the same rights as those with certificates.

Lobby groups like Proshare, a City outfit that was formed to promote individual share ownership, have run out of steam. When the last edition of this book came out, Proshare was a lively and vital organisation; it now seems to have lost its energy, and its web site is poorly maintained and often out of date.

Despite this dispiriting trend, just under one in four Britons hold shares, compared with less than one in ten in 1979. Sixteen million people have invested in the British government's tax-efficient ISA schemes, though not all of them are equity related. Given that private share-ownership had been all but wiped out by the disastrous economic policies of the immediate post-war Labour governments, these figures are remarkable. While the initial take-off occurred during the privatisations of the Thatcher government in the early 1980s, a further surge took place when many mutual insurance companies and building societies turned themselves into public corporations, providing windfall shares for their policyholders and members in the process.

Although the percentage of shareholders in many other countries is much greater, Britain is sixth in the league table. Australia, with its fast-growing economy and prosperity, is now top, with just over half the adult community owning shares. Share-ownership in Australia is no longer the preserve of higher income earners and the tertiary educated: a plumber is just as likely to own stock as a lawyer. Australia's rise in individual share-ownership has shaded the United States into second place, where private ownership stands at 50 per cent. Canada is next with 46 per cent, and then there is a big gap to fourth place Switzerland (24), Britain (22), Hong Kong (20), Germany (18), and then South Korea (8).

The example of Australia is particularly interesting, because the Australian Stock Exchange has carried out detailed research into who its individual shareholders are, showing it is actually interested in them! Half the male population owns shares directly, and four out of ten women do so.[1] While the biggest share-owning groups are graduates and postgraduates, 45 per cent of people with trade certificates – plumbers, electricians, carpenters – do so. These private shareholders are not confined to the prosperous leading cities of Sydney and Melbourne, but spread across the nation, with 45 per cent of people living outside the five main cities owning shares directly.

These private investors had a high opinion of both the ASX and their brokers, with 87 per cent holding the belief that the share markets offer 'opportunities for everyone, not just big business and wealthy people'. They also showed prudence. More than half also said that although they liked owning shares, they would never be the major part of investment. And 86 percent said they saw themselves more as investors for the long term than traders. The research also showed that all but a small percentage regularly monitored their investments.

---

[1] Australian Share Ownership Study 2004, ASX.

I can find no evidence of any substantial and comparable and recent study in Britain, which is not surprising since it appears to me both the London Stock Exchange and the City generally have lost interest in individual share-ownership. When setting out to create a nation of shareholders Margaret Thatcher would have rejoiced had Britain gone down the path of Australia. Despite a promising start, this has not occurred, but, as we shall see, that does not mean that the stock market is not at the centre of British life.

Proshare used to run an annual survey of private ownership conducted for them by MORI, the opinion pollsters, which provided a wealth of information. The last of these was published in September 2002 and made fairly depressing reading. It found that trading activity had fallen away to only 3.2 trades per investor per year, citing market turmoil and crashes as the reasons. One factor in the ebbing confidence of private investors was a series of corporate accounting scandals, which left 62 per cent of private investors 'less trusting of all company reports and accounts'.

The survey also reported that the private investor was seeking less information on companies from television, friends and the companies themselves, 'perhaps in an attempt to avoid bad news and because of fewer purchases'. Obviously no one told them about hedge funds, discussed later! Proshare's chief executive concluded that there had been a significant dent in confidence and that private investors were keeping their heads down. Those that did so saw their investments recover and gain ground.

Some private shareholders, of course, have been very successful and ended up in the league tables of the super-rich. There are people like Bill Gates and Rupert Murdoch who are at or near the top of the Forbes 1,000 list of the world's richest people because of their personal holdings in businesses they have built themselves from scratch. There are others who have achieved wealth by using their judgement and astuteness in trading shares in other people's enterprises.

Another phenomenon in individual share-ownership has been the rise in the wealth of senior executives in business, who increasingly are rewarded with stock in their companies as well as in pounds or dollars. High-profile executive directors and managers of major corporations expect to receive considerably in excess of their agreed annual salaries as a matter of routine, and in most cases this is achieved through the issue to them of free executive share options in the companies for which they work.

The stories in the newspapers about exalted earnings for chairmen and chief executives – or multimillion pound pay-offs when they are forced out or 'retired due to ill health' – often fail to report that these share options are now an important ingredient of any manager's employment package. The theory is simple: the better the company does, the more the manager gets. And the better the long-term reward, the less likely he or she will be to resign to join up with a competitor. The level of remuneration that chief executives earn has now become a political issue.

These kinds of share options are not to be confused with those you can buy and sell on the markets, which are discussed elsewhere (see p. 42). They are awarded by the employing corporation, and those lucky enough to be given them get a certificate entitling them to buy up to a specified number of the company's shares at an agreed price after an agreed length of time. Normally, but not necessarily, the price is set close to the share price on the date of issue, and the right to exercise the option kicks in after a period of between three and five years. If during that time the price falls, the options are worthless and are not exercised. The executive gains nothing, but has lost nothing. If the shares rise sharply, there is a handsome paper profit and, if the scheme has Inland Revenue approval, tax is not normally payable on the capital gain until the shares are sold. If it is an 'unapproved' scheme, then capital gains tax is paid on the price on the day the option is exercised, whether the shares are sold or not.

Thus executive share options can be very lucrative, even if you are not responsible for the success of the company. Take the case of a senior executive in Pearson receiving 10,000 share options at the start of the 1990s, with the right to exercise them any time between 1995 and 2000. In 1990 the shares languished around the £2 mark, partly because the British market was still recovering from the 1987–8 crash and also because the company's management at the time was regarded as limp and lacking ambition. By 1998 the old management had gone, and a lively American, Marjorie Scardino, was brought in to refocus the company, whose shares had come out of the doldrums and risen to around the £6 mark. Mrs Scardino pledged to double shareholder value, and by 1999 had done better than that, with a valuation above £13. The executive with 10,000 1990s options could exercise his rights and increase his wealth by £110,000. However, by the autumn of 2001, the shares had fallen back to just above the £6 mark, and stayed at that level.

While the use of executive share options in senior management compensation has grown in Britain, their significance is small when compared to what has happened in the United States, where awards have increased to astonishing levels. Since America tends to set the trend in management rewards, it may be expected that the practice will become universal. According to an executive compensation company, Pearl Meyer and Partners, the compensation of American chief executives climbed 60 per cent to an average of $10.7 million a year from 1996 to 2004. Shares and options form a major part of these packages: in the 200 biggest American companies shares and options for chiefs accounted for just over one eighth of total equity.

Some CEOs do exceptionally well in good years. Merrill Lynch's Stanley O'Neal pulled in $32 million for his performance in 2004, most of it in restricted stock, vested over time, which means he could not cash out immediately. In the same year Morgan Stanley's Philip Purcell saw his reward package rise 45 per cent to $22.5 million. These two, and Goldman Sachs' Henry Paulson and Lehman Brothers' Richard Fuld have each earned more than $100 million during the first five years of the new millennium,

It is a winner-takes-all society, in which chief executives of most businesses get a disproportionate share of revenue, compared with anyone else.

The median bonus for chief executives at 123 companies with revenues of more than $1 billion was $860,000 in 2004, 31 per cent higher than in the previous year, most of the money coming in options. Of course the actual value of these options to executives when the money is vested and they are entitled to sell them is more often than not likely to be several times higher than the issue amount.

There are problems with these kind of mega rewards. One is that the rise in share prices may not be the result of individual effort, but rather be due to a general rise.

Another concern is that the incentives on offer from share options may be so great as to encourage top managers to pursue policies that may not be in the company's long-term best interests. Cutting costs goes straight to the bottom line, thereby improving immediate performance, but it may handicap the opportunities for growth if there are not sufficient trained and skilled workers when you need them. Measures designed to build short-term share value can demoralise employees and damage service levels, as evidenced by British Airways' experience.

It is also likely that chief executives will become predatory in acquiring rival corporations because of the share benefits that will accrue to them if they can swallow another large company. The fact that their corporation may have to borrow heavily to do this is overlooked or even ignored. Against this it is argued that a motivated chief executive is less likely to go in for wasteful corporate extravagances if his reward package depends on shareholder value, and certainly some leaders make a point of practising frugality in headquarters buildings and corporate travel. Others, however, do not, and still display a lust for the trappings of power. There seems to be no clear pattern.

The feel-good factor that these men and women must experience is not necessarily shared by all of those who have to get out of bed each morning to go to work for them.

Yet many ordinary employees do enjoy similar benefits to their bosses, albeit on a much less grand scale. Employee share ownership has been growing rapidly in Britain. There are more than three million Britons participating in employee share schemes run by over 2,000 companies.[2] In the United States there are 10 million workers involved in company share plans, and 16 million people also save money to buy shares at cheap rates in the companies for whom they work. None of these schemes are obligatory. France seems to be the only country, at least in Europe, to have passed a law which dictates that every firm with at least fifty employees must establish a company savings scheme. The law is obligatory on employers, not employees, who have the right to choose not to save in this way, although it appears that almost one in four do so. Perhaps the most lucrative example of company share generosity is Microsoft, which from its early days has had a policy of offering share packages in exchange for lower salaries. In 1996 the shares rose ninety-fold, and this astonishing increase made many employees very rich.

In Britain not all workers are in the type of scheme enjoyed by their bosses, though some are. These favoured schemes allow companies to provide selected employees with the right to buy shares within three and ten years of options being granted at the price prevailing at the time the option was granted, usually referred to as the strike price.

Most employees, however, are in what are called profit-sharing schemes, better known as free shares plans. Under these ingenious plans, companies can reduce their taxable profits by subscribing to a trust fund whose trustees buy shares in the company and distribute

---

[2] Employee Share Ownership Centre, 2005.

them to employees. There are rules, the most important being that membership of such schemes must be open to all employees, both full- and part-time, who have been with the company for at least five years, though many firms accept those with shorter service. Another rule is that employees must be given shares on similar terms. This does not necessary mean an equal number of shares for all, though it can do. More likely is an allocation arrangement based on a percentage of salary.

Less popular but still generous are save-as-you-earn schemes. Here employees are given the right to buy at a future date a limited number of shares in their company at a price fixed when the option is granted. They are then obliged to commit to saving a fixed amount per month with a recognised financial institution, such as a building society, and have to do this for a period of either three years or five years. The least that can be saved is £5 per month and the most £250. At the end of the period employees then have the choice of keeping their savings plus interest, or using them to exercise the options and buy the shares. No tax is payable on the benefit of being able to buy the shares cheap. As with free share schemes, the save-as-you-earn schemes must be open to all employees with five years' service.

Percentage of shareholders by age in employee share schemes

Age group	Percentage
16–34	45
35–44	28
45–54	24
55–64	15
65+	10

Source: Mintel Share Ownership Survey, 1999

Those in employee schemes, however, are overshadowed by private individuals who make their own decisions. They can be found everywhere. When I was a junior reporter my senior colleague was a man who lived extremely modestly in a caravan in the small Norfolk market town of Fakenham. By appearance he was shabby and poor, as befits the image of a district reporter for the local paper. But each day he bought and studied the *Financial Times*, and spent half an hour on the phone to his broker buying and selling shares. By the time he had retired from the *Dereham and Fakenham Times* he had made much more money from the stock market than from his modest pay as a newsman.

Most individual investors are soloists, making their decisions daily, weekly or monthly, based on their own hunches and beliefs. Many take advice from stockbrokers or other financial professionals. Increasingly, though, investors are seeking out like-minded individuals and working together in investment clubs.

Day Traders

A day trader is a speculator or gambler, not an investor, since, as the name implies, shares are bought and sold with a view to making a profit within the trading day. By definition you will never keep any of the shares you have bought.

Many people who call themselves day traders because they buy and sell stocks most days do not fit the description. What they are doing is more like week-by-week trading, in which you attempt to spot an undervalued stock with a view not to keeping it for the long term but to selling it after it has seen a rise of perhaps 10 per cent. If your judgement is wrong and the price falls, you will probably put a stop-loss on it if it drops 10 per cent below the purchase price. A stop-loss is a standing instruction to your stockbroker to sell your shares once they have fallen to a predetermined amount. Using this technique, you will hope to make money by having more gains than losses. The accurate description for this activity is frequent trading. Frequent traders benefit from much lower dealing costs from online brokerages, although they still have to pay the same stamp duty.

Real day trading means never holding shares overnight. Day traders have to pit their wits against professional traders in London, New York and elsewhere, who will have much more sophisticated systems than most individuals can afford. These differences can be overcome if the day trader has the ability to undertake detailed technical analysis and an iron will to take profits when they are there without being greedy for more, and to accept losses before they grow larger. At the end of the day he or she will have bought and sold many stocks or derivatives – sometimes buying and selling the stock several times in large volumes – and the trader will close out positions and take profits or losses.

There are people who have exchanged well-salaried jobs with guaranteed pensions and a company Mercedes to sit at home, wearing jeans and sweater, day trading at a computer terminal. It may beat wearing a suit or commuting on the London Underground, but it can be gruelling in other respects. You need to be able to think mathematically and work systematically. It requires total concentration, an ability to grasp fast-changing situations and, if you have a relationship, an understanding partner. You cannot go out and walk the dog or attend your child's school concert when you have exposed positions on the markets. The core skill is to understand the trend for the day in any given stock or derivative you are following, and then to be able to quantify the degree of resistance to the trend. How much could it rise or fall in the remainder of the trading day? This assessment is made all the harder in that most share price movements take place within minutes of the markets opening, often meaning that the scope for further gain or loss is minimal.

Advice is not hard to come by, and there have been many books devoted to day trading and related activities such as technical analysis and charting. None of them are much of a substitute for hard experience, which should be gained by attention to detail rather than instinct. According to one expert:

> One certainty exists. If you allow your trading decisions to be driven by intuition or gut feelings, then losses will result. Day trading can really be very consuming. You will need to follow the markets on a minute-by-minute basis. As a day trader you will be making trading decisions on your assessment of technical issues, rather than fundamentals that are more relevant to the longer-term investor. Also never lose sight of the fact that you will be competing with professional traders in securities firms and investment banks who will be trading with a greater degree of market information than is available to most other participants, and that electronic trading means you will be devoid of any nuances, feel or flavour of the market.[3]

Long-term day traders say they often buy and sell within a four-minute time span. The most active day traders in the United States deal between 200 and 300 times a day. So those with slow internet access, or no Internet access at all, should not take it up. Anyone serious about starting as a day trader should experiment first before giving up his or her salaried job. A good way of finding out whether you have the ability to make money this way is to conduct notional trades first. You can do this in the evenings using US stocks and

---

[3] John Newman, head of business development, Sweden UK Ltd, 11 May 2001.

derivatives if you have an online account which allows the buying and selling of American stocks. Remember though not to process the trade once you have got the market quotes. Remember also that in the long run it will not be possible to make money using the average online broker for day trading.

Effectively you will need a mini dealing room in your home office. That means investing in a Bloomberg terminal or equivalent that will allow you real-time prices, and access to what is called Level II information. This is the same information the professionals have, an immediate read on how markets in each stock are moving, and an indication of the weight of buyers versus sellers and the prices they are prepared to pay. For those reluctant to invest the £12,000 a year or more that may be necessary, try advfn.com's professional service, which costs a mere £25 a month.

Some day traders do not like the idea of working in isolation or surfing the web with a noisy toddler biting their ankles. There is an alternative, but it means a return to commuting. For the gregarious enterprising frequent trader, some brokers have opened day-trading centres in the City. A seat and a terminal can cost as much as £1200 a month, but you will get the feel that you are working in a real dealing room, great for those dealers who have been made redundant.

Frequent Traders and Short Sellers

Frequent traders buy and sell often, but not every day. Frequent trading can be fun and profitable, and the expansion of online brokerages on the internet has made this activity a possibility in any household equipped with an average computer and internet access. It is possible to be a frequent trader through telephone dealing, but the charges are higher and the services slower and less user-friendly.

Frequent trading would be more popular still if online brokers permitted or encouraged short selling, because this would mean that traders could bet on the price of shares falling as well as rising. Short selling is a technical term that describes the practice of selling a share in the belief that it will fall in price in the near future. You don't need to own the stock to do this. When it does fall you buy the stock back at a lower price, thereby gathering a profit. Since many people seem to find the concept of selling something they do not already own hard to grasp, let me explain with an example.

Gabrielle believes strongly that BT shares are set to fall further, so she sells 2,000 at the quoted price of £4. If she actually owned the shares she would send the certificates to her broker, and within a week would receive a cheque for £8,000 less brokerage commission. But she does not own them, and cannot produce proof of ownership. If, within the three-day settlement period, BT shares fulfil her predictions and fall by 50 pence to £3.50, she will buy the shares back at a cost of £7,000, thereby closing out the contract. She will have made £1,000 profit less commission and stamp duty, and her only cost will be these deductions. Expressed in percentage terms, her profit will be just below 1,000 per cent in less than a week. However, if she is wrong, and the price of BT rises, she will be forced to buy the shares she does not own, pay for them and deliver the certificates. Assuming the price goes up by a similar amount to the previous example of a price fall, she will have lost £1,000 plus commission and stamp duty. In percentage terms the loss, including opportunity costs, will, however, only be about 30 per cent.

When investors trading stocks in Britain had just under two weeks to settle, the risks involved in short selling were significantly less than they are now, with only three days allowed for settlement. Short selling today is a very risky proposition, and one that is increasingly being discouraged by most brokers catering for the private investor.

Saving for Old Age

Young people find saving for old age a yawn, and many of them do not do it, unless persuaded or forced into a company pension scheme. Things tend to change at middle age, when long-term partners and families become a basic part of everyday life. Those with aged parents living in penury because they saved little and became dependent on a government pension collected weekly from the post office have come to realise what retirement might mean, especially if it is forced upon them prematurely through redundancy.

The result has been a rapid growth in personal savings and pension schemes, with most of the monthly savings ending up in a pool of money invested in equities, bonds and unit trusts. Most people have chosen to leave the management of these schemes to professional fund managers, but some manage their own portfolios within tax-efficient mechanisms created by the Government to encourage thrift.

These are ISAs (Individual Savings Accounts), which at the time of writing allow a saver to put away up to £7,000 a year in a savings plan, which is shielded from tax. Equities, bonds or unit trusts sheltered within an ISA are not subject to capital gains tax provided the plan is kept in being for at least five years. Nor is any income tax payable on the dividend or interest generated by the investments, and this revenue may be reinvested in the plan.

Personal pensions are a different concept, although money put into them also ends up being invested on the markets or in property. There are several kinds of personal pensions, but the most important in recent years have been AVCs, personal money schemes and stakeholder pensions.

AVCs
Additional voluntary contributions (AVCs) are mostly for employees who are already in company pension schemes, and who wish to top up their contributions to receive more upon retirement. Most of these schemes are run by company pensions departments, but it is possible to take an AVC independently. Contributions are fully deductible against tax, although the percentage of salary that can be shielded from income tax is limited. However, if you are a higher-rate taxpayer, deductions are allowed against the highest rate of tax. So, at present tax rates, £10,000 a year contributed to an AVC will mean a tax saving of £4,000. Put another way, if you save £6,000 into an AVC, you will be getting £10,000 of contribution value.

The problem with AVCs comes on retirement day. Some AVCs perform poorly, and if the hard-earned money you put away has been managed badly then the fund created will not be as large as you had hoped. Worse still, at the time of writing British law requires that you invest your whole retirement fund in a poor financial instrument known as an annuity. The company providing the annuity will take the pool of money saved under the AVC and pay you an income for life. If you live to be a hundred, then you may feel the benefit, although the life company will normally pocket all the money generated by way of dividends, interest or capital gains. If you die young, perhaps at three score years and ten, then the money remains with the insurance company and will not be passed on to your heirs. A simple example will serve to reveal the iniquity of annuities.

Your AVC fund on maturity is £100,000 when you retire at sixty. A company offers you a taxable annuity of £7,560 a year. This is 7.5

per cent return on your savings. You would get 5.5 per cent by putting the money on deposit at the nearest Tesco store, slightly less than the annuity, but upon your death the £100,000 would form part of your estate rather than vanishing into the coffers of the life assurer faster than your coffin is conveyed into the fiery furnace. Had you been able to put your money into a respectable corporate bond fund, you would be getting an income of £7,000+, with your capital intact. Steer clear of annuities if you can.

The last Conservative government planned to abolish the inequitable law compelling those with AVCs to buy annuities, but never got round to it. The Blair government has considered abolition, but Chancellor Gordon Brown, under considerable pressure, one suspects, from his friends in the large Edinburgh-based life assurance industry, has decided to refer the issue to a committee of inquiry. An argument for annuities, often repeated in the financial press, whose publishers gain huge revenues from life assurance companies, is that, left to their own devices, AVC holders might become reckless and spend all the money on extravagant living, travel or foreign property. Having enjoyed tax relief on their savings, it is argued, pensioners should use their AVCs with prudence, a word much in favour with the present Chancellor. However, if that were truly the argument, then people should be given the choice of putting the money into national savings, an ISA or an alternative long-term investment vehicle. The reality is that annuities are an additional form of death duty, except that the beneficiary is not the state but the life assurance industry.

Many people who have made additional savings through AVCs would have been better served by paying the tax on their incomes and buying property to rent. For them it is too late. However, those now faced with the option of subscribing to an AVC should read the small print, study annuity rates and hope that before their fund reaches maturity date the law has been changed.

Personal Money Schemes

Personal money schemes are mostly used by high-wealth individuals or the self-employed, and work in two ways. Traditionally individuals have signed up with a life assurance company as the pension provider, and contributed premiums every month or every quarter, leaving the institution to invest the money at its discretion where it thinks fit. An alternative is to instruct the institution to act as your pensions provider, but to create and manage your own portfolio of stocks, bonds and unit trusts within it. With the financial service industry's love of acronyms these schemes have become known as SIPPs, or self-invested pension plans. The trouble with SIPPs is that most assurance companies expect you to invest at least £25,000, and the charges for the minimal amount of work the assurer has to do are high.

Stakeholder pensions

In contrast to the 'mother knows best' attitude towards annuities, where reasonably well-off retirees are not thought capable of looking after their own savings, the Treasury and its political masters have recently introduced the concept of stakeholder pensions, which are designed to encourage Britons to take more responsibility for funding their old age. Just why the politicians and Whitehall mandarins believe that those on low or modest incomes are more likely to be able to manage their savings better than those who had the wit to put aside additional chunks of their earnings has never been satisfactorily explained. It is all the more perplexing since by introducing stake-holder pensions the Government is forcing the pensions and life assurance industry to lower charges to consumers, while at the same time permitting these same institutions to rip off retirees who have no choice but to buy annuities.

It remains to be seen whether stakeholder pensions take off. An immediate advantage is that they have no initial charge and the buying and selling price for acquiring or disposing of units has to be the same: there is no bid-offer spread such as ordinary investors suffer.

7   Investment Clubs

The message is clear. Ignore the ups and downs of the markets and pick individual winners. Do your homework; ferret out companies that will continue to make first class profits no matter what happens in the big world outside.
    Terry Bond, development director, Proshare Investment Clubs

Women like to gossip. They like to swap ideas and to speculate – that's why they make good investors.
    Margaret Lee, secretary of the investment club, The Optimists

It might have been an episode of *The Vicar of Dibley,* or the village fête committee ruefully considering an annual event that has been washed out by the summer rains. Yet the flickering screen of a laptop and spreadsheets strewn across the table in the back bar of an Essex alehouse showed that something much more serious was on the agenda.

It is mid-evening, and the regular meeting of the Dirty Harry Investment Club is underway at the Harry public house in Leigh-on-Sea, a suburb at the tip of the Thames estuary. Dirty Harry is one of more than 10,000 clubs in Britain alone, and it is fairly typical in that it meets monthly on licensed premises, has twenty members and mixes investment with pleasure, while taking the former seriously.

On this particular evening the monthly performance presentation from the honorary treasurer is decidedly downbeat. A portfolio that cost the twenty members just over £20,000 one year earlier has almost halved in value, with some stocks shedding 90 per cent of their purchase price.

Not that the atmosphere is glum. In the face of adversity, Essex man's humour can be characteristically defiant. Barry Lake, the treasurer, better known as Bazza, hands round his analysis, which shows a minus on almost every line. 'We've lost another £245 today, boys,' he says. 'I am thinking of putting in expenses for red ink.'

However, one of the securities has actually risen a few pence because previous profits forecasts turned out to be too pessimistic.

'It's a very sad indication when profit warnings are good news,' comments Bazza drily; like other members, he has seen his losses rise to above the £500 mark.

The Dirty Harry Investment Club was formed in late 1999 with a defined goal: maximum capital growth. Its members, most of them men, nearly all come from the Southend area, with a wide variety of occupations represented. There is a banker, a money broker, a company director, a retired chief executive and a probate lawyer. There is also an electrician, two truck drivers, two policemen, a quantity surveyor, an insurance man and a customs officer.

At this meeting several absentees are noted, which does not please the chairman, Mark, who wants their non-appearance recorded in the minutes. Perhaps when markets fall, members lose interest, I ponder, as we turn to a detailed examination of the portfolio. First, Baltimore Technologies, the rising star with which the club kicked off their investments two years earlier, buying 186 shares at £5.35 each. Tonight Baltimore shares stand at 44 pence, less than a tenth of the purchase value. 'Not worth selling,' says Bazza. 'It will all go in brokers' commission.' He adds: 'Let's face it, we put too much into technology. We have been looking at the wrong sectors; other sectors have risen. And anyone who says "I told you so" gets beaten up.'

A cheer goes up as the landlord arrives with more pints of beer and bags of crisps, along with soft drinks for those whose turn it is to drive. The twenty members put in about £10 a week, and the club has £750 in the bank which it could invest after this meeting, after detailed discussion and deliberation.

How it works
Individual members keep watch for buying opportunities and at the monthly meetings suggest additions to the portfolio. They table the proposed acquisitions and then present the case for each of them, backed up by their own research. After discussion and regular reference to web sites like adfin.com, the members reduce the suggested acquisitions to a short list of three by a paper vote. At this stage the assumption is made that the club will buy stocks. Once the short list has been selected, it is open for any member to make a formal proposal for action. Assuming no one does this, the portfolio will remain intact. It may be that a proposal is tabled for certain shares to be sold, and one or more of those on the short list bought. All proposals are put to a majority vote and acted upon the next morning.

Six stocks are now put forward for debate. Bazza nominates Canary Wharf. It is one of those ventures which 'began like the Channel Tunnel', but two of the three new towers were topped out (that is to say, fabricated to its highest point, though not necessarily completely finished) and the company is now running on a 55 per cent profit margin and buying back its own shares. 'They are solid and are going to climb within the lifetime of our club,' says Barry.

Mark likes Shell. 'They are also aggressively buying back their shares; as a result the earnings per share are rising.' He reminds us that Shell pay solid dividends, and that a third of the company's turnover is in America. 'I think Shell will be considerably higher than they are now,' he says, adding cautiously: 'I do not see any reason why they should dive.'

Bazza puts the case for Manganese Bronze, the manufacturer of London taxicabs. 'They forecast a loss this year, but an improvement next year,' he says, pointing out that net asset value is about twice the present share value, and that this could mean they are ripe for takeover.

As discussion continues late into the evening, other stocks debated include Land Securities ('running a 69 per cent profit margin') and Halma ('a 700 per cent rise since 1975'). Mark, though, thinks the club should lift its stake in Biocompatibles International, which has lost 47 per cent of its value since it was first acquired at the top of the market in the starting portfolio. 'There is nothing wrong with the company,' he argues. 'Everything we bought it for is still there.' He explains how he believes the company's growth strategy is still intact, despite a recent profit warning, and points out that the US Food and Drug Administration has just approved one of its key products. A United States company has also just invested heavily in convertible loan stock.

It is time to vote, and at the count Biocompatibles gets the most crosses on the ballot papers. Tony puts forward a motion proposing that the club liquidate three of its worst-performing tech stocks, BATM, Parthus and Reflec, and invest a further £1,000 into Biocompatibles. The members agree they will wait until next month before considering further purchases. The vote is carried by a narrow majority.

They close the meeting reflecting on a successful summer barbeque and passing a warm vote of thanks to the member whose home was used as the venue. The Dirty Harry Investment Club enjoys its social side too. Some members move off to an Indian restaurant for a curry, and I head for the last train to London reflecting that there must be few clubs where it is possible to derive so much enjoyment from losing money. But then there is always the hope that one day there will be a crock of gold at the end of the rainbow.

Investment clubs do not operate in isolation, though there is nothing to stop them doing so if they wish. When the first edition of this book was published in 1986, there appeared to be only five clubs. One of these was at West Houghton in the Lancashire industrial belt, where a group of women had decided to get out of British Telecom shares to buy Marks and Spencer, because 'it's always busy'.

The 10,000 clubs that have sprung up across the country since then are well organised and meet regularly, with over half of them having assets of more than £5,000. The average club meets monthly, usually on a weekday evening in the first half of the week. Half of them meet in public houses and wine bars, though there is also a partiality for ethnic restaurants. Many important share purchases have been hatched up over a curry and a beer.

Every few months, members of registered clubs have the opportunity to meet each other at a series of investment seminars organised in the regions by Proshare Investment Clubs. It was set up by the City establishment in 1992, which then lost interest in it and sold it off to a commercial web site.

After some quiet and ineffective early years, when it encountered opposition from both the educational establishment and the more staid and complacent elements of the City, Proshare blossomed into a significant force for the encouragement of private investors. It did this by concentrating on three sectors – youth education, investor clubs and assisting companies with employee share ownership schemes.

I enjoyed the company of a large number of investor club members at one of Proshare's weekends in Bournemouth, the manicured south coast resort. The enthusiasm was palpable. Why else would several hundred people forsake the spring sunshine for a basement conference hall of a three-star hotel? But there they were, early on a Sunday morning, staring at a big screen which proclaimed: 'Time is the Great Healer'. The audience, predominantly greying and middle-aged and beyond, heaved a collective sigh and for a moment I imagined I had gatecrashed a diocesan retreat.

Here, though, the God is Mammon, and the preacher is the perky editor of *Shares* magazine. He is at full throttle. 'When you are at your most frightened, you should be optimistic,' he intones, 'and when you are euphoric, you should be scared.'

The 250 members of the audience scribble this down, for they are scared and these are words of wisdom. Most of them have seen previous profits in share trading eroded, many lost money in the dotcom crash of 2001 and some are 'ninety per centers', investors who have lost all but one tenth of their original investment capital.

Meeting club members, I was struck by their diversity and knowledge. There was a most impressive ethnic group from south London who had formed their club six months earlier, making regular monthly contributions but deciding not to commit to their first purchase 'until we have learnt enough to be confident we know what we are doing'. How different from so many people who are bulldozed into bad money decisions by commission salesmen.

Many are young groups, like the Stab in the Dark (SID) club, which meets monthly in the Black Horse public house in Denshaw, near Oldham. The average age is just above 25, and the group has a varied portfolio which until the time of writing was outperforming the FTSE index. The club uses what it calls a share champion system whereby each of its members takes on the obligation to become an expert in one of the stocks held. The champion has to report to the other members weekly on the web, as well as at the monthly meetings.

SID also operates a carefully thought-out stop-loss system to limit the impact of bad decisions or sudden shocks. A stop-loss is a price which an investor sets to limit the fall he is prepared to take in a share's value. It is an essential tool for any investor, particularly for a person who does not follow the markets on a daily basis. Each share's champion sets a danger mark halfway between the price paid and the stop-loss, at which the future of the stock in the portfolio is discussed. Here is how they make it work:

> The mechanism that we have agreed on at Stab in the Dark comes in two parts:
>
> 1. We calculate the initial stop-loss at 80% of our investment plus £12 to cover disposal costs (spread over the number of shares held). For example, if we buy 500 shares in Company X at 100p each and the cost of purchase is £15, the investment is £515. The initial stop-loss would be set at $((£515 \times 80\%) + £12)/500 = 85p$. I accept that it is a little mechanical, but it does reflect the initial risk we are prepared to accept in share-price fluctuation.

2. We also set an 'alarm' price which is set somewhere between the stop-loss and the current price of the share. This price is set by that shares champion through discussion with other members. The reason for the alarm price is to prompt some discussion on reasons why a given share has fallen to, or below, the alarm price. A sale of the stock could therefore occur well before it reaches the stop-loss if we consider the future looks bleak for that particular share.

To sum up, we have the stop-loss, which means that if a share drops below this figure the share must be sold. We also have the alarm price that is designed to force discussion on a share if the price drops below this figure. It is then the responsibility of the share champion to propose the stop-loss and alarm prices at the monthly meetings. Normally if the price is falling below our original purchase price the stop-loss will stand at its original level (unless extreme specific circumstances justify considering a review). However, when the price is increasing and we are in a profit situation, which is where it gets interesting . . .

An intriguing feature of the club scene is that there are many all-female clubs, and sometimes they outperform those that are exclusively for men. In Campsie, near Londonderry in Northern Ireland, The Optimists have lived up to their name and won a major award at the end of their first year of operation, and in 2001 were Proshare Investment Club of the Year. The club was established by a group of women who decided they wanted to learn more about finance, and the twenty members discovered they had a natural aptitude for investing. According to secretary Margaret Lee: 'For the first six months we simply tracked various shares and watched the market until we had a good understanding of how things worked. The fact that we were cautious seemed to pay off.'[1]

The club meets over a meal and drinks at the White Horse pub in Campsie once a month. The women each contributed £250 to set up the portfolio, and the monthly subscription is £20. Each member is expected to come up with a share recommendation every month, and then they all vote on which to buy. They have had success with penny shares and with big-ticket stocks like Vodafone, but lost money on Tottenham Hotspur. Says Margaret:

Women tend to be very thorough and the level of information that comes into our meetings is really quite astonishing. We are good listeners, so everyone gets their turn. And that means we

---

[1] *Mail on Sunday*, 2 May 1999.

have twenty brains all putting forward different investment ideas. We all get a real buzz out of it.

Some aficionados belong to several clubs. At the Bournemouth weekend, I ran across Barry (Bazza) Lake from Dirty Harry's, but found him talking about the Brass Monkeys, the H and G Club and the St Leger Club. The St Leger turned out to be a group that meets only once a year, on the day of the St Leger race, and picks just one stock on which it will gamble for a year. And the Brass Monkey? According to Bazza:

> It started with the suggestion 'Monkey and Pony' as we all started with a 'monkey' (£500) and were putting in a 'pony' (£25) a month. Sally thought that was silly, and suggested 'Brass Monkey', as we were hoping to make some brass out of the deal. Quite honestly, we were getting bored by this time and the £10,000 we had to spend was burning a hole in our pockets, so 'Brass Monkey' it was.

It would be good to be able to report that all the investment clubs that were created in the excitement of the bull market of the 1990s are alive and thriving. Unfortunately they are not. Many of them have been wound up, or simply fizzled out as a result of the participants moving on and finding other interests, new partners, new jobs and new neighbourhoods. Many of the disbanded clubs have left litter behind, in the form of discarded web sites and underperforming portfolios.

Some of this is the inevitable attrition of groups of people bored with a costly hobby, but the City must bear its share of the blame. It has collectively lost interest in small shareholders. Proshare, the City organisation, founded and funded by the London Stock Exchange and others, has been broken up, with its education side sold to the Institute of Financial Services, while Proshare Investment Clubs has been taken over by a financial web site which appears to view them mainly as a way of gaining clients. At the time of writing the Proshare web site was part working, part out of date.

The majority of internet addresses (urls) of share clubs listed as still being operational return 'not found' pages, while some have been directed to bizarre destinations. One of them took me to a BMW dealer in the area where the club once operated; another to a hard porn site offering sex services.

Schools

Across Britain a number of schools have investment clubs, but the importance of stock markets in the national and European economy is not taught properly in schools, if at all. Teachers have been as slow to embrace it as a subject as the City has to communicate it to secondary school pupils. Both are at fault, and there has been little encouragement from Whitehall.

There was a period when it seemed this would change. Pioneering work was carried out by Peter Hogan, now the principal of Llandovery College in Mid Wales and previously a teacher at schools in Leeds, Sunderland and Derby.

In Leeds he took an approach which is not dissimilar to *The Times'* Portfolio game. Pupils were given a notional amount of cash, with which they could 'buy' shares quoted on the London Stock Exchange. They could buy and sell on a daily basis, using the prices quoted in the *Financial Times* as the guide price. After a period their portfolios were valued, and the pupil who had made the most gains was declared the winner. However, Hogan found that the novelty of a game that was not for real soon wore off, and believes that games that mimic the stock market have limited benefits. 'It's a bit like dressing up in the football kit of a Premiership team, and then going to have a shower', he told me.

I tried the idea out when teaching financial journalism at City University in London. Playing the game properly was hard work and the students were not that keen to embrace it, given there were no tangible or scholastic rewards. Nevertheless portfolio games and competitions of various sorts are run in schools in Britain and elsewhere.

A number of banks and other financial services groups – but not the London Stock Exchange or the City of London Corporation – clubbed together to form a charity, the Personal Finance Education Group, which took on board some of Hogan's ideas and today provide material and support for teachers who want to introduce the subject into the classroom. It is a help, but it lacks national cohesion, and the result is that most British children leave school without any idea of what the stock markets do or why they exist.

The LSE does run respectable courses at its building in Throgmorton Street, but the average school could not afford the high fees charged per student, and they do not appear to have a DVD which does the job. The educational work of the once proactive

Proshare has been taken over by the Institute of Financial Services, which also runs courses for profit. It is a sorry tale of one more opportunity missed by the City.

8 How Shares are Bought

A weak sun rises over the strip of stone and cement that runs alongside the Thames from Blackfriars to Docklands in London. On the river itself there is little traffic, a far cry from two centuries earlier when the Pool of London was alive with clippers and merchantmen bringing goods and spices to what was then the capital of the English-speaking world. On this morning the only craft moving are the barges that transport waste from the City of London's depot in Lower Thames Street to be dumped on Essex marshlands close to the sea.

This grey scene is reflected in the glass-walled offices that now house the heart of stock market trading in London. With the London Stock Exchange no longer providing a fixed centre for dealers to buy and sell, trading is all electronic, conducted from dealing rooms the size of football fields in clusters of buildings at Canary Wharf in Docklands, at the Broadgate Centre near Liverpool Street station, and in other office blocks in the City and other parts of London. The Square Mile round Throgmorton Street is no longer the focal point of the stock markets.

At Barclays Capital, sited at the Old Mint, where in the days of the Industrial Revolution gold and silver coins were once minted, the morning meeting is underway. The head of European equities makes no attempt to put a brave face on the gloom everyone feels on this particular day. The previous afternoon saw the FTSE 100 index fall to its lowest level since the global financial turmoil of October 1998.

'It started as Black Monday again,' he says, 'the FTSE dipping below five thousand after the weekend press had been very negative. We saw some bargain hunting, and a bit of a recovery, but the market is all over the place.'

One by one his colleagues play their part. Present are the chief strategist, the acting head of UK equities and specialist analysts. A Japan specialist seeks modest comfort in the news that Japan is at long last moving ahead with plans to privatise its railways. But the news from America is the familiar story of job losses.

Analysts report on profit figures that have just been published –

ahead of the start of trading in accordance with the normal custom. Retailer Next has unveiled a 16 per cent increase in sales. 'The top end of expectations,' says the retail analyst, 'but there's concern as to whether this can be maintained. We've got it on hold and we will maintain it at that.' A similar judgement is made on results from Friends Provident, but concern is expressed about the management of Scottish Power's United States operations. 'But the price fall may be overdone so we have upgraded it from reduce to hold.'

Tuned into the conference are other centres like Barclays Private Bank in Mayfair, and parts of the organisation based in Peterborough and Glasgow. The meeting lasts twenty-five minutes, and then the participants disperse, ready to advise clients on their portfolios.

Across the markets in London and elsewhere, similar meetings are taking place. Most market professionals are at their desks by seven or even earlier, long before the commuter trains begin to deposit their cargo of office workers. Many of the young men and women striding through the Italian-marbled entrance halls of the securities houses have flushed faces and carry sports bags, evidence of a thirty-minute workout in a nearby gymnasium while most Britons are still in their beds. Before the morning meeting they will have flicked through the *Financial Times*, glanced at the other newspapers and looked at Bloomberg or CNBC on the office television screens.

Some of the meetings, like that at Barclays, are designed to get business moving through the trading desks by persuading clients – many of them large investment institutions – to buy shares in the markets. This happens either by providing advice to those who call about their portfolios, or by equity and bond salesmen making buy and sell recommendations to clients.

In other meetings more directly related to the day's trading, there is a degree of tension between the analysts and the market makers, the men and women who set the price at which their employers will trade shares. More often than not, the market makers ignore the logical arguments of the analysts. Analysts, some of them trained in accountancy, a few of them former financial journalists, are steeped in knowledge of the companies in which they specialise and often have an almost scholarly approach to their work. Market makers are traders, and carry with them the air of the Cockney barrow-boy, many of them speaking in estuary English. Most are street smart and have to make split-second judgements over share values.

While the analysts retreat behind their glass partitions to write their reports, the market makers dealing with all but FTSE 100 stocks sit at their terminals keying in the prices at which they will buy and sell the shares in which they trade. The atmosphere is like a television portrayal of the newsroom of a big newspaper, though a trifle more tense, with more fever and bustle.

Most people appear to be on the telephone, their fitful dialogues always punctuated by taps at a keyboard, which reveal an array of coloured numbers on the bank of computer screens that dominates their desks.

Every few minutes someone gets up from his high-back swivel chair and shouts out a message – or, plastic coffee beaker in hand, wanders across the floor to talk with a colleague. For the most part these dialogues are friendly and unobtrusive, but the occasional sharp-edged rejoinder reminds the observer that this is a place where serious money is at stake. It is as well to get up and walk around, not only to stretch the muscles but also to avoid keyboard fatigue. Sometimes the latter can have dire consequences, as when in 1998 a Salomon Brothers trader slouched on his keyboard, firing off an order to sell $1.2 billion worth of French government bond futures. Realising his mistake, he bought them back immediately, but his temporary aberration had already cost his company several million pounds.

My description is of the equities floor of one of London's largest securities houses, where each working day tens of billions of pounds' worth of shares change hands. Most trading floors look the same. Large stakes in major companies are bought and sold; small allotments in privatisation issues are traded; money is won or lost.

Down on the floor, on the central desk, the lead salesman touches the flickering light on his telephone panel that indicates a call is waiting, picks up the phone and rests one foot on a drawer of his desk. The caller is a fund manager from one of Britain's largest life assurance companies. He is looking to pick up a million shares in one of the big breweries. The salesman keys into his computer the first three letters of the company's name, and the screen reveals to him that the price of the stock is higher than it has been for several weeks. But it also shows that the posted price is only available for the purchase of 50,000 shares or less. Buying a block twenty times that size could be difficult.

'Leave it with me, we'll see what we can do. The price is good, so someone might be prepared to sell,' he tells his client.

After ringing off, the salesman, a man in his early thirties, shirt-sleeved and displaying wide Wall Street braces, makes a few more keystrokes. In quick succession, two graphs appear on the screen – one of them portraying the movement of the share price of the brewery group over a five-year period; the other tracking it against the progress of the *Financial Times* Stock Exchange 100 share index, popularly known as the Footsie. The graph shows that although the shares have been rising, they have been outperformed by the index.

The salesman smiles, reflecting that one of the brewery's major shareholders may well be prepared to sell, given the higher price of the stock and the prospect that by reinvesting elsewhere there will be a more profitable return. He keys in a few more strokes and a printer at the end of the desk produces a sheet of paper with a breakdown of the company's major shareholders, in order of size of holding. Most of the names on the list are investment institutions, life assurance companies competing with the salesman's client, pension funds and unit trust companies. But there are also some international companies and a handful of wealthy individuals. The salesman calls over a junior colleague and tells him: 'See if you can do anything with this. We need a million.'

The young man returns to his desk, picks up his telephone and starts making calls. Within forty minutes he is back. 'I've got them,' he says, glowing with pleasure at his swift if unexpected achievement. The salesman whoops with joy, hits his client's number on the phone pad and passes on the good news. He then walks over to market makers sitting at another, larger bank of computers and asks them to execute the deal. The salesman is well pleased. His firm's commission on the transaction will be about £150,000. A small percentage of that goes towards his annual bonus.

Share prices vary according to who is buying, a little like the market for airline tickets. You can pay £1,200 for a fully flexible economy return ticket to New York and find yourself sitting next to someone who has paid £225 for the same class of seat, the identical meals service and the same quarter-bottle of rough French red wine.

Such differences exist in the British stock market. Different investors buy the same share at prices which vary depending on the day or minute, the number bought and the system used to buy them.

A class system exists. As you might expect, those with the most financial clout get the best deals. There are effectively two trading systems. The premier system is for those trading large blocks of shares in Britain's top 100 companies. These are traded on the Stock

Exchange's order book system, known as SETS, an acronym for Stock Exchange Electronic Trading System. This matches orders placed electronically by prospective buyers and sellers, partly replacing the quote-driven system where deals were done by telephone.

Buyers and sellers of large blocks of stocks can advertise through their broker the price at which they would like to deal, and then choose to wait for the market to move in their favour, or execute the deal immediately at the best price currently available. Only members of the London Stock Exchange can enter orders directly into SETS.

Under the system, investors wishing to deal will contact their broker by phone or electronic mail and agree the price at which they are willing to buy or sell a particular stock. The broker will enter the order directly into the order book, and it will be displayed anonymously to the entire market.

For example, the broker could open his screen on the stock and find an investor wants to sell 4,000 shares at once, at the 'best price' available. At the time, the best buy order available is for 17,800 shares at 938 pence. The sell order for 4,000 shares will automatically trade against the buy order – leaving 13,800 shares at 938 pence still on the order book. The second the order is executed, the trade is automatically reported to the Exchange and the market informed immediately.

This is only one type of share trade using the order book system. Another common deal is the limit order. Here the investor posts specific details of the proposed trade – the number of shares, the price and the date upon which the offer will close. These limit orders sit on the SETS electronic order book until either they are matched or they pass the expiry date. There is also the execute and eliminate order, which is very similar to an 'at best' order, but with a limit price specified.

Automatic execution through the order book takes place between 08.30 and 16.30. From 08.00 there is a half-hour period during which orders can be added or deleted in readiness for the trading day. In the half-hour between the end of the trading day and 17.00 there is a housekeeping period during which orders that have not been executed may be deleted if brokers do not wish to leave them on the system overnight.

Most individual share owners and those investing in medium and small companies have to use the second division market-making system, which means that we buy and sell shares at a price set by a trader in a busy dealing room. Since we cannot contact these market makers direct, we have to go through a broker, paying commission as well as a dealer's spread – the difference between the prices for which he will buy and sell a share. Market makers set the prices for all transactions other than those booked through SETS. Although the London Stock Exchange had hoped that most of the FTSE 100 trades would be conducted through SETS by the new millennium, the market makers and their spreads are still in evidence.

The job of a market maker is sedentary. They sit at their terminals all day, their only exercise swivelling in their chairs to shout across to a colleague or taking a thirty-minute break to visit a gymnasium or squash club. Not all market makers can trade all shares; their bailiwick is those sectors in which their firm has elected and been authorised to make a market. Like the jobbers of the past, the market makers will typically specialise: for example, in media stocks, the leisure sector, industrials, banks and so on. Once bid and offer prices have been entered, the market maker is obliged to trade at those prices, although of course he can alter his figures at any time in response to market conditions – in other words, after he has seen what competitors are doing. Shares are traded on a computer system known as SEAQ, which stands for Stock Exchange Automated Quotations System. This covers more than 3,500 securities and is divided into three groups of stocks – alpha, beta and gamma.

As the name implies, alpha stocks are the most actively traded shares, and market makers who buy or sell them must immediately enter the trade into the SEAQ system. From SEAQ the trade details are passed instantly to the London Stock Exchange's electronic information service, which is available to traders, brokers and investors.

Take the example of an investor purchasing 500 shares in British Petroleum: how does the SEAQ system work? His broker or licensed financial intermediary will call up the BP page from the system and see an array of offers from more than a dozen market makers, each of them identified by a code. One line will say 'ML 36–40 1 × 1'. This means that Merrill Lynch, are prepared to buy BP at £10.36 and to sell at £10.40, and that their figure applies for purchases or sales of 1,000 shares or fewer. Another line might say 'DMG 36–41 1 × 2', indicating that Deutsche Morgan Grenfell will buy at the same price as Merrill Lynch, but that they will only sell BP at £10.41, and then only in units of up to 2,000.

Another page on SEAQ will reveal that ten minutes earlier there had been a large transaction of BP shares at £9.38. Assuming he wants to trade, the broker calls the dealing desk of his own or another firm and asks to buy BP at £10.40. If the broker's firm is also listed as a market maker in BP, the broker will try and keep the deal in-house by persuading his own colleagues to match the Merrill offer, which they may or may not be willing to do. When the bargain is struck, the market maker enters it into the BP SEAQ page; other market makers, noting the transaction, readjust their offers accordingly.

Deals in beta stocks are concluded in exactly the same way, except that not all trades are logged, and there are fewer market makers, perhaps only two or three, who will usually be in firms that have decided to specialise in a particular sector, such as electronics or insurance. In the case of gamma stocks, only indicative quotes are provided, so that any broker anxious to consider a purchase has to call the market maker and negotiate a price, often based on volume. Many of the market makers in the gamma section may be regional brokers, who know companies in their area well and are better placed to hold the book than a large London conglomerate.

For the technically minded, the SEAQ system operates on two dedicated mainframe computers, designed to respond to entries within one second, update information at a peak rate of twenty items per second and handle up to 70,000 transactions an hour. In the event of a computer crash, a major fire or bomb outrage at the Stock Exchange, all the records would be saved, for parallel computers operate in another part of London and, for double protection, in the United States.

While equities represent the most interesting aspect of stock market activity, and offer the investor the greatest degree of risk and reward, it is important not to overlook the bond markets. There is a substantial market in buying and selling bonds, the prices of which vary according to how far out of line their fixed interest rates are with the standard rates of interest applying at the time in the economy. If interest rates are falling, then bonds with a higher rate will be sold at a premium to their basic price. As with equities, prices are set by market makers, drawn from twenty-five firms.

Indices

When listening to the radio or watching television, the one aspect of the financial markets that regularly gets reported is the ups and downs of stock market indices.

Indices reflect the overall value of all the stocks held within them, and in many cases are calculated on a minute-by-minute basis. In Britain the most popularly quoted index is the FTSE 100, known colloquially as the Footsie, which covers the hundred companies with the largest market capitalisation. The BBC often refers inaccurately to this index as the 'One Hundred index', presumably because it is reluctant to plug the *Financial Times*, although it never seems to have the same problem with sporting titles that incorporate the names of commercial sponsors, such as the Barclays Premier League.

As a company, FTSE is autonomous and independent of the London Stock Exchange, although the exchange and the *Financial Times* are co-owners. The company actually calculates thousands of indices each day, with more than a hundred of them, including the FTSE 100, being updated in real time. Many of these indices are based on mathematical values, such as the FTSE 250, the FTSE All Share or the FTSE 30. Others require value judgements as to which stock should be included. One of the most controversial is the new FTSE4Good index of 'socially responsible' companies. The selection criteria for this index covers three areas: working towards environmental sustainability; developing positive relationships with stakeholders; and upholding and supporting universal human rights. FTSE claims that 'there is no other socially responsible index quite like it. Independently defined and researched, FTSE4Good sets an objective global standard for socially responsible investment.' The company keeps adding and deleting companies according to its own criteria.

There are also FTSE international indices. The FTSE Actuaries World Indices cover all major and some smaller stock markets, expressed in terms of the local currency, dollars, sterling, yen and euro. There is also the FTSE Eurotrack 100, which covers major mainland European companies. British companies are included in the Eurotrack 200.

The Dow
The pre-eminent index in the United States is the Dow Jones Industrial Average, one of many indices generated by the Dow Jones Company, publishers of the *Wall Street Journal*. The DJIA is usually

referred to simply as the Dow, and like the FTSE 30 in Britain it is a formula based on the stock prices of the thirty major industrial companies. The formula adds up the stocks' prices and then divides them by a certain number to derive the average. Consequently the higher-priced stocks will have a greater effect on the average. Other Dow indices include the Transportation Average (twenty airlines, trucking companies and railways), the Utility Average (fifteen gas, electric and power companies) and the Composite (all sixty-five companies in the previous three).

The S & P and the NASDAQ Composite

Another widely used index because of its greater spread across the United States economy is the Standard and Poor's 500. This comprises a broad spread of 500 companies, broken into smaller industry segments, and also includes forty financial companies. The NASDAQ Composite has an even wider spread and includes a large number of technology stocks.

The techMARK

This market is designed to provide a home for high-tech companies that might otherwise have been lured to Germany's Neuer Markt or even NASDAQ in the United States. Since its launch by the London Stock Exchange in 1999, techMARK has become an international market for innovative technology companies and for shares in businesses at the cutting edge of technological innovation.

techMARK is open to all innovative technology companies, irrespective of their size, industrial classification or location. The LSE has abandoned its earlier requirement of £50 million capitalisation as a qualification. For the purposes of techMARK, the definition of a technology company is 'one whose business growth and success is dependent on the development of one or more technologies or on the development of products or services which require significant technological innovation'. All companies applying to techMARK are individually assessed by the Exchange with advice from an independent panel of experts.

The DAX

The main German stock market index is the DAX, which is based on the thirty most actively traded German blue-chip stocks. It represents over 60 per cent of the total equity capital of German exchange-listed companies, and trading in these shares accounts for three quarters of the market volume. Another index, the FAZ, operated by the leading German newspaper *Frankfurter Allgemeine Zeitung*, is also an important pointer, being more broadly based than the DAX.

There are many other indices across the world, including a series covering Europe.

Internet Brokers

An increasing proportion of individual share owners buy and sell through internet brokers, most of which offer competitive prices on commission and allow you to sit at your home computer logged in to their systems, where you can buy and sell in seconds at the prices set by the market makers associated with the company providing the online service.

Many of these internet brokers offer an array of other services, including access to prices, company news, historical performance graphs and comment. Some of them will offer telephone advice at extra cost. There are many opinions as to who offers the best service. The brokerages are fiercely competitive, and if it was just a matter of cost then the solution would be to pick those that offer to trade shares for a minimum charge of £10, no matter how large the trade. This is a huge reduction on the old percentage charges, where a sale of £100,000 worth of shares would once have cost £1,000 or more in commission.

But as in most services, cost is not the only factor. Accessibility is important. You need to be able to log on to the broker's web site quickly and trade immediately. You do not want to be getting messages like 'page unavailable: please try later' because the broker's server is locked up. Accuracy is also important. You do not want to find that you have sold all the shares in one company in your port-folio, rather than the 20 per cent you specified. This is a worryingly common type of error with some services.

The oldest of the online brokerages in Britain is Barclayshare, formerly Charles Schwab, set up in Birmingham. At one stage Schwab was conducting almost half of Britain's online trading. More recently it has encountered stiff competition.

The stock market's class system also extends to the provision of information. Anyone can buy the *Financial Times*, of course, and it can and should be mined for information. But real-time share prices and other up-to-the-second market information is only available on services for the privileged few who wish to buy them, which usually means the professionals. Computer services with real-time prices and up-to-date news cost in the region of £10,000 a year. At the next level down are internet services and television programmes such as those provided by Bloomberg and CNBC. These are free, as are services like the BBC's Ceefax, where the share prices, however, are far from current, just updated from time to time.

Paperchase

Once shares have been bought or sold, settlement takes place. This is carried out in what is called the 'back office' of the stockbroker, reflecting the old days when dozens of clerks would huddle in the basement or another unsalubrious corner of the office and issue hand-written statements seeking payment for shares bought. Once the shares had been paid for, the clerk would inform the registrar of the company whose shares had been acquired, and he would send out a share certificate. Share certificates were and are valuable documents, like property deeds, to be kept in a safe or bank vault. The amount of clerical work involved was considerable.

Three developments put an end to all that. The first was the rise in volume of trading and the tendency for many shares to be sold after only a short period of ownership. This resulted in tremendous pressure on back offices, and long delays in handling the paperwork. The second was the arrival of electronic trading, and the use of sophisticated systems. It made sense to try and integrate settlement procedures into dealing systems, and to reduce what had become an almost unmanageable paperchase. Unfortunately, this proved not as easy as was first thought, and, particularly in London, caused numerous problems and headaches. The London Stock Exchange spent tens of thousands of man hours and huge sums of money developing what was called the TAURUS system, but it flopped, and was replaced by another system called CREST. Slowly, over the years, CREST was made to work.

The third development was a move amongst frequent investors away from paper certification. They became used to the concept of having their share ownership registered electronically, and those with accounts with online brokerages such as Barclayshare accepted that their holdings could be placed in electronic nominee accounts. Effectively the brokers held the shares, and in return for forfeiting the rights to certificates, investors enjoyed lower commission charges and detailed statements of all transactions. It has worked well, although from time to time some online brokerages make mistakes, and those who use them are well advised to keep their own records and check them against broker statements. The London Stock Exchange has now introduced its own scheme whereby small shareholders can have their shares registered electronically there, rather than have a paper certificate. This excellent scheme is free of charge to those with three stocks or fewer; after that, there is a modest charge.

Stamp Duty

Stamp duty, a euphemism for an additional tax, is payable on all share purchases in Britain, and the rate is 0.5 per cent. The United Kingdom is one of the few countries where this tax is levied. Stamp duty is also levied in the United States, but at the modest rate of 0.003 per cent.

Each year, the Treasury pockets between £3 and £4 billion from stamp duty, so the Government's reluctance to drop a tax collected for it by brokers is understandable, though undesirable. It is undesirable because it is a tax on savings, not spending, and because it discriminates against those who trade their shares in Britain rather than elsewhere. Wealthy investors and institutions can trade shares in large companies in New York and avoid the tax. Speculators can use spread betting – betting on future stock movements in the same way one bets on racehorses – and avoid the tax. It is a strange world where betting shops are treated much more favourably than stock markets.

A study by the Institute for Fiscal Studies found this tax had dampened share prices.[1]

---

[1] Stamp Duty on Shares and its Effect on Share Prices, Steve Bond, Mike Hawkin and Alexander Keenm, 2004.

9 Global Markets

I would rather be vaguely right than precisely wrong.
                                                    Warren Buffett

*Risk arbitrage is not gambling in any sense. Traditional stock
investing is much closer to gambling than is risk arbitrage.*
                                        Ivan Boesky, *Merger Mania*

*The New York Stock Exchange is perhaps the most substantial
and perfect financial temple in the world.*
                                                    John Rodemeyer

Wall Street is the term used to describe the financial district of New
York. Like the City of London, it occupies only a small area of the
business capital of the United States. Wall Street is in Lower
Manhattan, facing out to the Statue of Liberty, and the stock market
grew up there in support of the merchants and bankers who, two
centuries ago, established themselves on the tip of the island, when it
was the pre-eminent business centre of America.

In those days Wall Street was the city's most important thorough-
fare. Cargo ships were moored on the nearby East River, and the
commodities they brought were traded in offices and warehouses on
what became known as 'The Street'. As in London, everything in the
area was destroyed by a Great Fire: the one in Wall Street occurred
in 1835, and the damage stretched from the present site of City Hall
to Battery Park.

The New York Stock Exchange is the world's largest. On an
average day 1.46 billion shares, valued at $46 billion, are bought and
sold, encompassing the stock of the most powerful companies on
earth. It was founded on its present site, the block bounded by Wall,
Broad and New Streets and Exchange Place, in 1863. It has been
rebuilt several times, culminating in the construction in 1984 of
Renwick's $2 million marble-fronted building, highlighted by eight
lacquered columns and a rococo cornice. The first New York Stock
Exchange was more like a gentlemen's club than a business centre.

There were 1,100 members, and its books and records were as closely guarded as those of a Masonic lodge. There was an honorary president, with few duties, and two salaried vice-presidents, but they had little to do except open and close trading at the morning and afternoon sessions.

The Exchange conducted its business by way of auctions, not dissimilar to those used by Sotheby's in the fine art market. Sellers would hand in their shares to the vice-president, who would guard them rather like a cloakroom attendant at a large hotel. They would be auctioned in blocks, and sold to the highest bidder. Inevitably, as with real-estate auctions, some deals took place outside the room, usually in the street, and a number of sub-exchanges grew up, often handling specialist shares.

One of these developed into an exchange of its own, operating from another building in Lower Broad Street. It was known as the Open Board, so called because access was available to anyone prepared to pay a $50 membership fee. Once inside, there was no auction, no organisation and no records kept; buyers simply met potential sellers and dealt. The Open Board operated six days a week, and stayed open as long as there were sufficient traders on the floor. Out of this chaos developed the ticker, a trail of paper printed from telegraph machines which simply listed the latest prices at which stocks were traded. As access to the ticker spread beyond Wall Street and New York to other American cities, further share-trading exchanges grew up, using the ticker as a guide to prices.

This development was viewed with some alarm by the elders of the New York Stock Exchange. Although the ticker services generated more business, their activities were outside NYSE control, their prices were sometimes wrong and they led to the proliferation of rival trading locations. So from 1885 onwards, reporters of ticker companies were barred from the floor of the exchange and forced to purchase the information. Within five years the New York Stock Exchange had control of the ticker and was able to insist that Western Union, the telegraph company that distributed it, should restrict its access to licensed brokerages and other approved buyers.

By this time business had grown to such a level that the auction system could not cope. What took its place was a sub-system of specialist auctions within the trading floor. Legend has it that a broker called Boyd broke his leg and, finding hobbling around the floor on crutches difficult, remained at one post to trade his shares.

After his leg had mended, he discovered that this mode of operation had become hugely profitable and stuck with it, thus creating the specialist market-making auction system that still exists today.

I can find no evidence that this story is anything but apocryphal, but something like it did take place, and provided the basis for present-day trading in New York, with its unique layout of market stalls manned by specialists. These specialists form about a quarter of the professionals working on the floor of the exchange. The others are the people they deal with – the brokers and traders. Some people believe that this system is old-fashioned, and that there is little use of technology. That is not the case. How could it be when $50 billion worth of shares is traded on an average day? In fact there are 5,000 electronic devices within the 36,000-square-foot floor area of the NYSE, as well as 8,000 telephone circuits. Electronics plays a part in every trade.

The NYSE, known as the 'Big Board', likes to claim that it is the 'world's fairest, most open and most technologically advanced marketplace'. Only member firms who own a seat on the NYSE can trade there. These firms can be huge corporations like Merrill Lynch or small entities owned by individuals. There have been the same number of seats, 1,366, since 1953, despite the large rise in share trading. Each of the brokers who are members of the NYSE has a booth. Some orders are telephoned in by the broker's distant offices or an outside agent, but most simply appear on screens in the booth, having been keyed in from afar by the person taking the order from a customer. The orders used to be passed to the firm's floor broker by way of a paper slip, but these days it is more usual to convey the information by pager, textmail on a mobile phone, or wireless telephony. The broker will then go to one of the twenty-two trading posts and seek out a specialist.

Each company whose shares are quoted on the NYSE is allocated to a specialist or specialists, who trade only in named stocks at a prescribed trading post on the floor. All trading in shares takes place at the designated trading post, which has a computer screen above it listing the shares in which its occupants will offer a market. These specialists act as auctioneers. At the start of each trading day they set a guide price for each stock under their remit, for both buying and selling. As market makers they are obliged to trade at these prices, though once a trade has taken place they can make changes. As soon as the ringing of the bell has signalled the start of trading, their auctioneering function begins, as the floor brokers gathered round the trading post will bid up or push down prices. Every time a bargain is struck, the prices are flashed on to the screens in the exchange and to the outside world.

The specialist's role does not end there. Some floor brokers will have been instructed by their booths that the firm's client will only buy or sell at a specific price – 'on limit' is the expression used. Fortunately for them, they do not have to wait, on a knife-edge, for the price of the stock to move to the set limit before acting. They leave their limit order with the specialist, who then will act as an agent and effect the trade if and when the limit is reached. This technique will have an important impact on the specialist's thinking, for if he knows that a large buyer is waiting in the wings for a stock to fall to a certain price, he will be more confident in his dealing.

In theory the market maker only changes his prices by notches: thus he is not supposed to react to any dramatic turn of events by radical shifts. In practice he is human, and will not want to pay over the odds for a share which is tumbling. Running for cover is not encouraged. On the other hand, when big institutions trade very large blocks of shares, it is unreasonable to expect an individual to hold out against a hurricane. The New York Stock Exchange attempts to keep market makers on track by policing price movements very carefully, and by encouraging competition.

The specialist will make his money on the difference between the buying and selling prices in the stocks in which he makes the market. But the job is not without risk. At the end of the day he has to balance his own books. If he is left with an oversupply or shortage of stock when trading ends, he has to hold it in his own account. An exposed position overnight can be highly dangerous, for example to those holding airline stocks on the day of the September 2001 calamity at the World Trade Center.

NASDAQ

In the spring of 1999 an event took place in New York which those who remember the era of Chairman Mao Tse-tung in China would have thought inconceivable. The Chinese premier, Zhu Rongji, paid a visit to the market room of NASDAQ.

The fastest-growing stock market in the world is not the Big Board but the NASDAQ, an acronym for National Association of Securities

Dealers Automated Quotation System. It was the first all-electronic market, it is the only stock market that can claim to be truly global, and it is the home of over half the companies traded in America. All trading is conducted through a sophisticated computer and tele-communications network – a network that transmits critical invest-ment data at lightning speed to more than 400,000 computer screens around the globe.

But back to 1999, and the Chinese premier's visit. The tour over, he presented Frank Zarb, chairman of the National Association of Securities Dealers (NASD), with a red bull, symbolising the hope that the buoyant United States market would continue to see a rising market for ever. Zarb replied with the announcement that he intended to open an office in Shanghai, China's business capital, as the 'beginning of a process to create for China a way to bring investors' capital to growing companies'.

NASDAQ has done precisely that for the United States, raising money for some of the nation's hottest stocks – Microsoft, Intel, Cisco, Dell, Sun Microsystems, Oracle and Yahoo. Nine out of ten companies making initial public offerings do so on the NASDAQ, which claims more securities listed than all the other American markets combined. It was set up in 1971 as the first ever specialist technology market, and led the way in electronic trading. Most of the world's leading technology companies list on NASDAQ, and some of the biggest, like Microsoft, choose to list only there, despite the greater pull of the NYSE. NASDAQ now has a market capitalisation of just under $2,500 billion, and all trades are transacted elec-tronically. Visitors to Times Square in New York cannot fail to be impressed by NASDAQ's Market Site tower, seven storeys high and the largest video screen in the world, updating itself in real time twenty-four hours a day.

No trading takes place inside this building, though visitors can see financial television programming from Bloomberg and CNBC going out live from studios there. However, there is a public exhibition, which, this being the United States, is called an 'experience' and gives visitors thirty minutes of exposure to a multimedia presentation of the stock market of the future. This is fun for both adults and children, and is an excellent attempt to give passers-by the feeling of how markets work. When I stopped by I could not help but contrast the efforts made by NASDAQ with the grey and unwelcome portals of the London Stock Exchange and its sullen security guards, whose inclination is to pounce on you the moment you have shuffled through the door. If you do not have proof of an appointment you will be sent straight back out into Throgmorton Street without so much as a brochure to study.

At its most simple NASDAQ is a giant computer facility where people who own shares can sell them to people who want to buy them, and vice versa. It is, literally, an exchange, which enables the buyer to find someone prepared to sell at a price he or she is prepared to pay. It is, if you like, a hi-tech, hi-speed, highly sophisticated version of eBay.

I will describe the process followed by a small investor who decides to buy 100 shares in Microsoft. The first task is to get a price – not the amount ($25) quoted in the newspapers, which will be 24 hours out of date, but the exact price at which the stock may be bought. This can be done over the phone or in person at a broker's office, but the easiest route is to use an online dealing service which handles American shares.

All that is needed is to key in the NASDAQ code for Microsoft, which is MSFT, and you will normally get five pieces of information.

Bid price: $ 24.85 > Bid size: 5,400
Ask price: $24.88 > Ask size: 500
Last trade: $24.85

What this tells you is that the last reported trade in Microsoft was at $24.85. At this moment in time someone is willing to pay that same price for 5,400 Microsoft shares. The ask price – known in Britain as the offer price – indicates that right now someone is ready to sell 500 Microsoft shares at $24.88. If you are ready to buy right now you could get your shares at $24.88, but you'd have to take 500, not the 100 you want. The difference between these prices is known as the spread, which is part of the cost off share ownership. When you trade in a second-hand car to a dealer you get less than he will sell the car for – that is his spread, which is likely to be much larger, but then only one item is traded rather than hundreds.

Let us now track what happens if you decide to place an order. You have two choices. One is to ask the broker to buy the stock at the best possible price, hoping that the firm will be able to get you your 100 shares at the $24.88 price despite the small size of your deal, but leaving him to pay a little more if need be. That is called buying 'at best'. Or you could place a limit order, whereby you tell the broker the most you will pay is $24.88, and you will sit and wait until you can get the Microsoft shares at that price. The chances are you will be successful, but if the market is rising you may be unlucky and then the order will fail.

However you place the order – online, by phone, or in person – your broker is legally obliged to execute it at the best price, even if you have set a limit that indicates you will go higher than the market price. The broker will direct your order to one of four places – to a market-making firm, to an electronics communications system (ECN), a regional stock exchange, or, if the broker is a large concern, to the NASDAQ system itself.

As Microsoft is a widely traded share, with millions changing hands each day, the average broker will probably use a firm of market makers – businesses that make a living by buying stock when others want to sell and selling shares when others want to buy. There are over 300 such firms in the United States. Just like the local supermarket, they often keep inventory on hand so as to provide customers with instant service. This inventory will consist of popular stocks rather than the esoteric, just as Tesco will stock Nescafé but perhaps not coffee beans from Papua New Guinea.

They make their money by buying at the low bid price and selling at the higher ask price, and although this spread is usually less than five cents a share, high volume means high profits. Big stocks like Microsoft have 50 or more market makers, so there is plenty of competition. Their quotes for each stock are displayed on the NASDAQ screen.

Some of the largest brokerages have in-house market makers, and will want to use them because they will get the market makers' turn as well as commission, but they are obliged to give customers the best price in the market, which usually means reducing the spread. Others channel all orders to a favoured market maker, who undertakes to match the best price available at the point of trade, rather than engage in an auction system. Others prefer to use an ECN, which is a facility that matches customer buy-and-sell orders in a computer. If you are a confident person you can open an account with an ECN for a subscription fee and bypass the broker.

In our Microsoft example, the buyer would place his order for 100 MSFT at $24.88, and it would be displayed on the ECN's screen along with all other bids and asks. Someone else logged in wanting to get rid of 100 MSFT at $24.88 would key in a sell order. The computer would recognise an exact match and execute the transaction. Because there is no spread these systems are of value to the frequent trader, who has only to pay an annual service charge for using the facility. This arrangement has some similarity to the British SETS, but whereas the latter exists only for the professional market, American ECNs can be used by small traders. It is another example of how the American market is more friendly to the individual investor.

The central computer system for NASDAQ is in Trumbull, Connecticut, but there is a full back-up facility in Rockville, near Washington, in case of failure. Trumbull and Rockville are connected by 80,000 miles of leased telephone lines to 3,400 securities houses, which display the prices at which they are willing to trade, as well as to report sales and purchases, and other market data. The NASDAQ system is always being refined and updated and is considerably superior to SEAQ. There is plenty of competition: a typical NASDAQ stock has eleven market makers hungry for business.

NASDAQ information is as accessible to the woman in the stock-broker's coffee lounge in Austin, Texas, as it is to the Barclayshare member in Liverpool who might want facts about the American market. There is nothing to stop individual investors subscribing. Those who pay a small subscription have access to the system through a dumb terminal and a black and white monitor. By using a word code on the terminal keyboard, they can obtain on the screen a representative bid and a representative ask price on the stock in which they are interested.

Images and Reality

There is nothing like a good Hollywood movie to create a false impression, and Wall Street has had its share, with the film of the same name and another based on Tom Wolfe's book, *The Bonfire of the Vanities*. Doubtless there are dozens of Gordon Geckos on Wall Street, though some of the worst offenders have gone to prison. There are also some very rich people in the Street, though most of them are not inclined to ostentation, preferring a sandwich lunch at their desk to anything more pretentious. It surprises many to discover that on summer weekends some of the Street's wealthiest choose to travel up to their weekenders in the Hamptons or Long Island not by helicopter or light aircraft, but by the standard bus service.

Wall Street has its carers too. I invited a friend from Merrill Lynch to lunch one Saturday only to find that he was spending the day with an unemployed teenager from the Bronx. He was one of many in Merrill's mentoring scheme, wherein high-salaried executives give one of their most precious commodities, spare time, to try to help those at the bottom of the heap. For every success story there was a failure, but at least they cared.

Perhaps the greatest test for Wall Street came on 11 September 2001, when two passenger airlines were flown directly into the upper floors of Wall Street's tallest buildings, the twin towers of the World Trade Center. Several thousand Wall Street professionals either died instantly or perished as they tried to leave the burning, tottering wreckage. They, and hundreds of valiant firefighters who lost their lives trying to save them, will go down in history as the victims of the worst terrorist attack the world has ever known. Some survived, but it was not a case of the rich looking after themselves. The *New York Times* told the story of John Paul DeVito and Harry Ramos, the senior officers of investment bank May Davis. DeVito managed to coax his twelve terrified employees down eighty-seven floors to safety. Ramos, meanwhile, stopped on the thirty-sixth floor to help a complete stranger. He was never seen again. His partner told the *Times*:

> If you had seen what it was like in the stairway you would be proud. There was no gender, no race, no religion. It was everyone unequivocally helping each other. I am sick and tired of hearing on Wall Street that the good guy always finishes last.[1]

Although loss of human life was the most tragic consequence of the acts of barbarism perpetrated that day, there was no doubt that the goal of the terrorists was to wreck Wall Street, the premier fortress of capitalism.

The next morning it looked as if they had succeeded. Several major finance houses had lost many of their staff, their offices and their computer systems. Those in adjoining buildings, like Merrill Lynch, Lehman Brothers, American Express and scores of others, were spared loss of life, but their buildings were uninhabitable and, in some cases, unsafe. The Millennium Hilton, a favourite of visitors to Wall Street, looked set to topple in the first strong wind. The whole of the Street – indeed, the whole area of Manhattan below Greenwich Village – was declared a no-go area for all but rescue and recovery teams. Trading

---

[1] *New York Times*, 16 September 2001.

on the New York Stock Exchange, the smaller American Stock Exchange and the NASDAQ was suspended indefinitely.

After three working days and a weekend, Wall Street was up and running again, after a truly remarkable effort. Merrill Lynch regrouped its top executives at the home of its head of communications in Chelsea Village, and then set up a command centre in an empty warehouse in Greenwich Village. Next day it phoned its staff and ordered them to other offices across the Hudson River in New Jersey. In the process it had to install new computers and new telecommunications and draw back all its records from a backup centre outside New York City. In this same period, Lehman Brothers took 665 rooms at the New York Sheraton in Seventh Avenue and refurbished them as offices for 1,500 brokers and analysts.

During the chaos that followed the disaster, the actual systems held up well. NASDAQ, whose headquarters are at One Liberty Plaza, directly across the street from the World Trade Center, evacuated its building as a precautionary measure, but switched its operations to its other centres and could have resumed operations on the morning after the disaster. Because there are more than twenty NASDAQ connection centres throughout the United States, with plenty of back-up, there was no technical reason for it not to open. Those trading rooms that could not connect were offered twenty-four-hour support as they established themselves in other locations. The reason why it did not open on 12 September was explained by NASDAQ's chief executive:

> It was a textbook example of effective cooperation among the government, markets and private industry. Telecommunication, power and employee access problems created enormous complications and risks in reopening the market. In addition there was unanimity among all participants that the equity markets should open as quickly as possible, but only when we could ensure that they could operate efficiently with proper liquidity available, without additional constraints and with universal access for investors. We also believed that, given the uncertainties, it was important for investor confidence that all equity markets open simultaneously.[2]

And so they did.

---

[2] Hardwick Simmons, CEO of NASDAQ, in testimony to the Senate Committee on Banking, 20 September 2001.

Europe Takes to Shares

Although there is evidence that a stock market flourished in Amsterdam at about the same time as London began share trading, the Europeans lagged far behind the Anglo-Saxons in developing equity finance. No one should be surprised by this: the mayhem caused to business and trade by two world wars meant that most people holding shares would have seen their values wiped out. Either the businesses or industries were obliterated or they were taken over by the state. Many thousands fled to America; others with savings put them under their beds or in the bank. Those Russians who owned shares prior to the Revolution had them confiscated.

Stock markets, known in Europe as bourses, were reopened after the end of World War II, but they could not be said to play a central role either in people's savings or in the financing of industry. Those functions were dominated by the banks, which, as one writer explains, re-established their earlier pre-eminence.

> The big continental banks evoke a much deeper dread than the British, partly because they have embraced industry with a closer hug. Their power goes back to the nineteenth century. The French Rothschilds helped to finance the railways in France and beyond, and their rivals the Pereires set a pattern for the 'universal bank', collecting savings from small savers and deploying the capital for the development and control of industry, which was followed elsewhere on the Continent. The French banks soon fell behind the German banks, who played a key part in the new industries, and used their deposits, and their customers' proxies, to establish controlling shares in the big companies. A German bank, as the saying went, accompanied an industrial enterprise from the cradle to the grave, from establishment to liquidation throughout all the vicissitudes of its existence.[3]

It was not until the winter of 1990, when the Berlin Wall came tumbling down, symbolising the end of the Cold War, that Europe began seriously to build effective stock markets. Now they are growing rapidly.

Fuelling the changes have been European Monetary Union and a wave of privatisations. Slowing them down have been the inevitable bureaucracy and processes that have accompanied the need to get cross-border agreements in a greatly expanded and very diverse

---

[3] Anthony Sampson, *The New Europeans*, NY Hodder, USA, 1968.

European Union. There has also been a certain reluctance in some quarters to embrace American-style financial systems, billed derisively by US critics as cowboy capitalism. That debate still rages, but the focus now is more on labour practices and social issues than the technologically-driven financial markets, which business leaders have embraced with enthusiasm, though many have qualms about American-style corporate governance.

The wave of privatisation came first, with Germany the prime mover in state enterprise sell-offs conducted as aggressively as those in Britain in the Thatcher years. The biggest of these, Deutsche Telecom, raised DM 20 billion in December 1996, with 690 million shares sold, creating a major global company. France followed suit, and many enterprises were privatised, but not to the same extent as in Britain. Some countries decided, with disastrous consequences, to retain their state-owned airlines, at a huge cost to the taxpayer, while also distorting competition in Europe. They also left their railways in state hands, regarding them as a public service, avoiding the disastrous mess of Britain's railways.

Then came the European Monetary Union, and with it a wave of mergers and acquisitions as Europe's giants sought domination in their sector. European groups like Axa and Zurich (insurance and financial services), Nestlé (food), Unilever (consumer products and food), BMW and Volkswagen (cars), Reed Elsevier and Bertelsmann (publishing and media) sucked up competitors in a rapacious bid for market share growth. Daimler Benz, itself a merger of two great automotive companies, merged with America's third largest car manufacturer, Chrysler, which then bought a big slice of Japan's Mitsubishi Motors. All these deals required massive cross-border financial advice and cash.

Europe's emerging bourses were not up to it and London failed to grasp its opportunity to become the dominant exchange in Europe. There are many explanations for this – lack of vision, poor leadership and the inability of some to see beyond the pound-versus-euro argument. There was also a tendency to see the battle for control of Europe's financial markets as one of location: the City of London versus the City of Frankfurt, a battle that still surfaces from time to time. There have been wins for London, as when DeutscheBank moved its investment bank to new headquarters near Liverpool Street station.

What many forgot was that location does not mean ownership, and that in an age of new technology, location does not matter that much. While the London Stock Exchange fiddled, the Europeans got their act together. The LSE had failed a few years earlier to grasp the full potential of the futures, options and derivative markets, and a separate institution, the London International Financial Futures and Options Exchange (LIFFE), was formed and operated very successfully.

In 2002 LIFFE was gobbled up by Deutsche Boerse AG, operator of the Frankfurt Stock Exchange, as part of a process of power grabbing that began when the euro was launched in 1999. Then there were 32 stock exchanges across Europe, most of them parochial and concerned only with the companies of the country in which they operated. At the time of writing the number is down to three – the LSE, still the largest by volume of shares traded, Euronext NV, a Dutch company which runs four stock exchanges across Europe, including the Paris Bourse, and Deutsche Boerse.

It seems only a matter of time before the LSE itself falls into non-British ownership. Unlike the individuals who owned the exchange before Big Bang, the present institutional shareholders have little loyalty to Britain, and are likely to take the best price. In early 2005 the Deutsche Boerse sought to buy the LSE, but offered too little to satisfy LSE shareholders and too much for some of the German board members, who staged a revolt. Had it succeeded, the German company would have achieved a dominant position in the European stock markets. Despite the failed bid, Britain's Office of Fair Trading continued to study the prospect of a takeover, in the belief that it was something that, sooner or later, would happen.

Like London, both its European rivals operate electronic trading systems which have cut costs and added value. Unlike London, both have effective futures and derivatives markets built into their systems.

The one thing that London has going for it is that its basic share market is deeper and wider than those in Europe, where the old traditions of finance persist among medium-size and smaller enterprises.

The family firm

It is the structure of European industry and its hangover from the past that limits the activities of the continental stock markets in a way that may still take many years to unravel. The main influence is family ownership of large companies with many interlocking directorships, something that simply is not a major factor in America and Britain. Rupert Murdoch's News Corporation is one of the very few Anglo-Saxon mega-corporations that is dominated by family interests, but neither it or Murdoch himself owns a substantial stake in a bank or a large non-media company. In Europe, such cross-ownership is commonplace. It is not unusual to find a major family controlling several industrial companies while also holding down a seat on a bank board. One academic study found that:

> The United Kingdom and the United States have 'outsider systems' of corporate control. There are large equity markets, dispersed ownership and active markets in corporate control. By contrast a majority of Continental European markets have 'insider systems' with small numbers of quoted companies, concentrated share ownership, and comparatively low levels of takeover activity. Germany is a good example of an 'insider' system. It has less than 800 quoted companies, compared with nearly 3,000 in the UK, and 85 per cent of the largest quoted companies have a single shareholder owning more than 25 per cent of voting shares.[4]

What this means is that there is substantial pyramid ownership. In half of Germany's companies one single shareholder owns 50 per cent of the stock, which gives them control of the company. The company they control then often owns 50 per cent of a second company. Work that out and you will see that it is possible to control the second company from on high by buying only 25 per cent of the equity, or 12.5 per cent if you go one further step down the pyramid. This could not happen in Britain, first because institutions, rather than operating companies, hold most stock in big corporations, and secondly because British law provides that once you hold 30 per cent of the stock of a company, you must bid for the remainder at the highest price you paid for the earlier share purchases.

There is a misapprehension that the banks hold large blocks of shares in German companies. They do not. A study in 2000 found that only 6 per cent of shareholdings in excess of 25 per cent are held by banks,[5] and that remains the case. What banks do have are proxy votes, often entrusted to them by family companies, which represent more than one fifth of holdings over 25 per cent. That is where they wield their power, particularly through blocking resolutions that might be damaging to their friends and clients.

---

[4] Julian Franks and Colin Mayer, *Ownership and Control of German Corporations*, September 2000.
[5] Ibid.

German companies, and those in some other European countries, are controlled by a two-tier strucuture. The first tier is what is called the supervisory board, which is composed of shareholder, employee and stakeholder representatives. Then there is the management board, which consists of full-time executives, headed by the chief executive. The supervisory board appoints the management board, approves the accounts and long-term strategy, and can intervene when there is a serious deterioration in the company's fortunes. The chief executive is not a member of the supervisory board, and does not normally attend its meetings. What is interesting here is that representation on the supervisory board goes hand in hand with ownership; in three out of four German companies where the shareholder is another company, the shareholder appoints the chairman of the board and one in four of all remaining members.[6]

Tokyo

Once trading on the Tokyo Stock Market resembled the crowd at a Premiership soccer match. The surging mass of dealers swayed to and fro, pulling faces and shaking their fists, sometimes shouting hysterically as they raised their hands in a kind of salute to capitalism. From time to time those involved in the mêlée were punched, pushed and kicked as 330 million shares changed hands on a daily basis.

Those days are gone. Since 1999 Tokyo and the other lesser Japanese exchanges have become becalmed in electronic systems similar to those deployed by NASDAQ in the United States and by exchanges in London.

Tokyo's recent history has not been helped by a series of scandals, ranging from simple market rigging and insider trading to the fall from grace of Nomura, Japan's largest securities house. Nomura, founded as a small money changer in the back streets of Osaka in 1872, was once the world's biggest stockbroker, and was forecast to swallow up both American and European rivals. While it is still a giant, it has spent much of the last five years restoring a reputation tarnished when it was forced to admit making illegal payments, totalling $50 million, to *sokaiya*, mob gangsters who made a good living from threatening to disrupt companies' annual meetings. It was ordered to stop trading for a month as punishment, and lost $36

[6] Franks and Mayer, op. cit.

million in revenue. Its revenues fell further when long-standing customers moved their business elsewhere.

The Ministry of Finance in Tokyo had threatened an even tougher penalty – a ban on trading for six months – but withdrew the threat when Nomura's president, Hideo Sakamaki, resigned in disgrace and was replaced by Junichi Ujiie, who undertook to clean up the company. Ujiie was untarnished because he had been out of the country running the United States operation when the crimes were committed. He immediately sacked twenty of Nomura's forty-three directors, including everyone at the rank of senior managing director or above, in doing so reducing the average age of the Nomura board from fifty-five to forty-eight. It was the biggest purge ever at any Japanese company.

Nomura and the two other leading Japanese financial houses, Daiwa and Nikko, are the main brokers in Japan, accounting for three quarters of the underwriting business and half of all trade on the Tokyo Stock Exchange.

Despite its problems, Nomura has sought to recruit English staff from across the globe. Its London office has been a very active investor in the British leisure market, at one stage buying up a number of the country's public houses. It has also been one of the largest recruiters of Oxbridge graduates, taking them to Tokyo for months of intensive training before posting them round the world.

I met a group of Nomura recruits on a visit to Tokyo a few years ago, and here is what they said:

> **Christopher**: I joined Nomura because I think their global expansion programme is absolutely phenomenal. I am sure they are going to come up as number one ahead of the others.
> **Catherine**: They are going to be very, very big. They are very ambitious, and the togetherness and the spirit really is obvious.
> **James**: They really believe in team work. I am also amazed at the degree of responsibility that last year's graduates have been given. (James held up a white Nomura carrier bag.) I have brought this to show you because it sums up Nomura's attitude. It says: 'Nomura makes money make money'. Now a British institution would probably have had a Latin ode.

Life is, I suspect, not as exciting in British exchanges, but the opportunities for bright graduates to work on the stockmarkets is expanding worldwide, particularly in Asia, where the key to success is to learn an Asian language, probably Mandarin.

10 Market Movers and Mavens

Our gain in wealth during 2004 was $8.3 billion . . . a
lacklustre performance.

Warren Buffett

Within seconds of a takeover bid being announced, a company's profits tumbling, a central bank lowering or raising interest rates or the share price of a company moving up or down on any of the world's major markets, investors everywhere in the wired-up world will hear of it. Financial news travels faster than anything else.

Usually the professional investors hear first, and pay for the privilege. They also have the benefit of the instant interpretation of a highly specialised team of analysts and chartists. Even so, the ordinary investor is not far behind the professional in the information chain, thanks to the internet. Government regulators have also contributed, although the objective of levelling the playing field is still far from being achieved.

Earlier, I discussed at length how shares are valued, and now it is time to look at the forces that change these values. It will quickly become apparent that there is no one group of movers and shakers, as the conspiracy theorists of the anti-capitalist movement would have you believe. Share movements are not dictated by a secret cabal of business leaders meeting on an American or European country estate guarded by hitmen and Rottweilers. Nor do exclusive summits such as the annual meeting of the World Economic Forum in Davos dictate the shape and flow of the markets in the days or weeks that follow their annual 'talkfest' in the Swiss Alps. I have participated in many of these summits, and while they are valuable networking events that make it possible to exchange views and predictions with hundreds of influential decision-makers, there is little or no evidence that they are the instigators of successful collusion and market manipulation. Markets are moved by a variety of factors.

No one predicted that global financial insanity would prevail in 1998 and 1999 in the valuations of some internet stocks. (They should not be described as technology stocks, because there is little that is technological about them.) Equally, only a few predicted that the internet bubble would burst as swiftly as it did. The Asian meltdown that followed the collapse of the Thai baht in 1997 was not foreseen by the Central Intelligence Agency, the International Monetary Fund or the World Economic Forum, despite the very substantial knowledge of these organisations and their staff or members.

Investor sentiment, the most powerful force in price movements, often reflects inexplicable shifts in the public mood. The bear market that coincided with the arrival of President George W. Bush in the White House in January 2001 was fuelled by a quite sudden decision by Americans to stop buying things, particularly computers and other consumer electronics products. This was not because Americans earned less, because they didn't, and they also had Bush's promise ringing in their ears of more money in their pockets through tax cuts. Even when Bush swiftly delivered on his promise and pushed through the tax cuts, Americans failed to rattle the tills on Main Street and proved just as recalcitrant when the Federal Reserve reduced interest rates not once but several times. Investors talked of recession and sold stocks. The falling stock market created its own clouds of gloom and the economy slowed further. Equally illogical was the rise in American stocks that accompanied the re-election of Bush for a second term. Let us look at some of the main groups that influence the markets.

Governments, Central Banks and Politicians

Across the world, this group has probably the greatest single influence, but we need to be careful and distinguish between what governments do and what politicians say. It is a sad commentary on modern politics that all too often words are not matched by action. Before the euro was launched as a common currency for some member nations of the European Union, many of Europe's political leaders prophesied that it would become a strong currency, even rivalling the dollar. Those investors, particularly Americans and Britons, who bought shares or funds in Europe upon the creation of the Eurozone (the countries in the European Union which have agreed to operate a common currency) quickly found that any gains they made in share values were more than wiped out by the declining value of the euro. Only when the US deficit flew out to record levels did the euro rise.

Most finance ministers are sensible enough never to comment publicly on currency rates; those who do usually get it wrong. Beware of political leaders predicting the rise or fall of a currency, because the opposite will usually happen. Reuters, the news agency, now always inserts 'says' or 'predicts' in any report of this kind – 'Brown says', 'Chirac predicts', for example – so as to distance itself from the claim.

However, government actions are another story. Markets are moved by publication of a raft of government statistics, and by changes in interest rates. Changes in interest rates have the most impact. Governments in the United States, Britain and the Eurozone leave the setting of interest rates to their central banks – in other words, the Federal Reserve Board, the Bank of England and the European Central Bank respectively. The rise or fall of interest rates is the key instrument of monetary policy, and these three central banks are independent and quite capable of making decisions which can be and often are against the political inclinations of ministers. Tightening monetary policy by raising interest rates and therefore discouraging borrowing and spending and encouraging saving is a key weapon against inflation, but often results in job losses. When an economy is slowing down, lowering interest rates is supposed to stimulate spending and fuel economic activity.

Thus a drop of half of 1 per cent in basic rates, the yardstick by which all other rates are set, is usually seen as a stimulus for equities, while rising interest rates damage share markets. When the return on bonds, a more risk-averse investment, rises to a level that wipes out the average equity premium, which is the higher return one gets for greater risk, many investors move out of equities into bonds until the position stabilises.

In Britain, decisions on interest rates are taken by the Monetary Policy Committee, a group of economists and other experts chaired by the Governor of the Bank of England, which usually meets over two days each month. After the meeting the Governor announces the decision – no change or a rise or fall – and often holds a news conference. The minutes of the meeting, summarising discussions and shedding more light on decisions, are published at a later date.

Then there is the annual Budget, produced by the Chancellor of the Exchequer and delivered to Members of Parliament in the House of Commons in March each year. This is where changes in taxation are announced, as well as a progress report given on the nation's economy. The Budget is a peculiar ritual in Britain. It is preceded by weeks in which the Chancellor and his senior officials in the Treasury are in purdah – their description, not mine – and consider a variety of pleas from pressure groups such as the Confederation of British Industry, the Institute of Directors and the Trades Union Congress. It is rather like a shaikh's majlis, with the supplicants noisily proclaiming their needs and the Treasury mandarins nodding sagely and keeping quiet. The period of purdah begins early in the New Year at a large country house, and continues through long and sometimes argumentative evenings at the Treasury's mausoleum in Whitehall. By the time the Chancellor has packed his secrets into a faded red dispatch case and carried them into the House of Commons, the financial community is in a state of high expectation, fuelled by Budget leaks and media comment. By tradition the Chancellor sips at a glass of whisky as his message unfolds. Every piece of news is flashed on to television screens and the market reacts. The impact of the Budget has lessened in recent years because of the Chancellor's Autumn Statement, which provides another major economic assessment.

There are other British Government decisions that move markets, such as a new issue of gilts. However, foreign government or quasi-official events also have an impact. The two most watched by traders are the decisions of the Federal Reserve Board on American interest rates, where any change impacts global markets, and the deliberations of the European Central Bank, which governs interest rates in the Eurozone.

The Analysts and the Ratings Agencies

Once upon a time the analyst was the office introvert, who spent his day hidden from view in a corner behind a pile of dusty papers, fretting over obscure charts while his broking colleagues got on with the business of trading shares. Now, though sometimes still held in low esteem by a few of the more self-opinionated members of the trading desks, analysts are high profile.

They have their strongest impact with their estimates of companies' profits, and buy or sell recommendations on individual shares. Major companies report their results to the London Stock Exchange and other exchanges on a quarterly basis, and others half-yearly. These events are eagerly anticipated, and when results are published, usually in the early morning before trading starts, they nearly always lead to share movements, unless they are, to quote a much-used phrase, 'in line with analysts' expectations'.

The rules provide that companies publish their results through the main exchange on which they are listed before discussing them with anyone. What that usually means is that within seconds of publication, a company's chairman, chief executive or finance director – and often all three – will be hosting a breakfast for analysts who follow the company. Sometimes specialist company reporters from the broadsheet newspapers will also be invited, although more often this group has its own less detailed question-and-answer session, which usually concludes with one-to-one interviews between the chairman and business television channels. The comments to analysts and the media will also impact on the markets because almost certainly the company executive will be asked for a forward-looking statement.

After the meetings the analysts will head back to their offices to brief their colleagues on the trading desks, although if what they have heard excites them they will use their mobile phones. They will then enunciate their opinions to the outside world, through media interviews, newsletters and the internet.

In between results announcements, companies sometimes issue statements about their outlook, with the most important of these being profit warnings. A profit warning will always depress a company's shares, and may well impact on an entire sector.

Analysts usually work in sectors, such as telecommunications, media, oil and gas, or banks, in which case their focus is usually limited to a handful of major companies and their work highly specialist. These men and women tend to be as knowledgeable about a company as those in the company itself, and they are usually highly respected.

Fundamental research and field trips take up to two thirds of their time – and they spend a surprising amount of time on marketing activities, frequently talking to the media. This partly explains why analysts, especially those who appear often on radio and television, are not universally admired, particularly by the chairmen of the companies upon whose operations they comment.

Some companies also run away-days or weekend trips with analysts and selected financial journalists. Carlo de Benedetti, when chairman of Olivetti, favoured Florence, where the men and women from broking houses across Europe could sample fine art, good food and Tuscan wine. British Airways sometimes flies opinion-makers in the City to a variety of exotic overseas locations in the old but not mistaken belief that the further away from home, the closer the mind might be concentrated on the subject in hand. Many German companies favour a day in Rhineland vineries followed by a stiff morning of financial presentations at head office. Golf days for susceptible business editors are popular in Britain, while I have also heard of weekends spent 'curling' in the Scottish Highlands.

As and when they complete their detailed studies of the companies they watch, analysts will issue recommendations. These will not just be 'buy' or 'sell', but will include other terms such as 'strong buy' and 'hold'. These recommendations will be widely reported, and will usually lead to price shifts.

Securities analysts have now formed an industry in their own right, and have their own professional body. It is a highly competitive business, and one in which the rewards can be considerable. There are even annual contests for best analysts and broking firms, sector by sector. The best-known survey, the annual Extel Ranking of UK Investment Analysts, run by Thomson Financial, was started in 1973 by Continental Illinois and is based on a detailed questionnaire sent to investment managers of the major institutions. Only four out of ten bother to reply in detail, but this still makes almost a hundred, with over £600 billion of funds in their care, and the survey is self-perpetuating, as the winners can count on many a new job offer and a stream of telephone calls from journalists, merchant bankers, accountants and others anxious to tap their expertise.

A similar analysts' Oscar awards takes place in New York, under the aegis of *Institutional Investor* magazine, owned by Euromoney.

More detached from the markets are the credit rating agencies, of which Moody's and Standard and Poor's are the majors. They grade a company's financial health by a star system. Triple A is at the top, triple B is risky. Anything below that is classified as non-investment, better known as 'junk'. Both these agencies also rate country's debts – or the chances of creditors being repaid. Their approach is somewhat different from that of the mainstream stock market analyst, whose objective is usually to make a value judgement on a company's future prospects and profits. The ratings agencies are more concerned with the strength of a company's balance sheet, the level of its debt, particularly the ratio of debt to assets, and its ability to meet its liabilities to bond holders and others who have lent it money. Nevertheless, ratings agency reports are an invaluable guide for the equities investor too. Their ratings are an important factor in determining a company's cost of borrowing.

The Chartists

Unlike the 'health warning' section of financial services advertisements, chartists believe that past performance really is a guide to the future of share price movements, and go out of their way to prove that this is the case. Chartism goes in and out of fashion, and some of the best chartists – or technical analysts, as they are sometimes called – command respect and a large audience whenever they make a presentation.

The chartist is particularly interested in market peaks and troughs, and believes that these high and low points can be predicted with a reasonable degree of certainty. Expressions like 'points of resistance' are important. Just as it is possible to foresee that house prices cannot rise beyond a certain point (because the ratio of borrowing to average income becomes too high) or that prices can fall no further (because demand will rise from those on lower earnings), so stock market chartists are convinced that it is possible to assess a share's intrinsic value.

By carefully plotting price movements over a period of time – an easy process with high-speed personal computers – a chartist can spot a trend, and recommend a time to buy or sell. That is the theory; in fact, chartism is fallible. The chartists failed to predict the great stock market crash of 1987, but then so did most other so-called experts.

Those who wish to learn more about the charms of chartism would do well to go to their nearest business bookshop and browse through some of the many titles available. An easier option might be to use the *Financial Times* to plot the performance of the main indices, and to look at shares that, year after year, appear to better it. If you have a PC, there are some interesting and inexpensive computer programs that enable you to do this.

The Gurus

More colourful than chartists are those rich individuals who have made fortunes out of the markets – George Soros, Peter Lynch, Warren Buffett, Ron Brierley, to name but a few. They have an impact in several ways. First, anything they say is likely to move markets, and not one of them could be called shy. Secondly, their actions are watched closely by other investors, and mimicked. Thirdly, many investors try and build a portfolio that tracks that of the gurus, in the hope that they too can become super-rich.

Warren Buffett, affectionately known as the Oracle of Omaha, is America's leading investment authority. From a small and unpretentious office in Omaha, Nebraska, he has bought and sold shares to achieve a personal wealth of over $10 billion. Buffett, self-effacing and gracious, runs his investments through his company, Berkshire Hathaway. His 'buy and hold' investment strategy is, according to his friend Peter Lynch, built round 'determining the intrinsic value of a business and paying a fair or bargain price: he doesn't care what the general stock market has done recently or will do in the future'.[1]

How can the average investor employ Warren Buffett's methods? According to Lynch, Buffett 'never invests in businesses he cannot understand or are outside his "circle of competence".' Says Lynch:

> All investors can, over time, obtain and intensify their 'circle of competence' in an industry where they are professionally involved or in some sector of business they enjoy researching. One does not have to be correct very many times in a lifetime as Warren states that twelve investment decisions in his 40-year career have made all the difference.[2]

Buffett went out of fashion temporarily when he decided not to invest in the new economy and dotcoms. Some commentators wrote him off as out of touch, the once-great investor who did not 'get' the new economy. Buffett refused to accept the trendies' new metrics, epitomised by the use of acronyms like EBITDA, earnings before interest, tax, depreciation and amortisation. Such measurements were used to grossly inflate the share price of Vodafone, the British-based mobile phone company, which in 2000 soared on an EBITDA of £7.04 billion. The reality – its profit and loss – was a loss of £8.09 million. When reality set in, Vodafone's price collapsed. Buffett asked scornfully: 'Who do those who use EBITDA think pays for the capital expenditure that generates depreciation – the tooth fairy?' When internet stocks crashed, Buffett had the last laugh. In his 2001 annual letter to shareholders, he commented wryly that he had

---

[1] Robert G. Hagstrom, Jnr, *The Warren Buffett Way*, John Wiley and Sons, 1995.
[2] Ibid., Introduction by Peter Lynch.

'embraced the 21st century by entering such cutting edge industries as brick, carpet, insulation and paint. Try to control your excitement!'[3]

Buffett's yearly letters are required reading for those interested in investment, and can be found on Berkshire Hathaway's website at www.berkshirehathaway.com. His March 2005 letter was a classic, ripping into the Bush administration for allowing the dollar to fall and the current account deficit to widen to a 'staggering' level. This, as he put it, was 'force-feeding American wealth to the rest of the world at a rate of $1.8 billion daily'.

For many years Henry Kaufmann was one of the most influential voices in Wall Street. Armed with a doctorate in banking and finance, Kaufmann helped build up the research department of Salomon Brothers, the largest investment bank in America in the latter part of the last century. In the seventies and eighties his predictions on interest rates, inflation and other economic indicators were hugely prescient and widely followed. Paul Volcker, one of the more renowned chairmen of the Federal Reserve Board, praises Kaufmann for his 'depth of thinking'. An extract from Kaufmann's auto-biography illustrates this quality:

> Financial markets are in many ways a microcosm of the people and societies they serve. Though measured in sterile figures, they embody and reflect much of the drama of the human condition: from the quest for comfort, security and wealth to the impulses to take risk and ensure the future and to compete and cooperate. The extremes of market movement reflect the extremes of human nature and human emotion: from optimism and elation to pessimism and despair. In the financial markets, as in life, rationality prevails most of the time.[4]

Investor Relations Managers

Companies themselves like to publish more information then ever before about their operations, and the rise of the specialist broking press has been such that the financial directors of large companies,

---

[3] Berkshire Hathaway annual report, 2001/2002.
[4] Henry Kaufmann, *On Money and Markets. A Wall Street Memoir*, McGraw Hill, 2000.

and their public relations people, often spend more time wooing brokers' analysts than talking to financial journalists. Many companies employ an investor relations manager, whose job it is to keep both institutional investors and analysts informed of the more favourable aspects of the company. They now have their own body, the Investor Relations Society. Many of its members have lavish expense accounts, and jet in and out of two or more European capitals a day, expending great energy and charm on their subjects. Things can, however, go wrong. I remember the investor relations executive at Olivetti wringing his hands at an unfavourable broker's circular on his company written by a very presentable woman analyst, and crooning down the phone: 'How can you do this kind of thing to me?'

In recent years, increasing attention has been paid by the major European companies to soliciting investment in the United States, and those who have neglected this aspect of financial public relations have done so at their cost.

An example is provided by ICI, which maintains a full-time investor relations executive in New York to keep analysts at both institutions and broking firms up to date with the company's financial affairs. Some of the information is printed material, but another aspect of the job is to organise an annual road show to five American cities. There are also quarterly meetings allowing all major US analysts to meet the company's finance director and other top members of staff, and visits are arranged for those who wish to tour ICI's operations in Britain.

In recent years, the demands on company investor relations staff have grown considerably as institutions and analysts have sought greater insights and direct access to company managements, especially the finance director and the chief executive. The London Stock Exchange believes that these two executives should now expect to spend two months a year on investor relations, this time including telephone and face-to-face briefings with analysts, meetings and lunches with institutions and press contacts, post-results road shows, set pieces such as annual meetings, and hosting company visits by analysts and investors.

> Any company which does not provide it [access to senior management] will inevitably be seen as unresponsive and secretive, and will see its share rating suffer in the long-term. In essence the institutions usually own the business, and expect the management to reflect this by being available to report to them

. . . as a company becomes more international, involving road-shows across Europe and even the United States, the appetite for European stocks is growing rapidly. The finance director will also get constant calls from a range of brokers, asking him or her to come and meet their institutional clients and those visiting from overseas. Unfortunately it is very hard to turn any of these down – the problem being that you have a business to run at the same time.[5]

Investor relations is particularly crucial for smaller quoted companies. Why does it matter? 'The answer is simple,' says the LSE guide. 'There are 1,500 other smaller stocks out there all battling for attention. Compound that globally and there's enormous choice. You have simply got to get seen.'

Most companies use financial public relations firms and their corporate brokers to help them, but these people's services do not come cheap, with £300 an hour being a usual charge. Many financial public relations professionals are former financial journalists, and therefore can talk the language of both the finance director and the analyst. They also tend to be skilful at discussing the state of their clients' businesses without upsetting the regulators.

Two areas of investor relations call for considerable skill – correcting wrong price forecasts published by analysts, and handling company visits. The first needs a great deal of subtlety, because in advance of a company's results the person handling investor relations cannot give detailed figures for fear of breaching the FSA rules. He can break these rules even by a too-precise correction. If things go bad and the company publishes a profit warning, there is a danger the stock price will collapse. If he talks up the stock, he will be in trouble also.

Visits by institutions are even more difficult, because if their representatives do not like what they find, they will sell your shares. There is nothing personal in this; the institution is under pressure to perform within quite short time periods and will be vigilant for any sign of weakness. So visits to a factory cannot just be left to an amiable plant manager buying a steak and kidney pudding for his guests at a local pub. Preparation by the company's finance director – and his presence at the visit – is a prerequisite, and it does not look good if the man from head office demonstrates that he has not been to the factory, and is not known by the local staff. The finance

---

[5] *A Practical Guide to Investor Relations*, London Stock Exchange. April 2000.

director will also have to do some homework into the institution. What does their portfolio consist of? Why did they buy into our company? Do they have cash to invest further? Is there a new fund manager, and if so where did he come from?

Investor relations people spend a large part of their time courting analysts. It has become customary for companies, particularly large companies, to make life as comfortable as possible for analysts, transporting them *en bloc* or individually to expensive country hotels, where it is possible for them to socialise with directors and senior management as well as to talk shop. A thorough briefing of analysts immediately after a company's results are published can be crucial in getting a good press, for increasingly newspapers are dependent on the views of analysts for comment. Expectations can be lowered if profits are going to be bad, and vice versa.

Financial public relations companies like to think that they are a cut above their counterparts in the West End who deal with products and services, and they probably are. Their senior people certainly exude more style, and maintain larger expense accounts. Their role is also much more important. There are legal obligations on companies who make financial changes to inform the press, and someone has to ensure that announcements are hand-delivered or sent electronically round the City at the right time, usually before market trading starts or in the late afternoon. There can be no question of sending out details of an acquisition, or a rights issue, on an embargoed basis.

But City PR advisers are no mere messenger boys. In many cases they are the eyes and ears of a company chairman, and occasionally his voice. Some company chairmen are gregarious and well-connected individuals, able both to project a positive image and to be sensitive to public opinion. The majority are not. A good PR person will be able to keep the chairman and directors informed of shareholders' opinion, what the newspapers are saying and, increasingly important, an assessment of political, Whitehall and Brussels opinion. If needed, he will be able to lobby politicians on the company's behalf. In major takeover activity, or in rights issues, the public relations man will also become a valuable aide to merchant bankers and stockbrokers.

Brokers' Circulars

These days almost all the share-broking houses run their own publishing operations, providing material in print as well as on the web, though internet users will, of course, be able to read it first. Still, brokers pride themselves on being able to get their publication out fast. On Budget day, for instance, some broking firms, as well as a few firms of accountants, will have their analysis of the Chancellor's measures in the hands of important clients long before the newspapers arrive.

Brokers' publications fall into two categories. There are regular weeklies or monthlies which contain a detailed review of the major economies and their financial markets, and offer a number of recommendations. Their forecasts have a high reputation for accuracy, usually better than the Treasury's. Amongst the regulars are Morgan Stanley's and Merrill Lynch's monthly outlooks, which are always good reading. There are regular specialist publications also, such as Salomon Brothers' *Financial Futures* and *Options Analysis*. Then there are sector or subject reports, which look at either a company or an industry in great detail and come up with recommendations.

Financial Advisers

With such a wealth of information available, to whom do today's investors turn for knowledge, and from whom can they obtain the most reliable advice? It is an obvious question, and it is perhaps the one that is most frequently asked by those with more than a few pounds to invest. It is also one of the hardest questions to answer.

One quite correct answer is no one. In the end the investor, whether the chief investment manager of a large insurance company or a widow in Worthing, has to make the decision as to which is the best vehicle for improving the value of their savings. It is possible, even for those who do not consider themselves financially literate, to have cheap access to a great deal of information, and even that is sometimes of less use than a hunch or an everyday observation. For instance, anyone who has watched the development of Britain's high streets over the past ten years will have noted the rise of Tesco. You may not make a quick profit on Tesco shares, but they will grow.

But this is to avoid the real question. To whom can one turn? A bank manager, stockbroker, accountant, building society manager, perhaps. All have their place and purpose, but none of them is necessarily a good investment adviser. Today's bank managers prefer to lend money than to give investment advice, steering customers in the direction of in-house unit trusts, which have not been the best performers. Accountants are useful tax advisers, and usually save you the cost of their fee, but when one seeks investment advice from them, they can start talking about complicated accountant-run pension schemes for the self-employed and property trusts. Building society managers live or die by the balances on deposit in their branches, so it is not easy to accept their views as impartial. This leaves stockbrokers, who can be either good or bad advisers, but mostly are a mixture of both.

Regrettably, very few large stockbrokers seem to want to service individual investors, and an increasing number of firms will not deal with them at all, unless the clients are very rich. This short-sighted approach is in contrast to the interest shown in small investors in the US, where share shops are common. But it is typical of the patronising attitude of many in the City towards the average member of the British public.

Britain is still well behind the United States. There, sharebrokers take their business to the public, and in almost every prosperous suburb there will be one or more open-plan broking offices, laid out rather like a large travel or estate agent, where members of the public may call, enjoy a cup of coffee, and discuss their investments with a consultant. There is plenty of literature available, including both brochures and financial magazines; Wall Street prices run continuously on television monitors, and there is a friendly and unpressurised atmosphere.

It is a pity that one of the few equivalent places in Britain's high streets appears to be the betting shop. The emergence of independent financial advisers should have led to the development of money shops, but not very many exist. For the most part the advisers stick to insurance broking, leaving share dealing to the banks and big securities houses.

11 Getting Too Much: the Information Overload

It is not long since private investors rightly complained that they were starved of adequate and timely information. Even with a subscription to the *Financial Times* or other periodicals they simply could not get enough of it. They were at a substantial disadvantage to professional and institutional investors with information at their fingertips. These days an average investor on a limited budget can access the same information as that available to the professionals. The problem is there is so much of it that it is easy to become overwhelmed and confused by information overload.

There is only one way to cope with too much information, and that is to be selective, searching for quality and taking the time to assimilate only media content that adds value to the investor's decision-making process. In my view that means looking for analysis and comment that has an intelligent perspective, a good example being the daily Lex column of the *Financial Times*, or the acid comments by Neil Collins, the long-standing and excellent City Editor of the *Daily Telegraph*. There are other worthwhile columns in the press, but there is a lot of chaff, even in the *FT*, that has little import for investors.

A primary requirement is fast and easy access to prices, preferably in real time. These need to be set in a historical perspective. Good charts are important, as is perceptive analysis by a credible observer. Achieving this means accessing all forms of media.

Everybody has a personal preference. When I am in Britain during the working day I prefer to have Bloomberg Television quietly in the background, supplemented by online internet access to web sites like advfn.com. I read the *Financial Times* and the City pages of the *Daily Telegraph* and *Daily Mail*. At weekends I like the *Economist*, the *Observer* and the *Investors Chronicle* magazine. I do not bother much with mainstream television news, believing its coverage of business to be flimsy and superficial, despite recent expansion in this sector. This is a personal preference. Each investor should experiment to find the media that suits his or her portfolio.

Television

Most people in Britain use television as their primary source of news. But there are only two channels that provide active and full-time coverage of business and finance: Bloomberg Television and CNBC, an acronym which stands for Consumer News and Business Channel. Both are American-owned. Bloomberg's founder and owner is an extraordinary entrepreneur and Mayor of New York, Michael Bloomberg, whose main business is the Bloomberg terminal for professionals. CNBC, part of the American network NBC, is owned by General Electric. Both have substantial operations in Britain and can be seen on cable or satellite for a basic subscription of about £10 per month.

Of the two, Bloomberg's London-based channel has a much stronger focus on the United Kingdom. While it will carry frequent live reports from the New York Stock Exchange and NASDAQ, it never forgets that its viewers are British investors. It has separate channels for France, Germany, Spain and Italy. The strong team of presenters impress with their knowledge of the markets, and handle breaking financial news with competence and flair. Bloomberg also has split screens, which is an advantage. Just under two thirds of the surface is dedicated to the actual television output, mostly live financial news and comment. To the right of the screen is a panel containing the time, and the actual state of three or four share market indices. This panel is rotated every five seconds and includes both the value and the percentage change for the FTSE 100, the FTSE 250, the All Share Index, the FT Futures, the techMark, the DAX from Germany, the CAC-40, the Dow Jones Industrial Average, the NASDAQ, NASDAQ Futures and a variety of currency cross rates.

Thus in a couple of minutes a viewer can get a complete global take on how things stand. Below this and across the screen is the first of two tickers, which contains a scrolling list of real-time share prices for the major markets mentioned earlier. Beneath is a second ticker line of less prominent indices. The final strip, across the foot, scrolls breaking financial, company and sporting news. Many television professionals do not like the display, and there are some who find it confusing. However, there is no other broadcaster as effective as Bloomberg in providing current and pertinent information.

Other cable and satellite broadcasters that cover business with a number of daily programmes include BBC World, BBC News 24,

CNN and Sky News, but their output will not satisfy those who want to be able to access information whenever they want it. Terrestrial or mainstream broadcasters in Britain provide little of interest to investors. What business coverage they do provide is aimed at the general public. After all, that is their remit.

The Internet

The internet has to be the best primary source of information for those who wish to follow the markets; in fact, for many it will suffice as the only source. The web has the advantage of being available twenty-four hours a day, seven days a week, and most of its content is free, though there are some sites that charge and are worth the subscription. The issue for investors is which sites to pick on grounds of reliability and objectivity.

Again, each and every user will develop a personal preference, and these preferences will depend on whether you are a day trader, frequent trader, occasional investor, or just an interested observer. There are several types of site to be considered:

- pure news providers
- those that contain market prices, breaking news and other hard information as well as providing access to a number of investment tools to help you manage a portfolio. These sometimes call themselves portals, implying that they provide a gateway to other relevant sites
- those that are built out from print publications, where much, if not all, of the content is culled from the newspaper or magazine
- those provided by companies, with a special section for their stockholders
- web sites of official or regulatory bodies such as the London Stock Exchange, the Financial Services Authority, and NASDAQ

Another site worth a regular visit more for its commentaries than for facts and charting tools is that of The Motley Fool, an organisation that has strong anti-establishment credentials and regularly expresses profound scepticism about the marketing antics of the big players (www.fool.co.uk). While not as thorough as its United States parent, it contains many common-sense comments, such as this example two weeks after the 11 September 2001 disaster, when the perceived wisdom was to slash the value of insurance shares:

> In the current market then, as you might expect, one of the hardest-hit sectors is insurance companies. Clearly with such a major disaster there will be some gigantic payouts to be made yet the effect of this is not shared out equally amongst the companies. But the knee-jerk reaction of the markets is to cream them all at first, creating potential opportunity. There may well be companies out there that have virtually no exposure at all, hit by indiscriminate dumping of anything smelling remotely of insurance. This is where deep crisis players must look. Similarly those that have some exposure may still be oversold.
>
> Insurers are an obvious hunting ground, but look at banks that have fallen. This makes no sense at all and is a good example of a potential crisis situation. Why would Lloyds as one example be a poorer-quality share the day after all this than before? I cannot see any reason. If anything, banks may profit from the presumably enormous rebuilding programme that will be commenced by the ever-resourceful Americans who, as I know them, will not permit this tragedy to alter their way of life.[1]

Acts of terrorism such as the attacks on the World Trade Center and the Pentagon depressed all shares, and those companies in crisis before the event are likely to remain in crisis for some time. But good companies with solid businesses might be expected to benefit substantially in the medium term. The Motley Fool's logic made a refreshing contrast to some of the more apocalyptic comments to be found elsewhere.

All these sites have bulletin boards where investors can participate by exchanging tips and opinions about the stock markets. These sites have a wide following, although any tip offered on a bulletin board needs to be treated with caution. Some tips are genuine; others are ill-concealed attempts to ramp the price of a share. There have been instances when one person has sent a bulletin board several thousand e-mails on the same stock within a year. A harder scam to detect is when someone tries to ramp a stock using multiple identities, either concurrently or in a planned sequence. Another more subtle scam is to respond to any negative remarks about a share you favour with an upbeat comment. Most bulletin boards have technology in place to try and identify those perpetrating scams.[2]

Bulletin boards are fun to use, especially when enough people take

---

[1] www.fool.co.uk, 22 September 2001.
[2] *Investors Chronicle*, 30 March 2001.

part to make a session a genuine exchange of views. But no one should expect comments on share values to be any more reliable than those of soccer supporters' clubs on their teams' prospects.

Company web sites

Don't look to a company site to give you news about that company first. All price-sensitive announcements have to be made available to the market before being published on the internet. That said, many company web sites are rich in information about their businesses and products, and a great deal of research time can be saved by making use of them.

The best sites will always have the most recent annual report, company announcements and press notices, and speeches made by the chief executive, downloadable in pdf format. Pdf files can be opened by a piece of software called Acrobat, available free from the web site of its maker, Adobe, or for a few pounds from any computer store. The information can then be saved or printed out.

Some sites have special sections for investors and include news stories that have appeared in the financial press about the company. Event calendars are often published showing dates for interim and annual dividend announcements, industry conferences and trade shows. Others go even further by providing transcripts of briefings to analysts. Pearson has a particularly good web site for investors, and includes video and audio clips of long briefings for analysts given by its chief executive, Marjorie Scardino.

The Investor Relations Society runs an annual award competition for best FTSE 100 web site for private investors. Those in the short list for 2005 were Hanson, Imperial Tobacco Group, Prudential, Royal Bank of Scotland, Signet Group, and Whitbread.

Other notable corporate sites are those of Barclays, BP, British Airways, Reuters, Sainsbury's and Vodafone. Most of these are third- or fourth-generation sites, rebuilt and redesigned after earlier efforts failed. Unfortunately, many companies have sites that are, by comparison, still primitive.

Many United States companies encourage questions from investors by e-mail and hold timed briefings at which people may post their questions over the web and have them answered by a general forum. Further developments down the line are likely to be web-casting of annual and special company meetings, with proxy voting available on a corporate web site. This will create a much more level playing field for stock holders who may live far away from a company's home base. Also, information that might once have been restricted to investors in one country is now available to all.

The Financial Press

Newspapers and magazines are for perspective, comment and analysis rather than hard news, although if you are not interested in trading shares more frequently than once or twice a week, a selection of reading matter will provide much of what you need.

Amongst the dailies, the *Financial Times* is the newspaper the professionals read and is the only one that provides a complete range of share prices and detailed company news. It also has breadth in that it covers the major international companies as well as overseas economies and emerging markets. Alas, the *FT*, good as it is, is not without some weak points. Apart from the excellent Lex column, which has three or four short commentaries each morning, it is surprisingly thin on analysis, and does not have the kind of probing investigative stories one might expect from such a reputable publication. These essentials for investors can often be found in magazines like *Fortune* and in some other international financial dailies, such as the *Wall Street Journal* in the United States and the *Australian Financial Review*. The *Wall Street Journal* has a European edition, *Wall Street Journal Europe*, but unfortunately it is a poor relation of its illustrious American parent.

Among the broadsheet dailies in Britain, the *Guardian*. the *Independent*, *The Times* and the *Daily Telegraph* all have solid business sections.

Pure news providers

There are only a few of these, and they display an understandable reluctance to provide more than a small amount of their output free of charge to non-paying customers. The exceptions are AFX News and Bloomberg News, whose output is bought and recycled by many web portals, and whose web sites are an excellent source of breaking news. AFX is a wholly-owned subsidiary of the state-owned French news agency Agence France Presse, but is based in London. Its site, afxpress.com, calls itself 'tomorrow's newspaper today', and conveniently groups stories in sectors to make access to specialist subjects easy. However, it does not have the analytical content of a newspaper and is very much a basic service. Bloomberg.co.uk has greater depth, more analysis, access to share prices, delayed by fifteen minutes, and the opportunity to look at clips of interviews in video and audio. For those who prefer a more worldly view of global business and are happy to accept only limited coverage of companies and markets, reuters.com is also worth a look.

Business Portals

When the last edition of this book was published three years ago it was necessary to go to specialist portals to get a comprehensive view of the stock market. Popular at the time were FT Market Watch, thestreet.com, stocktrade.co.uk and advfn.com. Now all but advfn.com have gone, closed down by their owners.

In their place mainstream search engines like Yahoo have moved in, and provide a magnificent service. For the average small investor, unable to afford a Bloomberg terminal, it is hard to fault Yahoo. Yahoo Finance provides all the latest financial news and the latest prices and currency rates, and has a set of analytical tools which – given that they are free – are magnificent. For example it is possible to dig deep into a company and view its historical share performance, company announcements and other factors.

I have reproduced the Yahoo Finance page for British Airways, an interesting company which was a successful privatisation, had its share of problems, changed management and is slowly recovering in

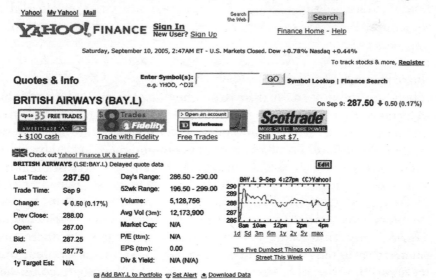

a tough competitive world. You get to its page by entering its symbol, BAY.L, in the box at the top. To the right is its latest share price and the percentage change from the previous close. Below are a series of useful numbers, such as the highest and lowest prices over a 52-week period and during the trading day. There is an up-to-the-minute calculation of key numbers such as the price earnings ratio, earnings per share and the last dividend payment. To the right is a chart of the price performance in the past few days – this may be adjusted to cover any historical period. To the left is a target number, which is the City consensus of what price the share could reach by the end of the year.

Another important service is analysts' estimates – in the case of British Airways the views of 20 analysts have been collated and an average forecast put up. There is also access to a series of brokers' reports, which can be downloaded, but at a cost of anything between £5 and $50 a time.

There is even a message board on which readers may post their own messages – some of them helpful, many of them barbed, like this one put up by someone identified only as 'conmaher' before Rod Eddington decided to leave his job as chief executive: 'Time to send Eddington back to the land of the Roos and get a real manager. He has done enough damage to this airline'

Advfn, which stands for Advanced Financial Networks, provides all this, and more. Just by registering you can get the free basic package which includes real-time share prices, actual share trades, access to its bulletin boards, charting packages, news alerts, company accounts data and watch lists. By paying £5 a month you can add a set of investment tools. There are other packages which enable you to access shares from overseas markets from Athens to Moscow. It is not surprising that Advfn continues to win annual awards for best financial web site. It has a superb set of graphing tools, and fully justifies its claim to be the first company to bring affordable, professional-level data to the mass market.

The only thing missing is analysis and comment, and here you need go no further than look to sites like ft.com and telegraph.co.uk. *The Times*, the *Guardian* and the *Independent* also have credible sites. Where ft.com scores is in the depth of its coverage of companies and markets, and the inclusion of material from its weekly magazine, *Investors Chronicle*, in its pay package. The *Investors Chronicle* tracks all UK listed companies, and is a magazine which has improved significantly in the past few years. As to the *FT*, you do not get a better testimony than that of Warren Buffett, who said it was essential reading.

PART III

Powering the Economy

There is a tendency in some circles to regard the stock market as a casino, frequented by punters ready to gamble a few thousand pounds in the hope of amassing a fortune. To hear some of the markets' critics, you might imagine it to be a globalised version of Las Vegas.

This nihilistic view of the markets ignores that their major role is to power the economy. Industries, whether manufacturing or services, could not function without the capital that is raised by the stock markets for both day-to-day operations and expansion. Gone are the days when business and industries were successfully run by governments.

In Britain power, telecommunications, energy, all manufacturing and most services are run by companies who in turn are owned by institutions and individuals through the stock markets. Railways, privatised by the Major government, are back in public ownership, and costing the taxpayer a fortune with little evidence of any improvement in services. Health and education, and postal services, remain mostly in the public sector, with little evidence of value for money in either.

Across the world the pattern is similar, with variations from country to country, but in most countries capital is provided by stock markets and banks, with most of the latter owned by shareholders.

How the markets work to raise capital is the subject of Part III.

12 Getting a Listing and Using the Stock Markets to Raise Money

Continuing obligations form an essential part of maintaining orderly markets and ensuring an acceptable level of investor protection . . .

FSA Handbook, 2001

You can't bring any old company to market and expect it to fly.
Keith Mullen, Thomson Financial

Almost every entrepreneur has a dream that he will be able to build up his own business as a private company, and then, because of its success and opportunity for further growth, be able to sell it to the market. For many the happiest solution is to find large numbers of individuals prepared to buy a total stake of, say, 47 per cent, so that the original founder and his family may retain control, while pocketing the cash generated by the sale. The lucky ones who do this become instant multi-millionaires, and are still able to hold on to the businesses they started and to run them in much the same way as before.

So how does an entrepreneur use the stock markets for his own benefit? The cardinal rule is that there should be some other reason for turning a private company into a listed one than simply to obtain a personal fortune. It would not be easy to bring a company to the markets if that were seen as the prime purpose. The most obvious attraction of going public is that obtaining a listing on any major stock exchange improves the standing of the concern and its products. There are not that many manufacturers of branded products or household names that are not public companies or corporations.

Apart from the benefit of obtaining a better image, becoming listed on a stock exchange also makes it easier, in normal times, to raise finance for expansion and development. Both investors and lenders have a strong preference for an enterprise that is not the play thing of an individual, or a group of individuals. Even though it is still possible for one man to hold the reins of a large public company, there are many more checks and constraints than on private companies, where clever accountants can play interesting games with the balance sheet. The accounts, and other indicators of performance, of public companies are closely scrutinised by meticulous analysts, who are always prepared to publish adverse comment where they believe it to be deserved. Thus most public companies are assessed with one objective – are they good investments? By contrast, the potential of private companies is not easy to assess, even when they are open to scrutiny.

Private company accounts are freely available only at Companies House, and for a small fee from the web, but they are usually at least one year in arrears. This alone explains why both institutional and private investors are reluctant to commit large sums to unquoted companies. What happens when the leading figures in a private company die? Their heirs may be hopeless businessmen, or may be forced to sell up part of their holding at an inopportune time in order to pay capital transfer tax. Father may drop dead just as the next recession is approaching; subsequent family feuding and a forced sale could leave the outside investors with little to show for their support.

Another strong advantage for an expanding business of being publicly listed on an exchange is that it helps in takeovers. Instead of paying cash for an acquisition, a company can often meet at least a part of the cost by offering a share swap, as in the summer of 1985 when Guinness offered shareholders in Bell, the whisky distiller, paper worth considerably more than the market price of their own scrip. When an efficient company is taking over a dull one, shareholders of the latter are often only too glad of the chance of such an easy escape route.

A further advantage of obtaining a listing is that the company attracts unsolicited funds. If they think you are doing well, any number of investors will buy your shares. Regular mention in the financial pages is useful publicity and, in the case of well-run companies, makes for easier relations with customers and helps when attempting to attract executive staff.

Going Public

When a company decides it would like to go public, it does this through an IPO, an initial public offering, a step which is not to be taken likely, because it is costly and also puts the business under a spotlight. In countries without stock markets there are no opportunities to do this, restricting the opportunities for local people to invest in their nation's businesses. In Western countries with large share markets there is a shortage of capital, so those seeking shareholders' funds have not only to open a window on their company, but also make it attractive to investors.

Perhaps not surprisingly, given the wave of regulation across the world and increased concern about corporate governance (the subject of a later chapter), there has been less appetite for IPOs in the new millennium. In Britain during the first three months of 2005, the number of IPOs was down to only 15, half the level of the previous year, and a fraction of both the volume and value of a decade earlier. Across Europe the trend was much the same, and even in the more entrepreneurial United States interest has slumped.[1]

So what does a company do, if it decides on an IPO? First it normally approaches a firm of investment bankers or a securities house through its accountant or trading bank. There is then usually a lunch or dinner, a getting-to-know-you session at which little more will be achieved than a general understanding of the nature of the business and its goals and aspirations. The directors of the company considering a listing will obtain some idea of how the listing, which is almost certainly a lengthy process, is to be planned.

The investment banker will also give an opinion as to whether the company will be able to meet the listing requirements of the Financial Services Authority. Once the job of the London Stock Exchange, the role of governing admissions is now carried out through a unit of the FSA, the United Kingdom Listing Authority, known as the UKLA.

The UKLA works from a thick rulebook that has become thicker as the European Community adds to listing requirements. A copy may be obtained from the FSA for £50, or can be downloaded from the web. The rules govern admission, the continuing obligations of issuers, the enforcement of those obligations, as well as draconian measures such as suspension or cancellation of a listing. However, the organisation is more user-friendly than the Stock Exchange, which used to send out frosty letters demanding an explanation if the rules were broken, always supposing its officials were alert enough to spot them. These days the UKLA staff tend to be younger, and work on the telephone.

---

[1] Thomson Financial

If an issuing company or its representatives have a problem, there are numerous specialised help teams waiting to provide an answer. If UKLA officials think that a company may be breaking or bending the rules they will call up the person responsible and discuss it with them, trying to put right or resolve the problem swiftly, before resorting to the prosecutor's office.

The FSA is particularly hot on its disclosure obligations, where it states the defining principle as 'to ensure that the information emanating from a company, its advisers or agents is given to the market as a whole, is timely, sufficient and relevant'.[2]

How the UKLA works

Once the formal application for a listing is made, the UKLA ticks off a huge checklist, seeking to satisfy itself that the company has met all its conditions. It will approve or reject listing particulars, and closely examine the prospectus drawn up by the company's investment banker, watching particularly for any statements that might lure an investor into an over-optimistic outlook. Don't expect the UKLA to accept at face value all of the information provided to it, even if a well-known City banker has signed it off. UKLA officials will be on the phone asking questions, or requesting a meeting at which a more thorough interrogation may take place. They will not be playing at being policemen, and don't have the capability or mandate to go out and carry out detective work. The role is more like that of an investigating magistrate, asking questions and expecting the supplicant to come up with the right answers. The UKLA also attaches considerable importance to the role of the applicant company's sponsor, and to other professional advisers, who will have to provide the assurance that the listing rules will be met.

Once the company is listed, it will join the ranks of all those scrutinised on a daily basis by the UKLA's monitoring and compliance group. People in this team will be on the look-out for breaches of the rules on price-sensitive information, and will not hesitate to call in directors or senior executives if they spot such a breach.

---

[2] UKLA Guidance Manual, Financial Services Authority, December 2004.

If directors on the board of a non-listed company thought they had an easy time, they will change their minds once they come to grips with the requirements for a full listing. Each one of them will have to sign an undertaking confirming that all the information the UKLA requires has been provided, and once the business is listed, all their earnings and share dealings will have to be recorded.

At this stage, there is likely to be some discussion on the identity of a sponsor. In Britain it is now a legal obligation for new entrants to the higher level of the stock market to have a sponsor, who may be either a company or a partnership, and who will guide the application through the regulatory hurdles discussed below. A sponsor is expected to have considerable experience of corporate finance, as demonstrated by its employment of senior staff with relevant backgrounds. It will have to show that at least four of its executives have been involved previously in providing advice to companies on a listing over a three-year period. It also cannot act for any organisation with which it might already have connections, for example as an investment or merchant bank, or stockbroker.

Preparing the Prospectus

Once contact has been established, and a decision made in principle, a partner in the securities house originally approached will seek a total brief on the company – particularly its management structure, strengths and weaknesses, labour force, present shareholders, competitors – and, of course, will also undertake a detailed study of full sets of accounts for the previous five years. Quite often this study will show that a listing is out of the question. In Britain, investors and fund managers are spoilt for choice, and any company that does not offer first-class prospects will not attract support. To go down the road towards a listing and issue a prospectus and then have to withdraw it would be a costly mistake.

Assuming, however, that the feasibility study shows a good prospect of success, the next stage for the stockbroker is to visit the company and its major plants or operations and to see it at work. This will usually be carried out by a senior member of the firm, under the supervision of a partner. The staff member will also try to visit competitors of the company, to seek another assessment, although the need for strict confidentiality makes this aspect of the study difficult. A firm of accountants, not the company's own auditors, will also be commissioned to carry out a thorough investigation.

All this will have to be done within three months, if a reasonable target for a listing is to be achieved. The next step is for the brokers to prepare a detailed proposal for the flotation, which will, in effect, form the blueprint for the day-by-day progress towards the listing. The brokers will suggest a price band within which shares might be offered – the decision on a firm price will come much later. They will set out a list of financial requirements which will have to be met and propose underwriters who, at a substantial discount on price, will agree to purchase any shares if the float is undersubscribed.

The company will usually be asked to pay off all major loans – for no investor is keen on picking up a load of debt – and to revalue all its properties. This stage completed, the next step is to decide how the capital of the company is to be made available to the public. In most cases, this will be through the issue of a prospectus, offering the shares at a price expected to be lower than the price at which the company will start its life on the exchanges. In the main European markets, such a prospectus is published in full in the *Financial Times*, and occasionally in other newspapers. The prospectus is, in fact, an offer for sale. It will detail the price at which shares will be available and name any proposed restrictions on voting rights. The terms of sale will be set out, as well as the names and addresses of the company's auditors, stockbrokers, bankers, solicitors and directors. There will be a full description of the company's products or services.

Isotron, a company providing an independent gamma radiation service in Britain, published just such a prospectus. It devoted thousands of words to an extremely detailed description of its technological processes and its business prospects. A large part of the prospectus was devoted to the curricula vitae of the directors and senior employees, right down to site managers. There was a chapter on safety procedures, while over a page of closely spaced print was devoted to publication of the independent report by accountants KPMG Peat Marwick. The reader was spared no detail, and the prospectus constituted an extremely thorough insight into the company.

Once the prospectus has been written, usually by the investment bankers advising the company in association with the stockbrokers, the approval of the local exchange where the shares are to be listed must be sought. This is much more than a formality, and it is quite normal for questions to be raised on matters of detail.

The terms of sale vary widely. Sometimes an underwriting firm of brokers will agree to buy all the share capital to be offered for sale on a given day, and then do their best to dispose of the shares to investors at a sufficiently high price to offer them a profit. Sometimes the shares will be offered directly to the public by advertisement; where this happens the underwriters will only have to take on the shares left unsold and, if the issue is a success, may end up with no commitment and a useful underwriting fee.

Finding an underwriter is usually not a major problem, for all brokers have a list of those they can call upon, whether institutions, investment banks or other financial groups. Underwriters do count, however, on the integrity and accuracy of a broker's recommendation. No securities house can consider accepting the job of arranging a flotation unless it is convinced it is a sound investment.

One way of raising the cash is through public tender – used by bankers J. Henry Schroder Wagg and Co. in the Isotron case mentioned earlier. Here 3,290,088 ordinary 25 pence shares were offered at a minimum tender price of 120 pence a share, the principle being that those prepared to offer a higher rate would receive the biggest allocation. Having received all the applications, Schroders were left with the task of setting a 'striking price', not exceeding the highest price at which sufficient applications were received to cover the total number of shares offered. A public tender was also used by Schroders and UBS Phillips and Drew in bringing Andrew Lloyd Webber's Really Useful Group to a full London listing.

Obviously public tender is a system favoured by highly successful, confident and relatively well-known companies. It is not to be recommended if oversubscription is thought unlikely. Since the price has been fixed beforehand, it also avoids 'stagging' – a stag being the individual who buys new issues in the confident belief that oversubscription will lead to the price rising sharply on the day of listing.

Whether stagging occurs in the majority of cases when the tender system is not used depends, of course, very much upon the price at which the shares are fixed for sale. Pricing can be the key to the whole issue. If prices are pitched too low, there will be a huge over-subscription, involving vast amounts of extra paperwork, the return of cheques and the difficult job of selecting the lucky applicants to receive shares. Where there is oversubscription, those applicants who are left out, or awarded derisory holdings, feel aggrieved, even bitter, while the stags will reap rich rewards. If, at the other extreme, the price is pitched too high, the issue will be a disaster, and months, even years, of work will be wasted.

Fixing the price is not easy, however, because most companies are the prisoners of current events. A series of air crashes, for instance, could damage the price of the shares of a manufacturer of jet engines. Inevitably, setting the price is left to the last possible moment, with brokers and bankers using their experience to judge market conditions as launch approaches. The forty days and nights before and after the day of flotation are the busiest, especially in the offices of those directly participating. It is not unusual for the major people involved to camp in their offices during much of this period, and certainly holidays are out of the question. While the final offer documents are away at the printers, they just hope that they have got it right.

Whether a company goes public through a full float or sale by tender, it is a costly business. The experts needed – lawyers, investment bankers, accountants, brokers and financial public relations men – do not come cheap, especially in the City of London. There are few ways of doing it cheaper, but one of them is to arrange what is called a placement. In this case, the stockbroking firm buys all the shares and sells them direct to its clients, avoiding the cost of dealing. This method is used in small new issues in London or where there is unlikely to be much public interest. But even here, the rules stipulate that more than a third of the company's issued capital must be in the placement, thereby preventing directors from using the system as a ploy to pick up some useful cash while still totally dominating the company. At least one quarter of the shares must also be sold to the public on the stock markets, which helps when open dealings start. A placement is considerably cheaper because the costs of advertising, printing and professional services will be much less, and there is no need for underwriters.

There is also the alternative of arranging an introduction, but this method of obtaining a quotation in London is only available to those companies that already have a wide distribution of shareholders, and where there is no immediate intention of anyone selling out. No capital is offered prior to listing, and it is therefore not necessary for the company to go through the procedures described earlier, or to issue a prospectus, although it is required to take out an advertisement to publicise the move. This method is most commonly used when a large foreign company decides to have its shares listed in London as well as on its home exchange.

The number of listings in any given period depends very much on the state of the market. When shares are falling, there will be fewer enthusiastic takers than during a bull market, though good issues will almost certainly succeed unless things are really bad.

Raising More Money

The stock markets were founded to raise money for industry and to provide finance for great national projects such as railways and canals. They did so with great success until the Second World War, and in the early post-war years it was where companies went for extra funds if they wanted to expand. Borrowing from the banks was, in Britain at least, considered expedient only for short-term finance. Borrowing from overseas – through instruments such as eurobonds, and more recently euro notes – was not popular. Why go further than Throgmorton Street?

Things began to go badly wrong with the capital-raising function of the Stock Exchange when successive governments in the middle years of the last century decided that the best way of paying for expensive public programmes was to tax the rich, which, to them, included almost everyone who did not belong to a trade union and pick up his wages in a brown envelope once a week. Denis Healey, a former Chancellor of the Exchequer, once talked of 'squeezing the rich until the pips squeak'. Income from share ownership was 'unearned income', and somehow thought of as less decent than interest obtained from a building society. Making a capital gain by selling one's own shares at a profit in order to pay for old age, school fees or even a trip to the Bahamas was regarded as extravagance, and therefore had to be discouraged through extra taxation. Company taxes were raised, making it harder for businesses to fund expansion. And in order to justify an ill-judged attempt to curb a free market for wages, 'dividend restraint' was imposed. With little point in investing either for capital growth or for income, investors followed the example of the trade union movement, and went on strike. In other words, they ceased buying shares.

The effect of the political onslaught on the investor in the 1960s and 1970s was to bring to an almost complete halt a stock exchange system which allowed development capital to be raised, pluralistically, by a large number of individuals and institutions, and to replace it with a more costly system of finance through banks. It seems unlikely that the trend will ever be completely reversed, but there has been an encouraging revival of capital-raising on stock exchanges, to the benefit of both saver and entrepreneur.

More recently, business school studies by Nobel Prize winners Professor Franco Modigliani and Professor Merton Miller show that the costs of debt and equity financing are comparable. The cost of debt – of course – is easiest to measure: it is the interest paid by the company on its bank loan or bond. Assuming the company is a highly credible and successful one, it will pay a premium of about 2 per cent over a bond issued by a creditworthy country like Britain or Germany.

The cost of equity is the dividend yield, which should be cheaper, but often is not. Dividends often depend on taxation policy. Raising money through the share markets from rights issues also strengthens balance sheets and prevents the kind of over-borrowing that has forced many large companies into difficulty.

Sometimes companies will want to use both methods. For instance, a British company may use a rights issue to fund a UK acquisition, but, if seeking to take over a European company, could use a foreign currency bond to match the currency of the target company's country.

What happens with a rights issue is that the holders of ordinary shares in a company are offered further shares at a discount, usually substantial enough to make it attractive. Under British rules, such new shares must be offered to existing stockholders in quantities proportionate to their holdings. This is known as a pre-emption right, which has been abandoned in the United States. A lively debate has been taking place in Britain over whether this rule is sensible. In many cases not all shareholders are willing, or even able, to take up the rights offer. So, under the present system, underwriters have to be found who will. As with new issues, pitching the price is crucial. If a rights issue is undersubscribed, there is a danger that the share price will fall, even if underwriters have been appointed, and this will defeat part of the objective of the exercise, which is to raise more capital.

The most important question for a company making a rights issue is to decide on the terms at which it will offer new shares. Normally this is done by offering the shareholders the right to buy a number of shares at a special price for each share they own. So, for example, a British brewing group raised over £500 million by giving its equity holders the right to buy one new share for every five they already owned. This is known as a one-for-five issue. In order to persuade shareholders to subscribe to a rights issue, the price has to be a worthwhile discount to the prevailing market price. But this does not mean that rights issues present shareholders with a bargain – an offer they cannot refuse. As soon as a rights issue has been completed, the price of the existing shares usually falls to reflect their dilution as a result of new stock on the register.

The small shareholder offered a rights issue is often in a Catch-22 situation. If he takes up the offer, he has to dip into his savings and increase his risk exposure to the company concerned; in other words an additional investment is forced upon him. If he does not take up his rights, he may sell them to a stockbroker for the difference between the rights price and the market price, but unless there is a substantial volume of shares involved, the commission is likely to be prohibitive. If, as often is the case, he does nothing at all, the company will automatically sell his rights for him, and pay him the proceeds.

Rights offers are usually contained in a long and arcane document preceded with the suggestion that if you do not understand it you should see a stockbroker. Many people, particularly those who have not paid close attention to their investments, or who have inherited equities, mistakenly throw these documents into the rubbish bin and lose out.

From time to time companies are forced into a rights issue. When a company runs out of cash and finds its bankers no longer prepared to extend credit it may have no choice but to make an emergency issue. This may be especially true when the creditors are knocking at the door. In these cases shareholders face a tricky decision: back the issue or watch the company go into receivership. Investors have to be confident that the new tranche of money will give the company a reasonable chance of survival, and will not go straight into repaying a debt from a bank or elsewhere. The old adage of 'throwing good money after bad' is very relevant here, because there is a very high risk of those taking up emergency issues losing it all.

A rights issue is not cheap, which is one of the main arguments against this form of raising additional capital. First there are underwriting fees, paid by the company seeking to raise the money to the investment bank or securities house managing the issue, and to those who have undertaken to buy any unwanted shares. These fees come to about two or three per cent of the amount of money raised. Then there is the paperwork – fees to lawyers, accountants and public relations consultants, plus the actual cost of printing and distributing the substantial amount of documentation necessary. Add to this the discount which must be offered to make the rights issue attractive – a figure of around 20 per cent is common practice – and it is easy to see why many a corporate financial director would rather go to see the company's bankers, or, if it were possible, arrange a placement.

An alternative to a rights issue is loan capital, which may be raised on the Stock Exchange through either unsecured loan stock or convertible stock. Loan stock is usually issued only by blue-chip companies. It might offer the additional inducement of convertibility to enable the holder to convert all or some of the loan stock at a later stage to equities. A company without a top rating would not find investors ready to buy it even at very high interest rates.

If a company is planning to modernise its plant to increase output and productivity, loan capital can be a particularly attractive vehicle. The interest paid is deductible before corporation tax is payable, so the company's tax bill is reduced. And as output, and hopefully profits, rise, so does the company's share price, making it beneficial for the shareholders to make the conversion.

As with new issues, there are several ways in which a stockbroker can obtain loan capital for his clients. He can arrange for a full prospectus detailing the offer to be prepared, published and advertised, and wait for the response, usually stipulating preferential treatment to existing shareholders. He may, if he chooses, place the loan stock with institutions direct – unlike placements with new issues, where a proportion has to be offered on the Stock Exchange. Or he may limit the offer to existing shareholders, an unlikely course because especially attractive terms are usually necessary to get full support. A placement is usually much more efficient.

Then there is the bond market, of which the eurobond market is the best known. Not long ago, only governments of stable and prosperous democracies and large international institutions such as the World Bank and the European Investment Bank would raise funds from the bond market, by issuing securities at good interest rates with maturity dates between ten and twenty years away. Mostly denominated in dollars, these securities offered large institutional investors an attractive hedge against the fall of sterling and against inflation. The introduction of the single European currency has brought a spate of euro-dominated corporate bonds to the market as companies begin to exploit a new capital-raising opportunity.

Taking AIM

Money can also be raised for small and medium-sized go-ahead businesses through the junior stock exchange, better known as AIM, an acronym for Alternative Investment Market. AIM is a British success story; in its ten year life, it has become the world's leading market for growing companies. Similar markets have evolved in Europe and the United States, and the concept has political support because small businesses have proved to be major sources of job creation, technological innovation and entrepreneurship.

AIM offers most of the benefits of the stock market, such as the opportunity for a higher public profile, and access to new capital and investors, but with a much simpler entry structure than going for a full listing. For instance, there are no restrictions on the size or location of companies who join, the length of time they have been operating, or the percentage of shares to be placed in public hands. AIM offers those who have a business case and can present it well the chance not only of raising capital for expansion, but also of becoming rich in the process. If the company does well, it will inevitably lead to an enhanced status with both customers and suppliers, though the reverse will be the case if things go badly.

The regulatory regime within AIM is less stringent and less bureaucratic than seeking a full listing on the London Stock Exchange through UKLA. There are a number of tax benefits. It is also much easier for a company on AIM to go for expansion via acquisition than would be the case if it were fully listed.

AIM was founded in 1995 as the successor to the Unlisted Securities Market, the London Stock Exchange's earnest but less than successful attempt to find a way of embracing start-up businesses, whose only previous recourse to funding had been to the banks or venture capitalists.

There were then only thirteen companies in AIM's first list. Now there are over 1500, for whom more than £11 billion has been raised. More than 100 are from overseas, from thirteen countries, with a market capitalisation of £13.3 billion. Of the thirteen founder companies, six graduated to a full listing, while four remain in AIM. Two were taken over, and one was wound up. One failure from thirteen is not a bad record. Share price performance has been mixed. One of the founders, Brancote, a minerals explorer, saw its share price almost quadruple before slipping back to offer a 250 per cent gain over six years. Others have fared less well.

The kind of companies that are listed on AIM are rich and varied. There are leading-edge technology companies. Many of the businesses are in the leisure industries, with quite a few football clubs, such as Charlton Athletic and Birmingham City, who over recent years have struggled between the television rich Premier League and the less well-endowed Division One. There are internet firms, privatised railways, recruitment consultants, wine importers and many restaurant groups, to name just a few of the sectors.

How it works

Companies seeking to list and raise money on AIM do not have to be British. Nor do they have to be of a certain size, or prove a lengthy trading history. But they must be public companies, registered under the laws of their country, and have published accounts which conform to internationally accepted accounting standards.

A company does have to show that it is 'appropriate' for it to come to the market and be publicly traded. It would be inappropriate, and disallowed, if the company's owners wanted to run it as a closed book, or as a relatives-only family business. Shares in an AIM company have to be freely transferable.

So before a company decides to join AIM, its owners must be prepared to accept the disciplines that go with being a quoted company, and be prepared to take into account the interests of outside shareholders. Directors must realise that a company's share price might be affected by factors beyond their control, and that flotation will inevitably lead to closer scrutiny of the company. This scrutiny will involve the media and share market analysts, who will run a slide rule over the company's performance and not hesitate to put a 'sell' recommendation out if they believe it is being badly run. This alone could dent an owner's worth. And if directors buy or sell shares, the transaction will have to be made public. These disciplines force boards to look at their public, media and investor relations, and hiring staff or consultants to do this can be very costly. The AIM company may not need to commit itself to road shows which take up the time of chairmen, chief executives and finance directors for a total of about three to four weeks a year, but even a minimalist effort in this area is expensive. A consultant working in this field does not come much cheaper than £1000 a day, which is almost as expensive as a City lawyer.

In making the decision to list on AIM, a company needs to tick off the following points.

❑ Do we need access to capital for growth, or can we achieve the kind of development we need with financing from our bankers or our own resources?
❑ Do we wish to create a public market for our company's shares, allowing anyone to buy at the market price?
❑ Do we want to realise cash for ourselves at this particular time, acknowledging there will be tax liabilities?
❑ Do we expect our company to have a high value?
❑ Are we prepared to face up to a heightened public profile, and critical comment, which may come at a time when we least want it?

If the answer to these questions is an unqualified 'yes', then it is time to proceed. Yet it should be said that there are many growing businesses that have decided to eschew any kind of listing, preferring to continue as private companies. One such group is Archant, which has a near-monopoly of the print media in East Anglia, owning, amongst others, the *Eastern Daily Press*, Britain's best-selling provincial newspaper. Over fifty years its owners have resisted generous offers for the company, preferring to maintain control and run it (successfully) in their own way as a private company. Whenever they have needed money for expansion or acquisition, they have found it themselves. The result is that the cities of Norwich and Ipswich are among the few places in Britain to enjoy the benefits of a strong local press not owned by a national or international conglomerate.

Once a decision is made to join AIM, the first step is to appoint two key individuals. One is called a nominated adviser or Named and the other a nominated broker, and both must be approved by the London Stock Exchange. These appointments are mandatory. The Named, who could be a stockbroker, accountant or banker drawn from a list of about seventy people, has the responsibility for deciding whether a company is suitable for the market, and for making sure it conforms to the AIM rules. Once listed, the company must retain the adviser to keep it on track and to make sure it fulfils its obligations, which include disclosing all material information to investors. The nominated adviser has to undertake to be available at all times to advise and guide the company's directors on the AIM rules. The nominated broker has to be a member of the Exchange, and, in the absence of a market maker, provides a means for investors to buy and sell the company's shares.

The next step is to produce an admission document – effectively a slimmed-down prospectus. It must include a full description of the company and its principal activities, the company's financial history and performance, details of the management, the directors and their personal business histories, and the names of substantial share-holders. This must be made available to all prospective investors without any kind of discrimination.

The cost of joining AIM is much less than a full listing, but can still be expensive. The modest annual listing fees are the least of the expense: the highest cost will come in the engagement of the nominated adviser and the other City of London professionals needed to keep the operation on track. Further details may be obtained from the London Stock Exchange.

Buying shares in AIM is clearly designed for professional rather than amateur investors, and is for the risk-taker who accepts that not all young and growing companies succeed. It is of particular appeal to the large number of fund management groups that specialise in investing in smaller companies.

AIM shares are bought and sold on what is called SEATS PLUS, which enables investors to trade with each other through the LSE. They can do this either through a market maker, if there is enough of a market to justify one, or by an order board, which publicly displays orders to buy and sell shares and enables trades to be executed automatically. The service also allows financial information about each company to be entered by the nominated broker, thus helping investors to evaluate the shares.

A comparable operation exists across the Channel in France, where the Nouveau Marché was set up in 1996 to cater for small and fast-growing businesses. This also has relaxed joining rules so that, for example, new companies do not have to provide three-year financial projections, but must provide quarterly results.

The problems of raising money for small companies in Britain are not confined to the equity sector; banks have also often failed to provide adequate funds at a reasonable price and on reasonable conditions. Despite attention-grabbing advertisements proclaiming their support for small business, the banks have been severely criticised in this area. Under pressure to improve their margins and the quality of their loans following the mistakes of the 1980s, the high street banks have demanded interest rate margins and levels of security that make it very difficult for a small business to establish itself. HSBC as good as admitted this when its chief executive suggested that the best way for the small business sector to move forward would be if there were some kind of government support or guarantee for small business loans.

Another new market in Britain is OFEX, which is for companies that are not yet ready to join AIM. OFEX is short for 'off the exchange' and is a low-cost trading company which enables investors to buy and sell shares in companies that are not listed. Technically it is not a market, even though it is frequently referred to as one. Most members are seeking to raise between £250,000 and £500,000 in capital and want their backers to have an opportunity to trade their shares rather than being locked in. The requirements for joining OFEX are nowhere near as onerous as those for joining AIM.

The main problem OFEX has is convincing investors that the companies it lists are worthy of attention. That means proving to investors that these companies are sound and well-run businesses with better than reasonable prospects. It has had, in its short life, many ups and downs, but in mid-2005 there were 133 companies quoted on it, with a market capitalisation of well over £1 billion. Two of the companies are football clubs: Arsenal Holdings and Queens Park Rangers.

In 2005 a new chief executive, Simon Brickles, recruited from a similar position at AIM, made several improvements, including a competitive market-making system, greater transparency, more disclosure and increased protection for those investing in companies that, for one reason or another, left the market.

Across the Atlantic, the NASDAQ market has provided the capital support for some of the most dynamic and innovative companies in the United States – Microsoft was founded in this way. A company seeking an IPO (initial public offering) in America will normally be advised by its investment bankers to offer its stock at 10 to 15 per cent below trading expectation in order to attract suitable support. The bankers will produce a highly detailed prospectus, with considerable attention paid to competitive advantages compared with other listed companies operating in the same field. The Securities and Exchange Commission (SEC) has a complex set of rules governing the issue of a prospectus, the foundation stone of which is full disclosure of anything likely to be relevant to an investor. But this rigorous attitude pays off; it gives the investor more confidence.

In the United States a prospectus must include information about products and services, manufacturing facilities, competition, and possible risks – as well as full financials – and omission of information, or inclusion of misleading information, can provide a valid cause for a class action lawsuit. Once a prospectus has been filed with the SEC, the officials review it and come back with comments, suggestions and criticisms.

Once a public offering has been made and the company is trading, it is subject to strict laws on corporate governance and the provision of information. There must be a minimum of two independent directors on its board. There is a total ban on the issuing of any preferential shares, or taking any action that would restrict or reduce the voting rights of ordinary shareholders. The company must also complete SEC documents 10-Q and 10-K, which require disclosure of a wide range of information, including executive compensation and securities ownership of certain beneficial owners and managers.

For small companies, the route to a listing is usually the NASDAQ Small-Cap Market, which has about 1,200 smaller companies listed. The requirements for listing on this market are substantially less than those for NASDAQ itself, and it is used as a conduit to the main exchange.

Obligations of listed companies

Once listed, whether on AIM or on the full market, the company's obligations have only just begun. Nor is the UKLA – and its parent body, the FSA – the only authority or institution with which companies have to deal. There is the Accounting Standards Board, the Panel on Takeovers and Mergers, the London Stock Exchange and a number of others.

One of the most onerous of the rules that have to be obeyed to the letter involves the dissemination of information. The lax and carefree ways in which companies could leak or publish stories about their activities are gone for ever. So are many of the practices once beloved of company public relations people and financial journalists. The editors of the well-padded business sections of Britain's Sunday newspapers love to get exclusive stories, partly for competitive reasons but also because there is very little financial news around on a Saturday. This led to the practice of the 'Friday night drop', whereby a financial public relations firm would deliver a brown envelope to a favoured business editor containing the elements of a story about a client company or one of its competitors. Almost inevitably the story was market price-sensitive; in other words it would move the company's share price the following Monday.

When it was the regulator, the London Stock Exchange turned a blind eye to this practice, even though it clearly broke the code that said that price-sensitive information should first be disclosed to the exchange itself so that all investors were treated equally. The FSA has been determined to put a stop to the Friday night drop.

It is now a legal requirement for listed companies that all price-sensitive information be distributed only to authorised and approved media outlets, and these outlets, which include Bloomberg, Reuters and other agencies, are obliged to make it publicly available in short order. These approved agencies are called PIPS, or primary information providers, and have replaced the monopoly once enjoyed by the London Stock Exchange's own Regulatory News Service (RNS).

Companies have also to watch for unusual price movements in their own shares and report these to the London Stock Exchange and the UK Listing Authority, whose supervisory unit will investigate, if need be. The disclosure rules also have a number of implications for a company's everyday contact with analysts, brokers and the media. Companies talking to analysts can only brief them on information that is not price-sensitive or is already in the public domain.

So what does a company do when it feels that the market itself, or one particular analyst, has misjudged its share price? It is possible to 'send out signals' through investor relations specialists to correct matters, but any semaphoring of this kind needs to be handled extremely carefully. Here is what the London Stock Exchange advises:

> Because analysts' forecasts are such a central determinant of the market's expectations, and are aggregated to form a 'consensus forecast', the finance director will sometimes find it necessary to call up when an analyst's forecasts get dangerously wide of the mark, and steer him or her the right way by reaffirming some of the company's previous public statements. This delicate process is made easier by the fact that analysts will generally send their note through for the company to check for factual errors on matters already in the public domain. However a company must not allow itself to be drawn into correcting any incorrect price-

sensitive information or assumptions. If the company decides it does need to speak to the analyst on factual corrections, then the call should be made quickly, because the analyst will not wait long before publishing.[3]

Sometimes unexpected circumstances can trigger an announcement requiring you, in the Stock Exchange's words, 'to move very fast indeed':

> If a company's share price does move sharply for no apparent reason, then that company and its brokers are likely to receive a call from the regulatory authorities to establish whether a leak of price-sensitive information may have occurred. If this may be the case, or there is a risk of a disorderly market, then your company will be required to make an announcement to the market. Similarly you could find yourself woken in the small hours of the morning by a call from your advisers telling you that the press is carrying a speculative story about your company. Much of the article may be wide of the mark – but it could contain just enough truth about your commercially sensitive negotiations to force you to make a rapid announcement.

A particular problem with newly quoted companies is that they drown in the hype that they have created, or that has been created around them by publicists and over-enthusiastic media. This was particularly the case when lastminute.com was floated in a huge bubble of publicity, much of it surrounding one of its founders, Martha Lane Fox, a fetching twenty-something-year-old with a good repertoire of one-line quotes. *Fortune* magazine added to the hype by emblazoning a rather sexy picture of Ms Lane Fox on its cover. Lastminute.com was slow to dampen down the hype with doses of realism, and investors deserted the stock in droves.

Biting the bullet can be difficult too. Some companies hold back on releasing bad news in the forlorn hope that it will get better. They get a lashing from the LSE:

> An early and full announcement of both the problem and the corrective action is not just a regulatory requirement. While obviously negative for the share price in the short-term it means the company can ensure the issue is aired on its own terms and in the right context. The alternative is a potential drip feed of bad press, with the company placed on the defensive and appearing

---

[3] *A Practical Guide to Investor Relations*, London Stock Exchange, April 2004.

indecisive and not in control of the agenda. Announcing a bit of bad news one week, and a bit more the week after, gives the impression – quite rightly – that the management is floundering.[4]

Raising money through a listing is arguably the most interesting stage in the growth of a business. While many small companies choose, rightly in most cases, not to take this course, the step of listing is an essential move towards joining the big league. It is also a process that is fraught with difficulty and expense, and should never be undertaken lightly.

---

[4] *A Practical Guide to Investor Relations*, op. cit.

13   Selling the Family Silver

It's like selling the family silver.
                         Former British Prime Minister Harold Macmillan,
                                        speaking in the House of Lords

*I am not able to say myself whether it will be worth all the
labour involved in privatisation. I do not know. I think we shall
find out only a lot later on.*
                         Sir Denis Rooke, former chairman of British Gas

Get it out . . . get it sold.
   Kenneth Baker, former British minister and one-time chairman
                                        of the Conservative Party

*Privat: Middle English proverb from Latin, privatus, not
belonging to the State, not in public life, deprived of office, from
the past participle of private, to deprive, release.*
                                        American Heritage Dictionary

Twelve Russians waited patiently in line for what, for them, was the
sale of the century. This was not the type of queue so familiar in the
Soviet Union in the 1960s and 1970s for bread, meat or items of
everyday clothing. The Muscovites had come to buy shares in one of
the country's best-loved concerns – the BBC, or Bolshevik Biscuit
Corporation, which, in earlier times, had held 12 per cent of the
Soviet market for cookies.

Each of them clutched a voucher worth 10,000 roubles, issued by
the Russian Government and entitling the holder to exchange it for
shares of equivalent value in any enterprise offered for sale by the
Ministry for Privatisation. Advising the ministry were dark-suited
experts from two Western financial institutions, Credit Suisse First
Boston and the European Bank for Reconstruction and Development.
As they advanced to bid for their shares, the shabbily dressed men and
women paid scant attention to the documentation set out on the
tables before them. But their questions showed their relish for their
proposed investment, as they asked: 'What will the return on capital

be?', 'What are your profits?', 'What are your marketing plans?'

That day in 1996 was the first time in Russian history that ordinary men and women had been able to bid for shares. Though the sale was not reported on television news bulletins in Europe or America, history was being made. Three years earlier, confounding Lenin's predictions, communism as practised by the Soviet Union and its Warsaw Pact allies had collapsed, leaving an economic shambles as serious as that faced in Germany at the end of the Second World War. New, democratically elected leaders sought to rekindle their economies by resorting to privatisation: putting the ownership of enterprises into the hands of individuals and private institutions rather than under the control of the state. Unfortunately, most individuals cashed in their vouchers, and it was not long before many of the significant enterprises in Russia were back in the hands of their former bosses, who used their not inconsiderable savings to buy control. Thus party hacks became oligarchs, conveniently shedding their Communist Party sympathies as they joined the world of capitalism.

Even so, privatisation has come a long way since it was pioneered in Britain by Margaret Thatcher's Conservative government on the idea of the management guru Peter Drucker – it is now a philosophy which has swept the world. One by one, governments have been divesting themselves of great state-owned corporations. Britain led the way in ridding the taxpayer of the burden – and the public servant of the responsibility – of huge utility businesses like power and gas supply, telecommunications and airlines. Now privatisation has reached Africa, Asia and Latin America.

Alas, in Britain a brilliant idea has been poorly executed, with the result that very few members of the public have ended up with more than a handful of shares. Instead of encouraging saving, privatisation bred stagging – making a capital gain by selling equity at a profit immediately upon acquisition. The issues were priced too cheaply, and the City made huge profits, leaving many ordinary families with the feeling that share-trading was not for them. Yet privatisation has not been without its achievements. Many of the private companies are much more efficient than they were as state corporations. There is no longer a dismal wait for a telephone to be installed, or for the electricity man to read your meter. More to the point, instead of costing the government and the taxpayer money in subsidies, the majority of privatised companies make healthy profits, and pay tax on them. Privatised companies account now for more than 20 per cent of the FTSE index. In Australia, Britain, France, Germany, Italy,

Japan, Singapore, Portugal and Spain, the top companies are all newly privatised.[1]

Despite disappointments, it is unlikely that the burst of interest in share ownership, particularly among the working classes, would have come about if the British Telecom float had not taken place, with its hype, touring road shows, television campaign and gimmicks like bonus shares and vouchers to help pay the phone bills.

Even more hype went into the sale in December 1986 of over four billion shares in British Gas, with the introduction to the nation's television screens nightly of an ubiquitous but enigmatic character called Sid. Clever if unsubtle advertisements by the Young and Rubicam agency urged viewers to 'tell Sid' about the opportunities for the public to buy shares in British Gas. One even had a pigeon fancier releasing his bird and saying, 'There y'are, my darlin', just go and tell Sid.' Right to the end of the campaign, Sid was never to be spotted; in the very last advertisement, a near-demented potential shareholder was seen climbing a mountain peak and peering through the mist crying 'Sid!' at a shape that turned out to be nothing more than a startled sheep.

The British public accepted the offer gratefully – and why not? As with British Telecom, the Government had priced British Gas attractively and with a forthcoming election in mind – those who sold quickly were rewarded with a capital gain in excess of 20 per cent, and those who held the stock could look forward to cheaper fuel bills with the prospect of gas vouchers in addition to normal dividends. For every hundred shares bought, investors received a voucher worth £10 payable over a two-year period.

Once British Gas was safely out of the way, the Government set about another major sale, that of British Airways. This was followed by British Steel, the nation's electricity industry, the water authorities and the railway network. The *Economist* saw it as 'the largest transfer of property since the dissolution of the monasteries'.

The worst privatisation in Britain by a long chalk was that of the railways. It was misconceived, and bungled from start to finish. For a full understanding of the debacle you would have to see David Hare's brilliant satire *The Permanent Way*, which played to packed houses from Soho to Sydney. As Hare depicted it the civil servants were languid and uncaring, the bankers, lawyers and accountants

---

[1] William Megginson (Professor and Rainbolt Chair in Finance, University of Oklahoma), *The Impact of Privatization on Capital Market Development and Individual Share Ownership*.

were greedy, and the Conservative government of John Major just wanted it done. The principle error was to split the unwieldy British Rail into groups that quickly became antagonistic towards each other.

The infrastructure was hived off into Railtrack, which garnished quick profits by selling off surplus property. The baronial British Rail headquarters in Marylebone became the Landmark Hotel, and numerous stations were remodelled into shopping malls. Meanwhile the track – the core of the infrastructure – was neglected and in disrepair.

The train operating companies blamed the track problems for delays – or blamed each other. There was little logic to the way these companies were set up, many of them running trains along the same route, with little regard for service. On the line between London and the Essex city of Colchester two companies, Anglia Railways and First Great Eastern, ran services but did not recognise each other's tickets, so that passengers could not always get the next train running.

Both used worn-out carriages, and Anglia used electric locomotives pensioned off from the London-Manchester service, which frequently broke down, thus delaying its rival's services and vice versa. A totally separate company ran freight services to the port of Felixtowe along the same track; their locomotives were even more unreliable.

All ran into the London terminal of Liverpool Street, which also served yet another rail company, WAGN.

A regular sight of an evening were hundreds of angry commuters staring at the departure boards only to find their trains home were cancelled or delayed. The train companies hurled insults at each other, and also at Railtrack, occasionally on the tannoys. A short distance away, in the comfort of their City offices, the investment bankers savoured their bonuses, based on the profits from privatisation.

The end for Railtrack came after a series of fatal rail crashes which exposed failures in maintenance, as well as incompetence by the Labour government, which had come to office blaming the Conservatives but had by this time been in office sufficiently long to be blameworthy also. By 2003 it became clear that Railtrack shares were worthless, and tens of thousands of private investors lost their money.

How Privatisation Stocks have Performed

Name	Date	Price	Price Oct 2000	Price Mar 2005	% change
BT	1984	130	727	200	153
British Gas	1986	135	173	414	306
BAA	1987	122	582	591	484
British Airways	1987	125	292	266	124
Powergen	1991	175	500	E65*	N/A
Scottish Power	1991	240	536	412	171
Railtrack	1996	380	1098	0	NTL[2]

Assessing privatisation in Britain is difficult. There have been benefits to the consumers in that some concerns are more efficient, better run and offer better value for money. The government has gained one-off revenue for each business sold and – the railways excepted – has seen subsidies reduced or eliminated. For the shareholder, as my table shows, most of those who bought privatisation issues have done well. The British Airports Authority has been an outstanding performer, with a near fivefold gain in share price. Even British Airways, billed by the City as a risk and experiencing bad times post 9/11, has been an acceptable investment.

Privatisation Methods

At this point it is worth stepping back a little to review in more detail how privatisations have been carried out. In theory, businesses that belong to the state belong to the people. Prime Minister Tony Blair, for instance, constantly refers to 'our National Health Service'. Many of the businesses that have recently been privatised were once before in private ownership, and then bought for our benefit through compulsory purchase, better known as nationalisation. The railway companies, Britain's post-war steel-makers and several motor manufacturers such as Austin, Morris and Rover were all bought for our benefit by left-of-centre politicians who used our taxes and borrowed funds to expropriate them from their owners. In the former Soviet Union and in Eastern Europe the state simply declared private profit illegal, and stole all businesses from their traditional

---

* Powergen is now part of the German group E.ON, and its share price is in euros.
[2] Near total loss.

owners. The politicians then ran these concerns as if they belonged not to the people, but to them. Most nationalised industries in Britain ran at a loss, so the taxpayer was called upon to make up the shortfall.

With the arrival of Thatcherism, the politicians decided to hand back to us businesses the people were supposed to own, but instead of giving them back, they made us pay for them. This meant spending tens of millions of pounds in fees to intermediaries in the City of London, which helped them through a sticky patch but which cost the rest of us dear. When we had spent our savings to buy these businesses back from ourselves, the Government decided to return some of the money back through tax cuts, so that we would re-elect them.

Share issue privatisations

Share issue privatisations have been the most common method of privatising state-owned corporations. They have much in common with an initial public offering (IPO), in that a detailed prospectus has to be drawn up, and approved, with all the same legal and disclosure requirements. They differ in that many share issue privatisations have been of very large businesses, such as BP, now one of the world's top three corporations, and a range of telecoms companies, including BT, Nippon Telecom and Telegraph, Deutsche Telekom, France Télécom, Telefonica and Telstra. As with large IPOs, shares are issued using a mixture of placement and offerings. Usually a significant proportion of a privatisation is offered to the public, with some shares reserved for employees. The remainder is placed with institutions. These institutions – or sometimes other institutions – also underwrite the privatisation; in other words, agree to buy the shares from the government selling the enterprise if there is not sufficient public interest. In practice, very few underwiters in privatisations have been called into action, as the majority of privatisations have been oversubscribed. Where this has happened, there have been two outcomes: allotments have been cut back, with the number of shares available to the public being rationed; or shares pre-allocated to institutions have been clawed back to increase the allocation to the public.

There are many reasons why the public may oversubscribe to a particular privatisation, but two predominate. The first is that although promoting the issue through advertising and other forms of publicity is normally banned, most privatisations have been accompanied by expensively funded advertising campaigns about the enterprise itself. In Britain, for example, the privatisation of British Airways coincided with hugely extravagant television and press advertisements promoting the self-styled 'world's favourite airline'. The same happened with gas, water, electricity and telecoms. None of the advertisements broke the law because they did not urge the public to buy the shares, but the City promoters have learnt the art of extracting maximum promotional value while staying within the strict legal limits. With such hype associated with the big-ticket privatisations, it is not surprising there was such great public interest.

Secondly, the price set for the great privatisations was always low enough to appear to be a bargain. Governments wanted privatisations to be a success, providing the public with a feel-good factor. The rapid rises in prices that followed most privatisations provided proof that many government businesses were sold too cheap.

Other forms of privatisation

Although share issues have been the most common form of privatisation in Britain, many other techniques have been used. Too numerous to mention here, they were outlined in my book *Selling the Family Silver*.[3] Two of them, however, stand out – selling the enterprise in whole or in part to an existing corporation; and issuing vouchers.

The voucher system was common in countries where the populace was thought not to have either the money or the interest in buying privatisation shares, but was entitled to benefit. There have been many variants on the Russian scheme described earlier. Suffice it to say that most voucher holders appear to have cashed in their shares, so that the equity designed for the public ended up with large investors. Essentially, though, this has also been the outcome of share issue schemes.

Privatisation: Privileges for the Workers

Few employees have fared so well as those working for privatised concerns in Britain, for in almost all cases they were offered privileged treatment on both price and allocations.

Let us look at just one example: the employees of Northumbrian Water, the most oversubscribed of the ten new water companies.

---

[3] Colin Chapman *Selling the Family Silver*.

Those who did not live in Northumbria were restricted to just 100 shares each, and even the customers were allocated only 200: hardly worth the bother, and almost a waste of time. Those who worked for the company, however, had every reason to smile, for they were entitled to apply for and receive up to 5,000 shares. Workers at the other water companies received the same preferential treatment.

The Northumbrian shares were priced at 240 pence, payable in instalments, but water employees were able to invest at a 10 per cent discount. When trading started on the share markets, the opening price showed a premium of 60 pence a share. A worker taking his full allocation would have shown a paper profit of about 84 pence per share.

The water workers – along with other employees of privatised concerns – have also enjoyed other special privileges denied to others, the most significant of which is exemption from the punitive taxation imposed on their counterparts who work for other companies seeking extra capital through rights issues. Although companies offering rights issues normally allocate employees' shares through the distribution of the so-called pink forms signifying a priority offer, those workers who take advantage of this have to pay tax as PAYE on the premium to the issue price when the share starts trading, as if it was income. Indeed, so unfair is this rule that most employees end up having this tax deducted from their wages before they are able to dispose of the shares. The workers of privatised companies face no such intolerable burden.

The 90,000 workers of British Gas were also given generous treatment, which cost the taxpayer a total of £54 million. Each employee was awarded £70 worth of shares, plus a further £2 worth for each year of service. Those able to invest their own money were given two free shares for each one bought, up to a limit of £300 worth of free shares. Those inclined to dig deeper into their savings could buy up to £2,000 worth at a 10 per cent discount. Pensioners were also each given about £75 worth of free shares. This was in sharp contrast to the parsimony of British Telecom, whose employee shareholders missed out.

In all the major privatisations so far, the majority of employees have taken up their entitlements, though many later sold or reduced their holdings. Foolishly perhaps, most employees sold their holdings on the market, rather than to work colleagues or trade unions, for had they adopted this latter course they could have wielded more influence in their companies. To some extent this happened in the case of British Airways, where 5,000 employees gave their union a proxy vote over their shares.

Sale by Mutual Consent

Just when the flow of British privatisation bargains had dried up another trend emerged. It was called – in another massacre of the English language by public servants – demutualisation. For years the building societies – among Britain's most established institutions – had competed with each other in a mad scramble for a prime space in the high streets. They had been operating, literally, for the mutual benefit of their members.

Building societies were created to enable people to buy houses. At its simplest, the concept of the building society movement was that some members lent their savings to the societies at one rate of interest, while others borrowed money at a higher rate to purchase their homes. The money accumulated because of the difference between the two rates, both of which moved up and down more or less in line with market forces and went to pay for expenses, or to boost reserves. While the societies noisily defended the level of management costs and the need to establish visibility in the high street through branch networks, many felt there were inefficiencies in the system. (Actually, the relative efficiency of many building societies pointed out the inefficiencies of the high street trading banks.)

This principle of mutuality also extended to a large number of life assurance companies. Their difference between income and expenditure also went towards building up lavish reserves, generous staff benefits for employees, especially senior management, and bonuses for policy holders possessing with-profits endowment policies. Quite often building societies worked alongside the assurance mutuals, encouraging individuals to purchase homes on an interest-only basis with the capital repaid on the maturity of the endowment policy. This inefficient form of home purchase was for many years encouraged by the Government, which made both the interest charges and endowment assurance premiums tax-deductible, thus conferring a substantial benefit to the higher-paid at the expense of those who could not afford to buy property.

As successive governments stripped away most of these tax benefits, both building societies and life assurance mutuals found they had to compete in the real world, and many of them did so very well. The Conservatives also introduced legislation to encourage competition in the financial sector, and many organisations from both groups felt they would be unable to hold their own against public liability companies.

Many, but not all, also felt they would be best able to compete by being on level terms and becoming fully listed public liability companies with the ability to raise funds on the stock market. One of these came from the East Anglian city of Norwich, where not only is it the biggest source of employment but in 1995 surprised the local community by offering a job to every school leaver with A levels in the county of Norfolk.

For all its humble origins, the Norwich Union, at the time of its flotation, was a global business with branches worldwide. Its approach to demutualisation was especially bold, because not only did it offer its members, those holding with-profits policies, a free windfall of shares worth between £800 and £4,000, depending on the size of policy, but it also raised about £1.8 billion of new money with an additional offer to policy holders. By the time it had joined the Stock Exchange and its shares were trading on 16 June 1997, it was one of Britain's top fifty companies, worth around £5.5 billion. By 2000 it had been merged with two other companies, Commercial Union and General Accident, to form Britain's largest insurance group, Aviva.

14 Mergers and Acquisitions: the Takeover Trail

That's what a dawn raid is – you hit at dawn.

Robert Holmes à Court

Hardly a day goes by without a major story about a takeover. Usually it is one large company bidding a multi-billion dollar sum for another, such as America Online's epoch-making purchase of Time Warner, a corporation which itself was the product of a merger and had also just swallowed up another corporation, CNN. These were agreed takeovers, but often a bid is unwelcome: that is, the directors and management of the targeted company would rather be left alone to run the business undistracted by the prospect of working for new owners.

What normally happens is that the firm of investment bankers working for the corporation that plans a takeover sends a printed letter, known as an offer document, to all shareholders of the target company, proposing to purchase their shares for cash or for stock in their own business, or a mixture of the two. Cash is usually more attractive because predators' share prices have a nasty propensity to fall sharply after acceptances have been returned, as in the case of America Online, where acceptance of that company's offer became more an act of faith in the new group's future than a quick profit.

This inevitably poses the biggest question that arises with any takeover – value. How do you value a public company? One simple answer is market capitalisation: the price of each share on the stock markets on a given day multiplied by the number of shares issued. Then all a bidder has to do is to pitch his offer sufficiently higher than the current price in order to persuade shareholders to give up their long-term prospects with the existing board of directors.

But is the stock market price the right one? As discussed earlier, the prices of shares are fixed not by any measure of assets or even current profits, but by the market's perception of value based on all the information that might affect a company's future cash flow. All the company's financial statements are digested and assessed against competitive forces by scores of analysts. Their collective wisdom is added to the judgement of traders and distilled into a share price. This sounds entirely plausible, but how can you then account for the fact that the world stock market as a whole on 19 October 1987 was worth only four fifths of what it had been the previous day? Or that on the same day ten years later the FTSE index was three times higher? Share prices can only really be the best guess at a value. An acquirer is not really buying the buildings, machinery and workforce – he is getting what he thinks these are capable of producing in terms of hard cash.

As the Wall Street arbitrageur Ivan Boesky, later to be convicted of and imprisoned for insider trading, put it in 1985:

> An analyst may fully understand a company he is following, may even be able to forecast its future earnings with unmatched precision. Does that mean he can forecast its future stock price with any precision at all? Of course not. Price-earnings multiples averaged as high as 25 or so in the heyday of stock trading in the 1960s. In the mid-seventies these multiples had fallen to 6 and 7. Any stock market price is buffeted by sweeping market forces that are virtually impossible to predict with any reliability. These forces are often important: the growth rate of the economy, the course of interest rates, the international value of the dollar, the inflation rate, an overseas war, a presidential election. They also can be distressingly unimportant: this week's change in money supply, the Federal Reserve Board's sale of securities, its reversal of that sale the next day.
>
> Nevertheless many large and significant public corporations have changed hands on the simple basis of share values. The predators have got what they wanted. The shareholders, presumably, were satisfied because they were able to take a profit and re-invest their money elsewhere. But the companies and their staffs that found themselves with new owners were not necessarily better companies for the transformation. In some cases new blood made them more efficient, and more effective use was made of their assets. 'Making assets sweat' is one of the main justifications for takeovers. In many others the acquiring company, its costs swollen by the expense of its own acquisition, has fallen apart.[1]

Not all of those carrying out takeovers continue to run the businesses they have bought. In many cases they sell the assets for

---

[1] Ivan Boesky, *Merger Mania*, Bodley Head, 1985.

cash. Asset-stripping became fashionable in the eighties and is a popular occupation of those who believe that the stock markets often underestimate the true value of companies. These people put their beliefs to the test by acquiring businesses and then breaking them up. This has frequently happened in the past when a company has a number of assets on its books – particularly property – which have not been revalued to reflect higher property prices. By disposing of the property, or by coming to a leaseback arrangement with a finance company, an asset-stripper can acquire huge sums of cash. By the turn of the century the activities of three generations of asset-strippers had sharpened up directors to the risk, though there is still a hard core of professionals on every continent who make money by spotting companies that are undervalued.

Despite the asset-strippers and the ordinary everyday risks in mergers, such evidence as there is shows that takeovers often succeed in their objective of achieving real growth for the acquiring company. A study published by McKinsey, the management consultancy, found that even cross-border acquisitions had achieved a high rate of success compared with other forms of corporate expansion.

McKinsey reviewed the overseas acquisition programmes of the top fifty companies in Europe, Japan and the United States – and found that 57 per cent were judged a success. However, almost all the success stories related to a company merging with another in the same business. Most of those involving moving into non-core businesses failed.

Legal Background and Takeover Rules

Before considering takeover tactics and planning, it is important to look at the legal background to mergers and acquisitions. In each country there are rules that govern takeovers. In some cases these rules are enshrined in legislation; in others they form part of a code, written or unwritten. In Britain there is a fudge between the two, with the further complication of intervention by the European Commission. Commentators – particularly those with no knowledge of the financial services industry – tend to assume that it is a free-for-all, with no rules and regulations, but this is far from the case in Britain or elsewhere.

The first point of reference in Britain is still the City Takeover Panel, a group of twelve City elders with a modest secretariat. There is a director-general, with two deputies, a secretary and a few other executives. The permanent staff provide interpretations of the rules, but contested decisions and disciplinary cases are considered by the Panel itself, with the right of appeal to the Appeals Committee, which sits under the chairmanship of a retired Lord of Appeal. The Panel operates under the watchful eye of the Financial Services Authority.

The Panel's most important contribution is the Takeover Code, and the interesting thing about this is that it contains a number of features designed to protect the small shareholder from the avarice of big companies. One of these features is the 30 per cent rule, which provides that once either a company or an individual has 30 per cent of the equity of another listed company, an offer must be made for all the remaining shares. Moreover this offer must be made at the highest price paid per share during the initial acquisition. To quote from Rule 9:

> Except with the consent of the Panel, when: (a) any person acquires, whether by a series of transactions over a period of time or not, shares which (taken together with shares held or acquired by persons **acting in concert** with him) carry 30% or more of the **voting rights** of a company; or (b) any person who, together with persons **acting in concert** with him, holds not less than 30% but not more than 50% of the **voting rights** and such person, or any person **acting in concert** with him, acquires additional shares which increase his percentage of the **voting rights**, such person shall extend offers . . . to the holders of any class of equity share capital whether voting or non-voting and also to the holders of any class of voting non-equity share capital in which such person or persons **acting in concert** with him hold shares. Offers for different classes of equity share capital must be comparable; the Panel should be consulted in advance in such cases.

Note the words 'acting in concert'. In the media you often hear of 'concert parties', which refers not to an expensive night out at Glyndebourne or the Royal Opera House, but to a group of like-minded investors clubbing together to win control of another business. The Takeover Code makes it clear that where this happens they are to be treated collectively as a single predator.

The object of Rule 9 is to prevent a predator buying a company on the cheap, especially where there is a wide spread of share ownership. Unfortunately, such rules do not apply universally. In many countries of the European Union, including Germany, France and Italy, it is possible to buy 50 per cent of a company without making an offer to all shareholders. This has created the network of pyramid companies discussed earlier.

Another rule in the Takeover Code provides that before an offer is announced, no one privy to the preliminary takeover or merger discussions is allowed to deal in the shares of either the bidding or the target company. Once an offer is announced, the share transactions in all the companies involved must be reported by all parties to the City Takeover Panel, the Stock Exchange and the press. Companies defending a bid must not do anything without shareholder approval. For those who wish to know more, it is worth obtaining a full copy of the Code.[2]

How it works

When launching a bid, those making the offer will make contact with the City Takeover Panel under conditions of strict secrecy. The bidders will almost certainly be advised by investment bankers, who are fully conversant with the rules, but the full-time staff of the Panel will also offer guidance. The staff work closely with the surveillance unit at the Stock Exchange to investigate dealings in advance of publication of bid proposals, the aim being to establish whether there has been any breach of the rules governing secrecy and abuse of privileged information.

As the bid proceeds, the Panel's executive monitors closely all developments. They check, for example, all documents and announcements issued, to make sure that they comply with the Code. They have access to the Stock Exchange's computer systems so they can monitor and reveal suspicious share dealings. They give rulings and interpretations both before and during transactions.

Sometimes the Panel itself is convened – often at very short notice – during a takeover, usually to deal with an appeal against a ruling made by one of the full-time staff. What would have happened is that if there appears to have been a breach of the code, the Panel staff invite the chairman of the company involved, or other directors, to appear before them. He or she is informed by letter of the nature of the alleged breach, and of the matters which the director-general will present to the hearing. These hearings are informal, there are no rules of evidence, and,

---

[2] City Takeover Code, obtainable for £15 from the Panel on Takeovers and Mergers, The Stock Exchange Building, London EC2P 2JX.

although notes are taken, no permanent records are kept. The principal against whom the complaint has been made is expected to appear in person, although he may bring his lawyer with him. At the hearing he is expected to set out his reply, normally based on a document which should already have been produced in reply to the director-general's letter. If the Panel finds there has been a breach, the offender may be reprimanded there and then, or may be subjected to public censure with a press release distributed to the media, setting out the Panel's conclusions and its reasons for them. In a bad case, where the Panel feels that the offender should no longer be able to use the Stock Exchange, either temporarily or permanently, the case may be referred to a professional association, the Stock Exchange, the Department of Trade and Industry or the City Fraud Squad.

In disciplinary cases – where the Panel is applying sanctions against an individual or company in serious breach of the Code – there is the right of appeal to a committee chaired by a judge. Panel rulings are subject to a judicial review, but only after a takeover is completed, not during its process, thus avoiding the possibility of litigation being called into play as a delaying tactic.

This system has the advantage of being relatively informal and flexible, but it has not been without its critics. Like so much self-regulation, its success rests on the credibility of those chosen to implement the Code, and their willingness to shame wrongdoers through bad publicity. But does it protect shareholders sufficiently? The Takeover Panel does not go public with all guns blazing very often, and even when it does, the resultant press release is unlikely to make the BBC Ten O'Clock News. Not every shareholder reads the *Financial Times*, and therefore the belief that shareholders are warned off by Takeover Panel actions may be false.

The Takeover Panel has also been criticised for not following its own credo by allowing stalking, a practice where predators canvass widely a proposed acquisition without making the financial commitment necessary to activate it.

If a firm fails to comply with the Code, or a requirement or a ruling by the Takeover Panel, the FSA will take enforcement action. The FSA is also responsible for applying European Union rules affecting takeovers, and in 2005 published a Market Abuse Code.

Two other bodies also have a major role in many takeovers, the

Competition Commission and the European Union's Competition Commission.

Both the national body and the European one work closely together, and each can and do block mergers if they consider them to be against their constituents' interest. The EU has even exercised its power to stop a merger between two United States companies.

In the summer of 2001 General Electric, one of the world's biggest companies, sought to acquire Honeywell, an electronics giant. The merger had not created a problem for United States regulators, but the Brussels Commissioner for Competition ruled it would harm European interests. One wonders what would have happened had American regulators sought to block the takeover of SwissAir by Lufthansa!

The acid test applied by the EU towards takeovers is to look at the post-merger scenario and ask a simple question, 'does the deal pose a threat to competition?' Needless to say the Competition Commission's staff do not rely on the words of the company making the takeover, but project the situation as they see it developing. Will there be a concentration of power? The most recent EU takeover code has this definition: A concentration which would significantly impede effective competition, in the common market or in a substantial part of it, in particular by the creation or strengthening of a dominant position, shall be declared incompatible with the common market.

Full details of the European code may be obtained from http://europa.eu.int/comm/competition.

Making an Acquisition

There are many and varied reasons for making an acquisition. The most obvious is that it is often much easier and cheaper than to start a new venture, except in the case of a product or service that is exclusive enough to depend for its success on the professional drive and energy of the entrepreneur and his team. If you have a product that will put your rivals out of business, you will usually be best served by generic growth.

But a takeover can be a useful route to expansion, particularly as it often enables boards to use other people's money to achieve their ambition. A takeover can enable a company to swallow up the competition, and thereby to increase profit margins. This is what happened with many of the large takeovers in the early part of the 20th century. Several of these were designed to set up large monopolies able to raise prices in basic industries such as steel, power and transport. Some of them were brought about by the legendary New York financier J. Pierpont Morgan. His biggest deal, in 1901, brought together eleven companies, accounting for half of America's steel industry, to form US Steel.

In many cases, a takeover may be the only way to fulfil ambitions of growth. Often it may be the result of egomania on the part of the chairman or controlling shareholder. There never seems to be a shortage of new owners for Britain's national newspapers, however precarious their finances may be. Prestigious department stores and breweries also seem popular targets. Sometimes the thrust of a takeover effort is to achieve a lifetime ambition.

Whatever the reason, there are usually only two forms of takeover: those that are uncontested, and those that involve a fight. But it is never as simple as that. There have been many occasions when a board of directors has decided to open merger discussions with a potential target rather than to proceed by stealth, only to find that the opposition is so great that all they have achieved is to give the other side advance warning to prepare for an assault. And there have been occasions when a contested battle has been so fierce and the cost of the operation so high that it might have been better to attempt to achieve the same result through negotiation.

Some takeovers are solicited. Many a company, for lack of progress or good management, feels that it would be better served if it were to be incorporated into a better-run, and perhaps larger, business.

With any takeover there are two stages: the preliminaries, which may take weeks or even months; and the active stage, when the bid is made and the offer digested and voted upon by the shareholders. Very few takeovers are the result of a whim; the vast majority are usually considered only after painstaking research involving the company's solicitors, accountants and investment banks, or other financial advisers.

Takeover specialists are at a premium in the City, and are paid enormous salaries. A senior director in the corporate finance department of one of the better-known British investment banks may expect to earn about £500,000 a year in salary and bonuses, while a junior director, who could be in his late twenties or early thirties, might receive £100,000 upwards. American companies pay more, but offer marginally less job security. For this, the specialists advise those either making or subject to a takeover on strategy and tactics, capital-raising where necessary, and public relations, often calling in outside specialists to assist.

When the pressure is on, most advisers would expect to work fourteen hours a day, as well as attending meetings at weekends. If their homes are outside central London, they would be lucky to see their families except at the weekend, and would almost certainly have to have a flat close to the City. One investment bank maintains an apartment for its directors above an expensive West End restaurant. However, if you are seen dining with a new client, word soon gets out. Takeover advisers have to work under conditions of great secrecy, for an essential part of the takeover game is to anticipate your opponent's next move, and to outwit him.

However, for the investment bank that can grab the lion's share of the business, the rewards are great, with takeovers in the European markets earning the largest portion of income.

Tricks of the Takeover Trade

In planning a takeover, it is essential to work out a strategy before making any announcement. This usually means weeks closeted with financial advisers, and it is a time when security is all-important. A stray document left in a photocopying machine, a loose word dropped to a friend in a bar, or even a minor indiscretion at lunch can lead to a leak. One paragraph in a newspaper can be enough to set the takeover target's shares racing ahead on the Stock Exchange, which could rule out a bid, alert rivals to the possibility, or create problems with the regulators.

Directors know full well that takeover strategy is not just a matter of obtaining enough shares in the targeted concern. In almost every case, politics and public relations come to the fore.

The predator in a takeover enjoys one major advantage: it can always count on the full support of its management team, which usually has much to gain from taking charge of a combined larger organisation. By contrast, the management of a target company often finds itself in a difficult, even ambivalent, position; its loyalties are to its present board of directors, but its future, as likely as not, will lie elsewhere. It also has the burden of dealing with worried employees, not to mention suppliers, distributors and others with whom the company has close connections. And it has to continue to run the business. It used to be the case that shareholders would usually stand by a business that had done well for them, unless those making the bid put up an irrefutable case. But in 1996, when Rocco Forte tried to persuade Trust House Forte shareholders to stick with him, they rejected his pleas and fell for the Irish charms of Gerry Robinson and his Granada group.

It is also true that the best defence against a takeover is to act before the enemy strikes; in other words, take action which will deter a predator from making a move, such as selling off subsidiaries which do not fit the core of the business, or explaining the company's strategy to analysts in such a way that the share price rises to reflect an accurate, rather than an undervalued, view of its stock. Once a bid is made, it is hard to do this, because any disposals or other capital restructuring have to be approved by shareholders.

When it is clear that a takeover bid is likely to fail, those who have conducted the unsuccessful bid need to be on their guard. Almost certainly the predator will have built up a parcel of shares in the company, and will want to unload them at the highest price possible. That will not be possible if takeover fever has subsided, and the predator may be facing a loss. In such a case it is normal to arrange a placement through brokers.

It has been known for an unsuccessful bidder to walk away from a failed acquisition with a large profit. Usually this requires barefaced cheek. This is what happened as a result of a visit on 20 November 1979 by the publisher Rupert Murdoch to his father's old office at the *Herald and Weekly Times* (*HWT*) newspaper group in Melbourne, Australia, where he cheerfully greeted Sir Keith Macpherson, the chairman and chief executive, with the glad tidings that his News Limited company was about to present the Stock Exchange with the terms of a A$126 million bid for just over half of the company. Since the offer valued *HWT*, the country's largest newspaper group, at A$100 million more than News, Macpherson suggested that the whole idea was ridiculous.

Perhaps it was; one newspaper later suggested it was like a snake trying to swallow a sheep. Murdoch, however, knew what he was up to. He wanted *HWT* desperately – ever since his father, whose genius had built up the paper, had died. But he suspected that he would not get it, even though News offered A$4 a share, a premium of A$1.26 on the market price.

His suspicions were correct. His bid caused panic at the head-quarters of another newspaper group 400 miles away in Sydney.

John Fairfax Ltd, a conservative family concern, had a minority stake in *HWT*, and its newspapers were bitter rivals of Murdoch's. Apart from the extra power Murdoch would gain if he controlled *HWT*, he would become a partner of Fairfax in two other major enterprises, Australian Newsprint Mills, the country's only newsprint manu-facturer, and Australian Associated Press, the national news agency, both controlled jointly by Fairfax and *HWT*. Fairfax instructed its brokers to buy all the *HWT* shares it could muster to thwart Murdoch, and the price rose quickly to well above the A$4 that Murdoch had offered.

Within two days Fairfax had laid out over A$50 million and had acquired 15 per cent of *HWT*. The shares stood at A$5.52. Murdoch knew that he was beaten, but astutely spotted a lucrative way out. Instead of conceding defeat, he instructed his brokers, J. B. Were and Co., to continue buying shares but on a much more limited scale. At the same time he commissioned another broker, May and Mellor, to unload the 3,500,000 shares he had already purchased. The Fairfax people, convinced that Murdoch was still a buyer, snapped up the lot, paying top prices, only to face the humiliation of hearing that they had been outwitted and that Murdoch had quit, using one of his own newspapers to condemn the Fairfax 'rescue' of *HWT* as 'two incompetent managements throwing themselves into each other's arms at the expense of their shareholders'. Maybe, but the real point was that Fairfax was determined to stop Murdoch at any price, and paid dearly for it. When the shares settled back down at a lower price, Fairfax had lost over A$20 million, plus the interest on the A$50 million laid out to acquire the stock.

Several years later, Murdoch got his prize, as a result of some spectacular blunders by Warwick Fairfax, a junior member of the Fairfax family, whose dealings in the junk bond market lost him the empire his grandfather had built.

The trick is that your opponent has to hate the idea of losing his beloved company so much that he will pay almost anything to keep it. In most contested takeovers the issue of who wins is decided by institutional investors, as the major shareholders. In Britain they are not quite as fickle as in the United States, but increasingly the institutions are under pressure to perform.

Corporate raiders

Politicians and others who do not know how markets work often condemn speculators as parasites. The canny speculator can also put economic frailties to the test, as did George Soros when he figured correctly in the late summer of 1992 that the pound did not have the strength to be locked into Europe's exchange rate mechanism. Corporate raiders achieve the same impact with companies, especially when they spot that the break-up value of a company, the sum realised when all its assets are sold, may be considerably more than its market capitalisation, or share value.

Investors in the eighties and nineties made a lot of money following corporate raiders, and still do so today. One technique, popular at the time, was called appropriately 'Copycat'. It involved studying the moves of renowned old-style raiders like T. Boone Pickens and emulating them. They were twenty-four hours behind, of course, but those who tracked the money masters in a bull market seldom fared badly. Those who wanted to limit risk used stock options. When this worked, they made big profits.

In the United States in which the leveraged takeover was once a favourite technique, a great deal of this activity was fuelled by borrowed money. A corporate raider would take a modest position in a large company, wait a short while and then offer to buy the entire stock by making a takeover bid. Where would the corporate raider's small company raise these billions of dollars from, you may well ask. The answer: use the company's own money, through junk bonds.

Where there's junk there's money

The man in the street might suppose that those proposing to take over a company have the wherewithal to do so. After all, takeover merchants have always been painted as piranhas swallowing the small fry. This is not necessarily the case.

In the late 1980s, many takeovers were achieved with borrowed money, and in some instances this money was borrowed indirectly from the company that the predator was targeting.

Let me explain. Company X wishes to buy company Y, but has insufficient spare cash on its balance sheet to do so. Nor does it have enough security to offer its bankers, and it does not believe it can raise cash from its shareholders in a rights issue.

So instead it issues junk bonds, which are no different from any other interest-bearing security except that they carry a substantially higher than average interest rate. These bonds raise the capital required to finance a bid, and are normally secured against the shares of the company targeted. An investor buying junk bonds normally does so on the basis that his money is only committed if the takeover bid succeeds. If it is successful the corporate raider issuing the bond can afford to pay the higher interest rates because he will have the assets of the newly acquired company at his disposal. In other words, the strength of the victim company's balance sheet is its own downfall. If the corporate raider fails and is unable to get enough shares in the company in his sights, it is a fair bet they will have risen in the market, and he will have made a sizeable capital gain.

The use of junk bonds was championed most heavily in the 1980s by the Wall Street broking firm Drexel Burnham Lambert, where its greatest advocate was Michael Milken. By 1985 $27 billion worth of junk bonds had been issued, most of them through Drexel. In 1970 there had been only $7 billion worth of high-yield bonds out-standing, and most of that was for quality offerings. By 1989, at the peak of the junk bond craze, $201 billion of junk had been unloaded.

Many people imagine that the holders of junk were avaricious investors, dissatisfied with the more prosaic returns available on ordinary investments. They were not. At the beginning of 1989, 30 per cent of junk bonds outstanding in the United States were held by insurance companies, 30 per cent by mutual funds, and 15 per cent by pension funds. Many of them lost their money as the companies in which the junk was secured turned down. Drexel went bankrupt, and Michael Milken went to gaol. Junk bonds went out of fashion.

Poison pills

The truth, of course, is a little different, through the occasional use of what are called poison pills, an intriguing piece of manipulation designed to prevent a deal being upset. Thus when the mining group BHP-Billiton trumped a Swiss attempt to buy Australia's Western Mining Corporation, a company that owned, amongst other riches, the biggest uranium mine in the world, it persuaded the board of WMC not only to accept its bid without a fight but also to swallow a clause which provided that if another corporation came along and offered more, WMC would have to pay BHP-Billiton a fee of approximately £40 million. By swallowing this poison pill WMC effectively put the takeover beyond contention, because had another mining giant like Rio Tinto entered the fray, their bid would have had to be more than £40 million above the BHP-Billiton offer.

Poison pills are frowned on by the regulators, but still occur. They became an art form in the United States, with the classic example coming when Merrill Lynch tried to outsmart the brilliant British entrepeneur, Lord Hanson.

In its heyday, more than half of Hanson Trust's income came from businesses in the United States. In August 1985, Lord (James) Hanson identified a major American company as a suitable case for takeover. The SCM Corporation was a solid if dreary conglomerate which manufactured outmoded typewriters, processed food, pigments and an assortment of other products. On 21 August, Hanson Trust offered $60 in cash for each share in SCM Corporation, valuing the company at $755 million, well below its market capitalisation. Robert Morton, an analyst, told me at the time that this was 'in the mould of Hanson acquisitions: SCM is exactly the kind of company he goes for, a company which has already undergone a great deal of rationalisation and sorting out, which perhaps has not been fully realised by the shareholders'.

The SCM management was horrified. Here was a lord from England buying their company at rock-bottom value. From all the precedents, it was clear that, before they knew where they were, they would be looking for new jobs. Fortunately for them, the board saw matters the same way, rejected the Hanson bid and refused even to talk to Hanson's US chief Sir Gordon White, despite several invitations to do so. It hastily called in its financial advisers, Goldman Sachs.

However, it was not Goldman Sachs that came to the rescue of SCM's beleaguered management, but Wall Street's largest broking house, the financial conglomerate Merrill Lynch. Merrill Lynch's capital markets division, headed by a young go-getter, Ken Miller, was hungry for new business and skilful in organising what have become known as leveraged management buyouts. Within a few days, Miller and his team had come up with a means whereby, at the stroke of a pen, Hanson could be thwarted, the SCM management could save their jobs and Merrill Lynch would receive a large fee.

On 30 August, only nine days after Hanson's bid, a new company was announced – legally a partnership between the SCM Corporation's management and Merrill Lynch, but funded by the Prudential Assurance Company of America. It offered $70 a share – $10 more than Hanson – for 85 per cent of the SCM shares, and promised to buy the rest out of SCM profits at some future date through the issue of junk bonds which, it was hoped, would also trade at about $70. A confidential Merrill Lynch paper described the deal as representing 'one of the most asset-rich leveraged buyout opportunities we have ever encountered'. For Miller, much was at stake: if he pulled off the deal it would be the first time that a leveraged management buyout had been successful against a tender offer for cash.

The wily Merrill Lynch team hoped that Hanson would withdraw, leaving them with the business, but they took steps to make sure they would still make money if he did not. A clause was written into the contract with SCM providing for a $9 million fee should the bid be topped leading to the termination of the arrangement. This was to be in addition to the basic fee of £1.5 million for fixing the deal in the first place.

Hanson had no intention of giving up. On 3 September, Hanson Trust increased its offer to $72 a share. Unlike the first offer, which valued SCM at a bargain-basement price, this was a much more attractive offer for shareholders. It was also all in cash. Accepting the offer would not involve the risk posed by the Merrill deal which, from the shareholders' point of view, meant waiting around for junk bonds and future profits which might never come.

It looked as if Hanson had won. But having made sure their $9 million fee was in escrow, Merrill's Miller and his team then came up with a much more ruthless way of frustrating the English lord's ambitions. They would strip out of SCM Corporation its two most potentially profitable businesses, in the belief that the Englishman would either lose interest or be left with a crippled company.

This tactic has become known as the use of the 'poisoned pill', although a more appropriate metaphor might be that of a scorched earth policy. In this instance, the SCM management and Merrill Lynch increased their leveraged buyout offer to $74 a share, but subjected it to a new condition: if Hanson or another party got more than a third of SCM shares, Merrill would have the right to purchase the two most thriving parts of the SCM Corporation – the pigments and processed food businesses – at knockdown prices. These businesses, described as the 'crown jewels', would then be run by the same SCM management. What was left in SCM would be hardly worth having. Merrill Lynch also took a retention fee of $6 million, investment banking fees of $8 million and dealer-manager fees of $2.75 million, in addition, of course, to the $10.5 million already paid.

The next morning Hanson Trust withdrew its $72-a-share offer, and spent $200 million buying SCM shares on the New York market; within a few hours it had acquired 25 per cent of the company. But on 16 September Merrill Lynch acted again. With the Manufacturers Hanover Bank working as agent, it put the shares of the crown jewel subsidiaries in escrow and apparently beyond Hanson's reach. At this point the lawyers took over, with the action moving to the New York District Court in Lower Manhattan. In the end Hanson Trust lost the case, but the verdict was reversed in the subsequent appeal. The English lord had won, but only after gritty determination.

Discussion in the United States since has ranged over whether the law courts are really the place to decide such matters, as well as whether the frenzy of takeover activity should be allowed to waste scarce investment capital, to inhibit innovation and to force managers to sacrifice long-term goals for the good of the quarterly balance sheet. And should management be able to conspire with its preferred bidder to frustrate a better offer for shareholders? Kathryn Rudie Harrigan, Professor of Strategic Management at the Columbia University Business School, talked to me about the increasingly common tendency for stock market takeovers to be decided in courts of law: 'It is just one more in a string of devices that managers and their investments bankers have come up with to avoid being taken over when they do not want to be.'

Is this new trend likely to be damaging to shareholders? Professor Harrigan thinks perhaps not, in that values are often forced up by what is essentially a game: 'It is a game, and it is a game that is played with great ritual, and is being played in many, many companies these days. It is often cheaper to acquire something than it is to build it from the ground up.' But she does believe that business will suffer in the end:

> I think it is damaging to the long-term health of the business, because when you are so busy satisfying these short-term requests of the financial community, who are looking for instant gratification from their investment, you often cripple the long-term ability of the company to be able to reposition itself to remain competitive in a changing environment.

Professor Harrigan also believes that the concepts of poison pills and crown jewels could be exported to Britain:

> The two capital markets are becoming very similar in the way that people operate within them, and the kinds of expectations they have of the companies whose equities they hold. And more and more of the equities are held by institutional investors, who have this kind of short-term expectation, and they want to see this quick pay-off on their investment. I think the kind of behaviour we see here, with these leveraged buyouts, will undoubtedly be appearing also in your stock markets.

Breaking Up is Hard to Do

Company divorces or break-ups, more politely referred to as 'de-mergers', have of late been as fashionable as takeovers. In the seventies, conglomerates were all the rage, large corporations stringing together a variety of businesses in totally unconnected industries. A good example of a modern conglomerate that still exists and thrives is General Electric, one of the United States' top five corporations, which until recently was headed by the legendary manager Jack Welch. Inside GE are corporations involved in electrical products like lighting, aircraft engines, corporate leasing, insurance, television and Hollywood studios. There is no logical link, but Welch's mantra was that GE should be either number one or number two in any business it was in, or not be in it at all. Where businesses did not make it, he looked for buyers.

In Britain, Pearson was once a conglomerate with properties as varied as Royal Doulton China, the *Financial Times*, Longman, Penguin, Tussaud's waxworks, Chessington Zoo, Lazards investment bank, some Texas oil exploration companies and the French Latour winery. Under the leadership of Marjorie Scardino, most of these businesses have been sold off, leaving Pearson as a more focused publisher, with particular strength in education following the acquisition of Simon and Schuster, the American market leader.

Very often, de-mergers are organised so as to restore focus to a company so that it can concentrate on what it believes it does best. In other cases they can become a useful way of raising money from a particularly successful and perhaps undervalued subsidiary.

PART IV

The 24-Hour Watchmen

Policing the markets to protect the consumer is now an obsession. There is little evidence the consumer benefits from the verbose rulebooks – or that the big crooks are being brought to book.

15   Policing the Markets

The financial planning industry is in many ways still in the days of the Wild West. The marshal hasn't ridden into town, there's mayhem in the streets, a lot of random shooting.
　　Scott Stapf, of the North American Securities Administrators'
Association

The principal way for investors to protect the money they put into the securities markets is to do research and ask questions.
　　Securities and Exchange Commission

As past and present cases show, consumers are often the first victims of market failures or financial instability. We have only to look at the fall-out from the bursting of last year's internet stocks bubble.
　　Howard Davies, former chairman of the Financial Services
Authority

At four o'clock in the morning of 23 October 1812, three men called at the Popincourt Barracks in Paris with the devastating news that the Emperor Napoleon had died beneath the walls of Moscow. It was a plausible story – news from the campaign front took three weeks to get back, and the French armies had just achieved a great victory at the Battle of Borodino that had opened the gates to the Russian capital. The men also said that the Senate had abolished the Empire and appointed a provisional government, and was calling on the 10th Cohort of the National Guard for support. Within hours, a huge conspiracy against Napoleon was under way, and the Emperor's leading supporters were thrown into prison.

This story, described by Italian author Guido Artom, in his book *Napoleon is Dead in Russia*, was the inspiration for one of Britain's earliest and most notorious examples of share-market rigging. In the early nineteenth century, only major news moved the fledgling stock market, and it took headlines like 'Napoleon Set to Invade' or, better still, 'Napoleon Dead' to cause a shock.

Since, even in the days before the telegraph, old news was no news, stockbrokers often placed faithful retainers in the port of Dover to listen to the rumour mill, watch the sea, talk to fishermen and report back regularly. So when, on 21 February 1814, Colonel de Burgh, alias Charles Random de Bérenger, turned up in Dover in a red uniform, claiming to be aide-de-camp to General Lord Cathcart and reporting the death of Napoleon and the fall of Paris, the news reached London at the speed of a pony and trap. Although foreign reporting was severely limited in those days, along with share ownership, there were those in London who had heard of the earlier, unsuccessful conspiracy against Napoleon and the subsequent execution not only of the plotters, but also of the soldiers who unwittingly carried the message. They were therefore very much on their guard against such stories. But Colonel de Burgh had an elaborate cover story, a detailed account of how Napoleon had been butchered by the Cossacks. He had also made a point of going directly to the headquarters of the Port Admiral in Dover to apprise him of the facts. Surely, said brokers, it must be true.

Prices on the Stock Exchange shot up, as the wealthy clients of brokers received the news, apparently confirmed by handbills distributed in the streets of London. They were not to know that these had also been handed out by de Bérenger who had himself taken a coach to the capital to collect his gains, estimated at about £10,000. It was, of course, all pure fiction, but note that those who lost out had been contacted by brokers, who were themselves often privileged possessors of inside information.

Not much changed in the following 175 years. Until recently it was those 'in the know' who stood to make rich pickings from speculative trading on the Stock Exchange. Latter-day frauds on similar lines to that perpetrated by de Bérenger were common in the early 1970s, during the so-called Australian mining boom. Reports of a nickel strike by an obscure, barely known and usually recently listed mining company would reach Sydney as a result of a tip from Kalgoorlie, a remote dusty gold town in Western Australia. Confirmation was impossible, but the word flashed round and the price of the stock shot up. I once worked on a magazine where the financial editor would return from lunch, very excited, and shout something like 'Bosom's Creek has struck nickel' before rushing to the phone to buy shares. Some brokers made a point of reserving shares for journalists, who could be counted upon to write favourably about a mining prospect which, more often than not, when the geologists' report arrived, turned out to be nothing more than a hole in the ground or a stick marking a spot in the desert. Fortunes were made and lost.

Much of the activity was 12,000 miles from the geologists' trowels. Each day, as soon as the London Stock Exchange opened, there was feverish activity as investors sought to cash in. Many had their fingers badly burned, and the two-year 'boom' earned Australian brokers a bad reputation which took years to live down. As one merchant banker who frequently visits Sydney put it: 'The Aussies saw it as a way of getting their own back on the Poms.'

Ramping stocks was not confined to those on the fringe of share markets. Writing in the *Observer* on 5 September 1971, under the headline 'Digging up the Dirt', I reported how an Australian Senate Committee investigation into the series of mining collapses and false claims in that country had severely shaken investors' confidence.

One thoroughly dishonest practice disclosed to the Committee was the purchase of huge blocks of shares in early trading by certain brokers, using their house accounts. By lunchtime, word would be round the markets that a particular share was on the move, and the broking house would unload its newly acquired holding at a substantial profit. Those shares that remained unsold would be allocated to clients for whom the firm held discretionary accounts, at a substantially higher price than the firm had paid for them, thereby enabling it to make a profit at its clients' expense. To add insult to injury, the clients would be charged commission.

The Committee's report makes interesting reading, even years after the inquiry. It scrutinised in detail the accounts of one stock-broking firm that had gone into liquidation, only to find that about 80 per cent of the firm's trading was on its own account, and that its income from commission amounted to only a minor proportion of turnover.

Let us move back to London, and to Thursday 13 June 1985. It was a typical summer Thursday on the Stock Exchange. Trading was languid, as is so often the case at this time of the year. Then came a sudden burst of activity, much to the curiosity of a party from a Norfolk Women's Institute that was visiting the public gallery that day. Someone was buying large blocks of shares in Arthur Bell and Sons plc, and their price rose by 14 per cent.

The visitors had to wait until reading their Saturday edition of the *Eastern Daily Press* to find out why. Guinness plc had made a bid for Bell on Friday the 14th, and on the eve of that takeover offer, someone had got wind of what was going on and had been buying Bell's shares furiously in the hope of a quick profit. Yet insider trading is strictly forbidden both by the law, which since 1980 has made it a criminal offence, and by the rules of the Stock Exchange. Despite that, as a practice, it is still widespread.

According to the magazine *Acquisitions Monthly*, the share prices of takeover targets rise on average between 20 and 30 per cent in the month before a bid. Over 90 per cent of prices move before a bid. One reason for this may well be that astute investors have spotted, from their own research, likely targets for takeover. Passing insider information is more likely.

To combat this, the Stock Exchange maintains a special squad of men and women at its Throgmorton Street offices to try to track down insider traders. This means questioning those suspected of using inside knowledge to make money, and putting the evidence before the Exchange's Disciplinary Committee.

New and powerful computers allow the squad to spot erratic price movements in London and on other major international markets, and they have the authority to question anyone who works for a member of the Stock Exchange, which, of course, includes a large number of international banks and other financial conglomerates. Their computers have instant access to all Stock Exchange trans-actions over the previous six months, and they may manipulate the database by asking over a hundred questions.

But just like detectives from the regular police forces, they rely more on hot tips from informants than on the craftsmanship of a Sherlock Holmes. The number of tips runs at about ten a week. Many of them come from market makers spotting something suspicious. Since market makers can lose thousands of pounds by incorrect pricing, they are very aware of phoney figures.

The Stock Exchange also has the backing of compliance officers employed in securities houses. These men and women make sure that both the Stock Exchange rules and their own house rules on share trading are strictly observed, and if they spot an irregularity in a transaction involving another firm, they usually report it to their opposite number.

Some companies are stricter than others in observing the code of conduct staff must obey when buying and selling stock on their own account. At most securities houses the phone transactions of all dealing staff are logged, so that investigators can, if they wish, find out who telephoned whom and when. Some firms have taken this a stage further and record the telephone calls of all staff.

A mixture of recorded conversations and the alertness of the London Stock Exchange's surveillance unit has already been responsible for trapping several insider traders. Just before the Mecca group bid for Pleasurama, the casinos and restaurant company, the members of the unit spotted that there had been an increasing amount of trading in Pleasurama. Their suspicions were further aroused when they received calls from market makers in some leading broking firms drawing their attention to the fact that something irregular must be going on. Compliance officers at several houses were phoned, and after a tape at Morgan Grenfell had been played, it was discovered that a tip had been passed on by a female member of Samuel Montagu's corporate finance team. This was the department involved in advising Mecca on its offer. The other banks then listened to their own tape recordings, and the woman plus two others who had used the information were unceremoniously sacked. The three had stood to make a useful sum of money from trading on inside information. That they were caught owes much to their own greed and the vigilance of the surveillance squad. If they had been more cautious and less avaricious, their dealings might well have passed unnoticed.

Even so, many insider traders escape detection. One particular problem is the use of nominee companies in offshore tax havens as the trading vehicle. The Stock Exchange team of former policemen, computer consultants, stockbrokers and accountants say they often follow good leads only to come up against obstacles when a block of shares is purchased by a nominee company. 'We can see no way at the moment of busting offshore companies without international cooperation,' I was told. 'All the old names are always there – the Cayman Islands and so on. But it is not only in the Caribbean or in Liberia that this problem exists – much closer to home, in the Channel Islands or the Isle of Man, we have just no hope of getting behind the nominee thing.'

At the time of writing, it is almost 20 years since the notorious Guinness scandal, but insider trading is still rife and largely undetected, even in very major takeover bids involving corporations of the highest reputation.

The Financial Services Authority

For years, the game of cricket was played in England only by amateurs, and control of the financial services industry was conducted in the same manner. There were a large number of self-regulatory organisations with strange acronyms and even more incomprehensible rulebooks. Essentially it amounted to the prefects controlling the boys with a somewhat light touch. However, as more and more scandals burst upon the City, and as it became clear that the old Stock Exchange motto of 'My Word is My Bond' was not a mantra that had a universal following, the politicians took over and passed laws to create a monolith, the Financial Services Authority (FSA). The FSA established itself comfortably in a tower under the shadow of Canary Wharf, and it is becoming increasingly clear that rooting out scandals and slapping miscreants on the wrist is only a minor part of its operations.

So wide has it spread its tentacles over the entire operations of the investment and personal finance industry, so all-embracing are its functions that Britain, once the least regulated of the major world economies, has become about the most smothered.

The process that led to the final creation of the FSA was a classic one – first an official inquiry, then recommendations for the establishment of a variant of the American SEC, a rejection of this in favour of a highly complex voluntary system, followed by a more onerous regime than anyone originally thought necessary.

When Tony Blair's revitalised Labour Party was elected to government in 1997, one of its first acts was to announce the establishment of the Financial Services Authority, headed by a former deputy-governor of the Bank, Howard Davies. The FSA took over banking regulation from the Bank and integrated the work of the Securities and Investments Board and all its subsidiary self-regulatory organisations. When Davies met the former chairman of the American Federal Reserve Board, Paul Volcker, the big American greeted him with a laugh and the comment: 'Big job, I just hope you can retain your sense of humour.' To his credit, Mr Davies did exactly that, with a series of speeches that mixed solid messages with wit.

The FSA is not a government department, nor is it publicly funded. Ingeniously, it is a private company whose income comes from levies on the businesses in the financial service industry, and from fines. Its aims are clear enough and defined by law:

- *Market confidence*: maintaining market confidence in the financial system
- *Public awareness*: promoting public understanding of the financial system
- *Consumer protection*: securing the appropriate degree of protection for consumers
- *Reduction of financial crime*: reducing the extent to which it is possible for a business carried on by a regulated person to be used for a purpose connected with financial crime

The FSA is politically accountable through the Treasury. The latter appoints the chairman and the board, which must have a majority of non-executive directors. The FSA has to provide Parliament with an annual report and hold an annual public meeting. There is also a committee of non-executive board members with clearly defined responsibilities, including ensuring the economic and efficient use of the FSA's resources and setting the pay of executive board members.

The first FSA chairman was convinced of the benefits of a single regulator.

> We believe this makes sense for us, given the growing integration of our financial markets and the growth of large cross-sectoral conglomerate institutions, which comprise banks, insurance companies, securities firms and investment managers under the same corporate umbrella. The longer we have worked with this single model the more convinced we are that it makes sense.[1]

Compared with the shambles of the regime that preceded it, there is a lot of common sense about the FSA. It cannot run amok, creating rules and regulations without regard to their practical impact on the various practitioners in the industry, and it has tried to create a regime that is cost-effective. It also appears to realise that there is no sense in having rules which cannot be enforced.

Another aspect of the FSA approach has been to adopt a risk-based strategy, identifying and assessing threats – for example, when it appears that a situation in a company or sector is likely to spiral out of control. But this approach did not enable it to identify a crisis at Equitable Life, until 2001 one of Britain's most prestigious life

---

[1] Howard Davies, chairman of the FSA, in speech to Grimaldi Forum, Monte Carlo,. July 2001.

assurance companies, where mismanagement led it to close its doors to new business, cut bonuses and impose higher exit penalties on those deciding to withdraw their money.

The FSA has also made major changes in the way financial services are sold. Until the end of 2004 financial advisers were divided into two – independent intermediaries who sold everyone's products, and tied agents who were on the staff of banks, insurance companies or investment groups and were restricted to selling only their employer's products. Now it is possible for advisers to sell from all the market, from a limited range of products or a single product.

But what they do have to do is to provide each customer with an FSA-designed 'key facts' document. This must set out clearly and unambiguously what is being sold, and at what price, and are displayed in such a way that a potential customer can compare like with like from competing firms. The statement also makes clear how much the adviser will be charging, whether by fee or by commission, thus ending for good the practice whereby many brokers misled customers into believing they were getting 'free' advice.

This is a welcome step.

One of the most controversial aspects of the FSA's new powers is its role in informing and educating the public. There are those who feel this is not the job of a regulator. Others argue, and I share the view, that given the poor record of the stockbroking community and the City generally in this area, it is good that someone has been delegated the task formally. It now has a great deal of study material in the 'learn-online' section of its web site.

Though politically accountable, the FSA has a raft of powers. These include information-gathering powers, powers to require firms to make regular returns or notify particular events, powers to commission expert reports – for example from accountants – and arrangements for direct reporting to the regulator by a firm's auditor or actuary.

The FSA has two main investigation powers. The first allows it to conduct general investigation of the affairs of an authorised person and its group, where there is good reason for doing so. The second allows investigations into a wide range of matters where there is the suspicion that particular offences have been committed or provisions of the Financial Services Act breached. The FSA can also go to court for a warrant enabling the police to enter and search premises in support of an investigation.

The Securities and Exchange Commission

The most feared and respected of the regulatory agencies – and the most important given the size of the American market – is the United States Securities and Exchange Commission (SEC), which protects the interests of America's estimated 50 million investors. Although its authority is technically limited to policing the securities industry in the United States, its tentacles are spread much wider, extending, for example, to the conduct of American investment institutions in their operations outside the country.

The SEC, with a current staff of just over 3,000, was established in July 1935, some six years after the Wall Street Crash of 1929. A Congressional investigation found that there had been stock manipulation on a huge scale, blatant dishonesty and insider trading, and the SEC was established with sweeping powers over the securities industry.

Now all corporations have to file quarterly financial returns, and much more detailed annual ones, with the SEC, as well as informing it promptly of any facts or important events which might affect the market for the company's stock. Federal laws require companies intending to raise money by selling their own securities to file with the Commission true facts about their operations. The Commission has power to prevent or punish fraud in the sale of securities, and is authorised to regulate stock exchanges. The law under which it operates lays down precise boundaries within which directors, officers and large shareholders may deal in the stock of their companies.

In its time, the SEC has notched up some notable successes in prosecuting corporate crime. In August 1968, it filed charges of securities fraud against fourteen Merrill Lynch officers and employees. In the end Merrill Lynch publicly consented to an SEC finding that it had used advance inside information from the Douglas Aircraft Company for the advantage of preferred institutional clients, defrauding the investing public of an estimated $4.5 million in the process – no mean sum at the time.

The Securities and Exchange Commission is a mecca for bright young lawyers who wish to make their name as determined investigators and then, as often as not, get out into lucrative private practice with the SEC name on their credentials.

However, while the SEC has a reputation as a vigorous force and has claimed many scalps, it is severely constrained in its activities by

a shortage of funds. Although it collects fees from registered investment advisers, it has to hand over a large share of the proceeds to the
United States Treasury. It has only about 300 enforcement officers to
cover the whole of the United States, and the section which deals with
the investment management and mutual and hedge funds industry
has an inspectorate of only about 60 people.

Although this latter group undertakes about 1,500 spot checks
each year on investment advisers, it is not surprising that many
confidence tricksters escape unscathed. Officially there are about
17,000 registered investment advisers in the United States, so on
average each gets a spot check once a decade, during which time
many will have sold their businesses on. But these figures include
only the registered advisers. The Consumer Federation of America
(CFA) believes that there could be about half a million people acting
as unofficial financial advisers, while even the Securities
Administrators Association accepts that there are 250,000. Many of
these not only claim to offer investment advice; some of them
actually manage clients' money.

The SEC also depends greatly on a number of self-regulatory
bodies to fulfil its task. For the most part stock exchanges police the
activities of their members, and each has an investigations branch.
The New York Stock Exchange, the American Stock Exchange and
the National Association of Securities Dealers (NASDAQ) all work
in close cooperation with the SEC.

The SEC's biggest coup was to catch Ivan Boesky, the self-styled
'king of the arbs'.

Arbs, or arbitrageurs, are people who buy stocks short-term when
pricing is in transition, in the hope of making a great deal of money
as they move up. They come to the fore in a takeover: after a bid has
been made, arbs buy as many shares as possible in anticipation of a
higher bid. When the higher bid comes, they sell. Arbs also work in
between markets, for example when a company's stock is quoted on
both the Australian and British exchanges. If the price moves up in
Australia they buy the stock in London hoping the price will rise
there also.

Boesky was brought to book after the Securities and Exchange
Commission netted Dennis Levine, a senior executive of a famous
Wall Street broking firm, Drexel Burnham Lambert, for insider
trading. During an extensive investigation and interrogation of
Levine, their quarry engaged in some judicious plea bargaining,
providing a large amount of information to the regulators. The

upshot was that Levine pleaded guilty, paid back $12.6 million in illegal profits and implicated Boesky. Like Levine, Boesky also 'co-operated' with the prosecutors, but he was fined $100 million, barred for life from working on Wall Street and ordered to dismantle his $2 billion firm.

Boesky was one of the biggest and best-known speculators in the feverish takeover business in America, using a phenomenal network of contacts to make huge profits through arbitraging. Like Levine, he also 'cooperated with the authorities', which is a euphemism for becoming a supergrass in order to keep out of jail.

16   Corporate Governance

*The remuneration of top dogs and fat cats is out of proportion
and excessive.*

Fritz Bolkenstein, European Commissioner

*There are ways executives are being compensated we did not
imagine ten years ago.*

Alan Beller, Securities and Exchange Commission

*Corporate governance is only about reducing the cost of capital.
It is not a moral crusade.*

Alastair Ross Goobey, chairman, International Corporate
Governance Network

The creation of the FSA in Britain and the further empowerment of
the Securities and Exchange Commission in the United States have
not prevented a wave of scandals on the stock markets, some of them
at least as disgraceful as some of the scams that went on before the
days of regulation.

Some of these affected a number of Britain's best known and most
respected companies. The oil company, Shell, and the *Daily
Telegraph* newspaper are two institutions that might be considered
to be pillars of the British establishment, but in the last few years the
chairmen of both companies have had to resign.

The Shell scandal was particularly disgraceful, and centred round
statements by its chairman, Sir Philip Watts, who was also a
luminary in the International Chamber of Commerce, a strong advocate of corporate governance and rectitude in business behaviour.

To the credit of some of the officers and directors of the world's
third largest oil company, when they discovered in 2004 that Shell
had deliberately overstated its oil and gas reserves, they commissioned an inquiry by an American firm of lawyers. This found –
amongst other things – that Watts had resisted attempts by the
company's exploration and production director, Walter van der
Vijver, to scale back the amount of oil and gas the company was
telling the world it was discovering.

The lawyers' report, which Shell made public, gave the details of emails that van de Vijver had sent to Watts. In one, dated November 2003, the exploration director told the chairman, 'I am sick and tired of lying about the extent of our reserves issues and the downward revisions that need to be done because of far too aggressive and optimistic bookings'. However, a month later, van de Vijver, responding to an internal report that suggested Shell's position on the reserves was a violation of United States securities law, wrote, 'This is absolute dynamite, not at all what I expected, and needs to be destroyed.' Both men left the company.

The Shell case is particularly fascinating because it happened despite many millions of pounds – and many more millions more words – having been expended on a new art form in business, commonly known as corporate governance.

Corporate governance is defined as the system by which business corporates are directed and controlled. Usually the system works through a set of laws or self-imposed codes being observed with care.

Yet despite these corporate governance guidelines and regulations, the Shell case showed a fatal weakness in the system; it does not provide for a situation where a strong-willed chairman wants to get his own way. The same problem arose in the case of the former proprietor of the *Daily Telegraph*, Conrad Black, who at the time of writing was facing prosecution in the United States, after it had been revealed that he had diverted moneys from Hollinger Inc., the company he once controlled when it owned the British newspaper.

The Black case gave birth to a new term in the stock market lexicon – corporate kleptocracy. It was spun by an investigating committee appointed by Hollinger International's board and chaired by former SEC chairman Richard C. Breeden, and it neatly encapsulates what it described as seven years' 'aggressive looting' of the media company by Black and the company's CEO, David Radler. According to the report the pair 'siphoned off' more than $400 million, 'making it their business to line their pockets at the expense of Hollinger almost every day, in almost every way they could devise.'

The Black case is too complex to detail here, but an excellent account of it can be found in a book by two Canadian journalists: *The Fall of Conrad Black*. Black's injudicious actions cost him dearly; he lost his newspaper titles, with the *Daily Telegraph* being sold to the Barclay brothers.

However, the Shell and Black scandals were minor compared to the one that shook the stock markets worldwide, involving the collapse of the American oil company Enron, which cost investors more than $30 billion and led to the creation of the rapidly growing corporate governance industry. The corporate behaviour of top Enron people made Gordon Gecko, the main figure in the film *Wall Street*, look almost harmless. A *Washington Post* writer described the company as 'an enterprise only lightly tethered to morality and decency.'

The creator and chairman of Enron, Kenneth Lay, was once feted in America as a business genius. He was a frequent visitor to the White House, where he was known as 'Kenny boy'. He was a 'global leader' regularly given prominence at the annual Davos summit of the World Economic Forum, a body which has as its aim to improve the state of the world. And he was a wonderful publicist for Enron, talking up the company's share price while its finances were in chaos and as he sold its shares. As this edition went to press, Lay was facing criminal and civil indictments.

As an editorial in the *Washington Post* stated:

> Enron's name has come to evoke more than just one company; it is a sort of shorthand for the systemic problems in corporate America, from loopholes in accounting rules to conflicts of interest among the auditors who supposedly enforce these rules, to boards of directors that fail to hold managers accountable.

The burgeoning new industry of corporate governance exists to protect shareholders and workers from more Enrons, but it has had mixed success, achieved only at great cost. The toughest action has been taken in the United States through the Sarbannes-Oxley accounting law passed by Congress in 2002, which created a new regulatory body to oversee the work of auditors and increased white-collar fines and prison terms as much as tenfold. It also forced companies to improve board independence. This last provision achieved little in preventing the Black scandal: Lord Black's hand-picked board of the great and the good – including former US secretary of state Henry Kissinger; Richard Perle, a foreign policy adviser to George W. Bush; Richard Burt, the former US ambassador to Germany; and the publisher Lord Weidenfeld – did little or nothing to prevent the unlawful payments being made.

Outside the United States, most countries, including Britain, adopted a system of corporate governance based on the observance of codes. These followed numerous studies on corporate behaviour over a period of about ten years, culminating in a long document produced by Derek Higgs.

Like the Ten Commandmants, these codes, if observed, offer a good basis for decent behaviour, but some are more important than others. The most significant – and controversial – surround the issue of executive pay, the need for independent directors and the role of institutional investors in companies in which they hold major shares. Rather than sitting on their hands, institutions are urged to be proactive when they spot something going wrong in a company in which they are invested, and to be much more transparent about how and when they vote or use other ways of chucking their weight about. Quiet, conspiratorial dinners are – in theory at least – out of order. Whistle blowers inside company managements who tip off share-holder groups and the media about wrongdoings should also be protected, with at least one board member nominated to listen to their complaint and to maintain confidentiality.

Executive indulgence

There is something nauseous about chairmen, chief executives and other senior managers receiving huge bonuses at a time when shareholders are suffering from lower prices and dividends and while employees are facing wage standstills, cuts in real pay and redundancy. Unfortunately the practice is widespread, but seldom justified. Few shareholders or employees jib at their chiefs taking home a generous bonus when things are doing well, but they do not understand why bonuses are still paid when the company is doing badly.

Executive indulgence has been a feature of the new millennium, and a series of shareholder revolts put it at the heart of the corporate governance debate. Some of these have focussed on high but lawful remuneration packages, such as huge amounts paid to Jean-Pierre Garnier of GlaxoSmithKline, Jack Welch, chief executive of General Electric and Sir Martin Sorrell of WPP, but no one criticised their work ethic. The activisists' objection to Garnier was not so much what he was paid each month, but the fact that the company's board had agreed a £22 million golden handshake if he left; the activists managed to persuade shareholders to reject the remuneration committee's recommendation.

There was indignation when Lord Black was indulging in a

champagne lifestyle at the company's expense when Hollinger's newspapers were losing advertising and the share price was tumbling. As Tesco and Wal-Mart continued to take business away from Sainsbury's in the battle of the supermarkets, there was profound disquiet at the remuneration package of Sir Peter Davies, the Sainsbury's chairman. When the chairman and chief executive of BT both resigned after the company's poor performance, they were given huge pay-offs that will ensure they are rich for life.

In each of these cases, and many more, institutional shareholders were slow to act and individual shareholders found they had little voice. Even when the institutions have acted against management excesses or incompetence, more often than not they act unfairly. When British Airways plunged from healthy profit to losses that nearly caused its demise, Robert Ayling, the chief executive, was made the scapegoat and paid the price. The company chairman, Lord Marshall, who had hired Ayling and endorsed his policies, escaped with his remuneration intact, but, of course, he had better City connections than the unfortunate Ayling.

The institutions appear to have done nothing about the self-aggrandisement of Richard Harvey, the chief executive of Aviva, Britain's biggest insurer. When Harvey arrived in Norwich to take over Norfolk's largest employer the Norwich Union was a household brand name across the world. The Norwich Union was merged with the Commercial Union into the ungainly CGNU, and its head-quarters moved to an expensive office block in London at a time when most insurers were cutting costs and moving to the provinces. Three groups of people suffered. The staff in Norwich saw jobs go and became demoralised. Pay rises were below inflation, and staff were asked to drive about 200 miles to Sheffield for meetings that started at nine in the morning; they were not allowed to stay in Sheffield overnight.

Shareholders, many of them former policyholders of the Norwich Union, saw the value of their investments slump. And policyholders who had taken out endowment mortgages found their annual and terminal bonuses cut to the point that they had insufficient funds to pay off their home loans and had to arrange further mortgages. But did Harvey suffer? Not a bit. His bonus rose and rose in value as he enjoyed his expensive new lifestyle in fashionable Belgravia. Harvey's salary has more than doubled since his Norwich days, and rose by 45 per cent between 1999 and 2002, about four times the rate of inflation.

According to the company's accounts for 2003, he picked up £718,000 in salary, £312,000 in bonuses and had his pension topped up with a cool £1.1 million. By contrast managers with more than 100 people reporting to them were paid less than £20,000, a bonus – if they were lucky – of £1,000, and had to contribute to their own pensions.

Harvey is one of several life assurance executives whose rewards were described by a treasury Select Committee as excessive, and whose companies were accused of not caring about their customers. John McFall, the committee's chairman, questioned how at a time when average pay rises were 3.5 per cent, such excesses were justified, when 'the industry has been going downhill like a slalom skier'.[1]

Corporate greed by fat cats is now enraging both public and politicians. The Chancellor, Gordon Brown, has made no secret of his contempt for company chiefs who are overpaid, while the European Commission has said the menace of overpaid boardrooms is high on its agenda. Expressing the view that the 'excessive pay of many top executives across Europe is an abuse of shareholder trust', the Commissioner for the Single Market, Frits Bolkestein, told a corporate governance conference, 'The remuneration of top dogs and fat cats is out of proportion and excessive.'

The British government at one stage threatened to intervene on fat cats' pay and pensions, but resisted pressure from the Trades Union Congress to do so after intense lobbying by the Confederation of British Industry and other business groups, including the City.

The other big corporate governance issue is the way institutional investors behave. All too often they do not turn up at shareholders' meetings, sometimes fail to vote, and cosy up to managements rather than criticising them. Not long ago the Anglo-Dutch consumer giant Unilever went public in complaining that its major shareholders often failed to vote. George Cox, head of the Institute of Directors, told a London Business School seminar that institutional shareholders were the least loyal of any group associated with a company, and too often were simply not involved.

Institutions have argued that their job is to protect their own funds and the people who have invested in them, so they need to be free to buy and sell as they please. Any rule or code that would require them to get involved in any way with the management or direction of a company would inhibit this freedom, so many prefer to keep their

---

[1] Treasury Select Committee, *Hansard*, 28 Jan 2004.

distance. It is a fair point, but a contrary view is that small share holders inevitably get outnumbered and outvoted.

Another issue in corporate governance is whistle blowing. The practice of whistle blowing first gained prominence in the United States three decades ago as a result of the activities of the consumer advocate Ralph Nader. Then the emphasis was on poor or defective products. After the Enron affair and other corporate scandals whistle blowing is being introduced into corporate governance legislation and rulebooks.

In Britain the Financial Services Authority has set up a dedicated whistle blowers hotline and email address where staff can spill the beans on what is happening in their companies under a pledge of anonymity. Protection is provided by the Public Disclosure Act of 1998. The interesting thing about this legislation is that the employee is protected even if the information proferred turns out to lack substance. The British have not gone as far as Canada, which has passed legislation whereby those who seek to intimidate whistle blowers face up to five years imprisonment.

Controlling the bean counters

All these issues have had an impact on the stock markets and have made public companies more transparent, while adding considerably to the corporate workload. But none of them are likely to have as great an impact as new rules that have been brought in as a result of the dishonesty of accountants. Perhaps dishonesty is too strong a word, but many of the scandals that have made headlines in the business press both in Britain and elsewhere could not have taken place without the involvement of a number of senior people employed by accountancy firms both large and small. The worst example, was Arthur Andersen's involvement in Enron.

Auditors have a fiduciary responsibility to make sure that company accounts are accurate, and to verify that the numbers that provide a snapshot of the state of the company are not distorting the picture. It is a tough and painstaking job, and well paid, so there is considerable competition between big accountancy firms to win or retain the business of large corporations.

Unfortunately this can lead to a conflict of interest. The auditors need to have a good relationship with the finance director of a company, while at the same time keeping an unswerving focus on the facts and figures of the business. Since historically boards have relied on finance directors for advice on auditors, it has been a temptation to present or manipulate numbers in such a way that suit him or her. Other past potential conflicts have occurred when accountancy firms with management consultancy arms have been seeking lucrative contracts for the latter. There have also been widespread differences in auditing practices in different countries, making it hard for even institutional investors to compare corporations in similar businesses based in different countries.

Their reputations damaged, accountants have worked with governments to clean up their act and, as a result, new accounting standards are being introduced which will have a major impact on stock markets. Companies which have traditionally presented their accounts in one way must, from 2005, present them according to these new standards.

The new standards are too detailed to present here, but it is worth mentioning a few which will have an impact, mostly beneficial, on investors and the stock markets.

One important new rule, known as IAS 19, provides that the cost of providing employee benefits such as sick pay, holiday pay, pensions, medical insurance, sabbaticals and potential redundancy pay should be disclosed when it is earned by an employee, not when it comes to be paid. This will result, in most cases, in employee costs shown as rising. The cost of earnings-related pensions, for example, must be provided for over an employee's working life, rather than when the money has to be paid out. This is particularly important when CEOs have contracts which provide for large pensions.

A similar rule applies to employee share-ownership plans, where the cost in future will have to be shown as an operating expense, rather than coming into the accounts only when finally paid for. Thus a truer picture will emerge.

Another interesting new rule deals with the treatment of intangible assets, by which is meant assets that do not have an obvious numerical value. These intangibles could include ownership of copyright, customer lists and customer relations, which are all worth something but have not been given a real value in accounts. Now they must be presented at cost. Curiously the rule does not extend to brand names or titles, such as newspaper mastheads, which must have an even greater value. Wisely perhaps, those drawing up the new rules decided that the best judge of the value of a brand like Birds Eye, the *Daily Mail* or Apple should be the market, not the bean counters.

Independent directors

Nearly all corporate governance codes place a strong emphasis on the need for companies to have a majority of independent directors, and for remuneration and audit committees – board groups that set the pay of top executives and appoint the company's auditors – to be chaired by an independent.

So who qualifies as an independent? Obviously directors who are executives in the company, such as the CEO, do not qualify, but beyond that deciding who is or is not independent gets tricky. In the old days directors were often appointed because they were pals of the chairman or principal shareholder, and therefore could be replied upon to vote the same way on important decisions. Sometimes they were cronies from the same West End club. Some chairmen, for example Conrad Black, liked to grace their board tables with the great and the good, whose names and reputation might add value to the company but who perhaps would be less diligent than some in poking their noses into a company's finances. Often relatives were appointed.

In theory at least, this has now stopped. The British code on corporate governance says that boards should be constituted with a balance of executive and non-executive directors 'such that no individual or small group of individuals can dominate the board's decision taking and prospects.'

This has stimulated a move for more professionalism, with many directors now receiving some kind of training. Many companies now use head hunters to find suitable independent directors, and retired business leaders are sought after for this role, provided they have the reputation to justify appointment.

But the new regulations and the activities of the FSA mean that being a director carries more responsibility, and some serious legal obligations. Except in top corporations, this has not yet been fully recognised, and research shows that many good people have less enthusiasm for the job. A survey showed that four out of ten boardroom members would be less likely to accept a new non-executive directorship.

In early 2005 even leading companies were only paying their independent directors an average of £35,000 a year for an average of 38 days' work, almost double the workload of a decade earlier. That works out at less than £1,000 per day, which is about one fifth of the charge-out rate of a City corporate lawyer or accountant. Unlike these professionals, many directors receive no secretarial backup or research help. There is still a long way to go before medium-sized companies have boards that are truly equipped to look after shareholders' interests.

17 New Game, New Rules, New Obligations

One hundred years ago the stock market *was* the City. The Square Mile of offices, the trading floor of the Stock Exchange, the dining rooms, coffee shops and bars, the tailors' shops and tinkers' stalls were the workplace of men and women who had a sense of the City's importance. They were at the heart of a financial world that sets its own boundaries.

Today that has gone. There is still much rejoicing City tradition, the City elders continue to dress up in their pantomine finery to welcome the great and the good to posh and pompous dinners in the Guildhall, where the port flows freely and gartered toastmasters preface each introduction with a thump of the mace and the words, 'My lords, ladies and gentlemen, pray silence for . . .' The unelected Lord Mayor – with a new appointee each year – still retains some independence from the elected Mayor of London, and celebrates getting the job by trundling through the streets in a horse and carriage one chilly Saturday in autumn as the office workers and school children clap and shout, 'Hip, hip, hooray'.

But the real City is not at all traditional. Behind the grey portals and rain-soaked windows, people work harder, faster and more competitively than ever. There are thousands fewer pretty secretaries and thousands more IT specialists, most of whom eschew any kind of tradition, especially a dress code. There are no bowlers to be seen, and the only top hats are worn *inside* the Bank of England by the pink-coated male 'waiters' that act as receptionists. At the City offshoot, down in Docklands, there is none of this frippery, and life is tougher because of the extra commute on a light railway that runs at overcapacity.

The other tradition that has gone is the Britishness of it all. The real power in the City now, for better or worse, lies in the hands of overseas interests, mostly American and European. The main futures market is owned by a foreign consortium, and by the time this edition is printed the London Stock Exchange may have gone the same way.

In early 2005 it narrowly escaped being taken over by the German Boerse.

This may or may not be bad news. The British motor industry is almost all in foreign ownership, and is thriving; it is certainly in much better shape than when much of it was run by the government. The only risk so far as the City is concerned is that many of the decisions about its future will not be taken in London. London, increasingly, is the European branch office of the United States, with all its attendant strengths, weaknesses, threats and opportunities.

Nor is the stock market of today the wicked place as described by the tea lady in 1802, but it has its moments. Despite the occasional scandal, wickedness is much less widespread, and the manipulation of markets is uncommon. Consumers have greater protection, and are more aware of the hidden costs created by commission agents seeking to sell them life assurance packages and financial services. But when scandals do occur there are few prosecutions, and very few of the perpetrators have seen the inside of a prison cell. The financial press is ever vigilant, but even the *Financial Times* failed to spot Enron.

The stock markets are still motivated by greed and fear, but a new game is being played, with a new set of rules. Curiously, given the all-encompassing nature of these regulations, there is more risk for the individual investor, not less. 'My word is my bond' and 'utmost good faith' have been replaced by caveat emptor, 'let the buyer beware'. The investor or saver may in theory enjoy greater protection, but at the same time is more exposed. He or she is like the home owner who installs a back-to-base burglar alarm but forgets to set it, or leaves the door open, or discovers, in an emergency, there is no police squad car within miles.

Whether playing the markets or saving prudently for a home or old age, individuals and families need to be much more wide awake than ever before. It is easy to make an error of judgement by picking the wrong stock, the wrong fund, the wrong adviser or a poor fund manager. What is important is to be able to recognise these errors of judgement quickly, and then to correct them at once. The watch you need to keep on your shares, bonds and other investments needs to be just as vigilant as the local neighbourhood watch. Those with money invested should never relax their guard, and this is as true of those who are in collective investments like unit trusts as the punter who buys speculative stocks.

Herein lies a problem. Stock and investment watch takes time, and requires some basic knowledge of how the markets work. Many people have neither. At the start of this book I described in detail a number of the factors that determine a security's share price, and hence its value. The proliferation of financial news, data and analysis has made it easy to make quick calculations on value, but the complexity of the judgements involved extend well beyond the merit of any one particular share or fund.

These days the future of currency values, interest rates, commodity prices and other economic factors as well as a company's actual performance come into play. A new investment skill has evolved around seeking out those stocks that are wrongly priced, and buying or selling them on the gamble that at some stage in their near future the market will determine their correct value.

Let me illustrate this with a simple example. A person in Britain with limited experience of the stock market may form the view that because the price of oil appears to be rising and because BP is a well-managed company its shares will do well. First we should not ignore the fact that these two views will already be factored into the prevailing share price at which he or she can buy BP stock. The market always looks at 'what will be', not 'what is'. Then we have to remember that the price of oil is designated in US dollars, and should the dollar fall in value against the pound, the notional benefit of the higher oil price might be much less in sterling terms. On the other hand, BP's treasury will almost certainly have hedged against such an eventuality. The investor himself can also hedge against the fall of the dollar. The investor may worry about the size and scale of BP's investment in Siberia: what happens if it goes bad? He can insure against a fall in the share price by buying an option to sell his BP holding at the price he paid for it.

Because of the complexity of today's markets, many sophisticated investors are turning to hedge funds, which do not depend on prices rising for success. There are more than 6,000 hedge funds in the world today managing about $600 billion of assets. These funds are just as likely to make money if the share and bond markets fall; their managers set profit targets and devise techniques to achieve that.

Many of these funds operate right away from the bailiwick of stock exchanges, for few of them are likely to buy ordinary shares, although they will stake a claim through options and warrants, and in stock market index futures. But their borrowed funds will come from banks and other investment groups, and these funds may be very large; so large in fact as to create a ripple in market trading when they are used. When hedge fund managers play the options markets, their activities can have a tsunami effect, sometimes reducing a company's value to such a low level as to make it vulnerable to takeover.

These unpredictable forces in the markets have made some queasy about the future. Worldwide there is a watch on the activities of hedge funds. But they are here to stay, are global in nature and have increased the speed at which the money wheel rotates.

It is more important than ever that our children learn about the forces that control the world's financial markets, Britain's role in these markets and their relevance to the workplace, family life and planning for old age. There is a big hole in both the public and private education system here. It is somehow thought beneficial to teach languages that are increasingly irrelevant in the world today, but not the language of money. Personal finance is on the agenda in some schools, but, for the most part, it is taught badly, as a branch of consumer education, by teachers who themselves are poorly informed.

The City has made some half-hearted efforts to deal with this, but those at the heart of the markets and at the cutting edge of the sweeping change taking place are too busy to be bothered with it. The London Stock Exchange itself has abdicated its responsibilities: charging £10 per hour per student for an introductory course that should be provided for nothing is living proof of that. The FSA does its best with a very limited budget.

Why is this so important? It is because most of the Earth's assets – and to some extent property beyond our planet – are, contrary to popular perception, owned not by rich individuals, but by us, the people, as shareholders and stakeholders. We may not know it, because these assets, which could be land and buildings, aircraft and ships, oil and other vast mineral resources, corporations and super-markets are, for the most part, in the hands of institutions numbered only in thousands yet in control of trillions of pounds. It's not their money, but they mobilise it, use it, provide it temporarily to some and deny it to others. Across in Wall Street the heads of these institutions are billed the masters of the universe. They have more power than any politician, certainly any British prime minister. We need to understand that and know how to keep an eye on them. If this book has helped to understand how and why this is so, it will be an achievement.

Glossary of Terms

ADRs American Depository Receipt; see depository receipts.

AER Annual Equivalent Rate. Usually specifies the interest paid from current, deposit or savings accounts. This new term replaces CAR (Compound Annual Rate), which denoted much the same thing.

AGM Annual General Meeting. The meeting of shareholders held each year to approve the accounts and to reappoint directors and auditors. Normally held twenty-one days after publication of the annual report. It must be held within eighteen months of the previous AGM. AGMs are often attended by private investors as an opportunity to question directors on a company's performance, prospects and results.

AIM Alternative Investment Market. The London Stock Exchange's market for smaller, younger and growing companies.

AITC Association of Investment Trust Companies. This is the industry body for the investment trust sector, and will provide investors with a great deal of useful information.

analyst Someone who studies particular stock markets or industry sectors and makes buy or sell recommendations regarding the shares of specific companies within them. Such recommendations are arrived at through a combination of research, economic statistics and visits to the companies themselves. See also **fund manager**.

Annual Report & Accounts The directors' report to shareholders, which sets out the details of the company's performance during the past year. Normally split into two halves, the important part is the back half, which contains the accounts. Once you have mastered how to read a balance sheet, you will find accounts a mine of information. Full details of directors' pay are included, along with much other financial information. The front half normally includes reports from the company's chairman and chief executives, but many of these are written by the corporate relations people and tend to be gratuitous publicity rather than useful information.

annual volatility Volatility is one measure used to assess the risk of a portfolio as it helps to describe the likely range of returns achieved by the fund. In statistical terms it is the standard deviation of the return distribution. Greater volatility of monthly fund returns means that there is a wider range of likely returns in the future, or greater uncertainty regarding the fund return. Most investors would equate this greater uncertainty with greater risk.

APCSIM Association of Private Client Stockbrokers and Investment Managers. This is the official body of stockbrokers and fund managers who specialise in providing investment services for private clients.

APR Annual Percentage Rate. The compounded rate used to give a standard comparison of the amount of interest you are likely to pay on loans, mortgages or outstanding credit card balances. This is a key figure, and should always be the one used to compare costs or returns on interest-bearing securities.

arbitrage The act of profiting from the difference in price when the same security, currency or commodity is traded on two or more markets at different prices.

assets Another word for real possessions. Net assets are the difference between what you own and what you owe. Sometimes investments held in a portfolio are referred to as assets. Assets are also items a company owns, such as land, machinery, stocks, cash and investments.

associated companies When one company has an interest in another company that represents more than 20 per cent but less than a majority of the voting rights in that company's share capital, then this is deemed an investment in an 'associated' company. The profits of the associated company are consolidated into the results of the company holding the investment. If the holding company has less than a 20 per cent interest, then only dividends received will appear in its accounts. If the holding company has over a 50 per cent interest, then the investment is deemed to be a subsidiary company, and its results and net assets will be fully consolidated in the holding company accounts.

at best order An instruction to a stockbroker by a client to buy or sell shares for the best price available.

audit A professional, independent examination of the accounts of a company. Accounts of all registered companies, whether listed or not, must be audited.

AUTIF The Association of Unit Trusts and Investment Funds, the industry trade body for unit trust and investment trust management companies.

balance sheet The statement featured in the Annual Report & Accounts that indicates the value of the company's assets and liabilities as of the end of its financial period. The balance sheet also provides details of the company's methods of financing.

base rate The core interest rate determined by the Bank of England in Britain, by the European Central Bank for those European countries in the European Monetary System, and by the Federal Reserve in the United States. Most other savings and borrowing rates are derived from base rate.

basket A contract or other derivative for the purchase or sale of shares, which comprise a pre-defined group of equities. It could be all equities in the FTSE 100, for example. You can also have a basket of currencies – for example the pound, euro and yen aggregated against the US dollar.

basket case Slang for a country that has debts exceeding its reserves, and is in need of international support. Sometimes used to refer to a company or companies in trouble.

bear An investor who sells a security in the hope of buying it back at a lower price. A bear market is a falling market in which bears would prosper.

bid-offer spread The difference between the price at which an investor buys unit trusts or shares and the price at which he sells them. The buying or offer price is usually higher than the selling price, and the difference between them may vary within the limits of a formula laid down by the Financial Services Act 1986.

bid price The buying price for securities in the market.

Big Bang 27 October 1986, the date when the rules of the London Stock Exchange were changed to allow corporate ownership and to abolish the role of jobbers as market makers on the floor of the Throgmorton Street building.

blue chip A popular term used to define a company regarded as being a sound and safe investment. The adjectives you normally associate with such a company are large, solid, well established, reputable and, perhaps, boring.

bonds Interest-bearing securities that entitle the holder to interest during their life and repayment of the loan at maturity. In Britain, but only in Britain, government bonds are called gilts, short for gilt-edged securities. American government bonds are known as Treasuries. The issuer promises to pay bond holders a fixed rate of interest for a fixed number of years. Those bonds with a life of five years or less are known as 'shorts', while those with ten years or more are called 'longs'. Bonds are traded on all stock markets and move up or down in line with interest rates.

broker A member of a stock exchange which provides dealing services with or without advice to the public, and which can also buy and sell shares on its own account.

bull The opposite of a bear. Bulls buy shares in the expectation of being able to sell them at a higher price. A bull market is a rising market. One of the longest bull markets in history came to an end in the year 2000.

call option The right, but not the obligation, to buy stock or shares at an agreed price up to a predetermined date in the future. One of the basic units of the futures markets.

capital An investor's savings and wealth or a company's share capital and reserves. Also sometimes used to describe a lump sum of money that is available for immediate use.

capital employed The funds employed by the company in its activities. On the balance sheet, the company's share capital, reserves and debt represent capital employed.

capital gains tax A tax on the increase in value of assets sold in a particular year. Operates as a handicap to personal investors as it inhibits them from selling shares when circumstances dictate that they should.

capitalisation issue An issue in which funds from a company's reserves are converted into shares that are issued free of charge to the company's shareholders.

cash The value of all liquid assets employed in a business, either as ready cash or invested in short-term securities that can be quickly sold and turned into cash.

cash-flow statement The statement in the Annual Report & Accounts that indicates the sources of all cash, from both operations and external means of finance, for the financial period. The cash-flow statement indicates how cash has been used for trading, capital preservation, investment and taxation purposes.

charts Graphs of share and market (index) performance used to determine relative trends and to identify likely future moves. Charts are key instruments in technical analysis. See also **technical analysis**.

City This term describes the London financial markets in the same way as Wall Street defines the New York financial centre. It used to mean the square mile within the operational control of the Corporation of London, but the term is now more generic to describe all of London's financial operations, including those in Docklands. It is similar in concept to the term 'Fleet Street', which means the national newspaper industry, though not one newspaper remains there.

commission The charge made by stockbrokers to individual investors for carrying out their buy or sell instructions. The charge may be either a percentage of the value involved or, for small deals below a stated and agreed value, a fixed amount.

contract note The paperwork investors receive from their stockbrokers confirming the terms of the deal that has been undertaken on their behalf.

convertible loan stocks Securities that pay fixed interest, but that can be converted into shares at a given price and at set times.

corporate governance The term used to describe the policies and procedures that a company's directors are expected to use in conducting the company's affairs and its relationships with shareholders. The directors are responsible as managers of the shareholders' interests in the company.

covered warrant A security issued by a party other than the issuer of the underlying asset, giving the holder the right to acquire a share or bond at a specific price and date.

creative accounting The term used to indicate accounting and financial reporting practices which, whilst not illegal, are intended to convey a circumstance or position that is either misleading or illusory, thus creating a perception of profitability or soundness that may not be wholly valid.

creditors, long All liabilities payable more than one year after the balance sheet date. This includes provisions, deferred taxation, loans, and debt (including convertible debt) repayable more than one year after the balance sheet date.

creditors, short All current liabilities payable on demand or within one year of the balance sheet date.

CREST The British electronic share settlement system that was introduced on the London Stock Exchange in July 1996.

current assets The value of the assets held at the balance sheet date that are represented by cash, or could be converted into cash within the next twelve months.

current liabilities The value of those liabilities at the balance sheet date that the company is obliged to settle within twelve months.

Debt Management Office (DMO) The part of the British Treasury that has responsibility for issuing gilts to fund the Government's borrowing requirement.

depository receipts Negotiable certificates that give evidence of ownership of a company's shares. Used to trade British and other non-American shares on the New York Stock Exchange, where they are known as ADRs.

depreciation The financial equivalent of wear and tear. Companies are allowed to deduct a certain amount from profits to allow for the decline in value of plant and equipment. Items like vehicles can be depreciated by 25 per cent of their value each year.

deregulation Removing or reducing restrictions in the hope that it will make a market more efficient.

discretionary account Account which allows a designated stock-broker or investment company to make investment decisions and buy or sell shares without consulting the account holder.

distribution The payments of any investment income generated by a fund. These payments may be made quarterly, half-yearly or annually. Investors can usually choose to have the distribution paid to them or reinvested in the fund.

dividend The sum paid by the company to its shareholders as their financial reward for investing in the company. Dividends are usually paid half-yearly as 'interim' and then 'final' dividends.

dividend cover The amount of money a company has available from its profits to cover the cost of its dividends.

dividend per share The income a shareholder receives on each share owned in a company.

earnings per share An important and widely used indicator of the return on equity investment. Mathematically, EPS is calculated by dividing the total amount of a company's net profits by the number of ordinary shares issued.

equity The part of a company's share capital represented by ordinary, or voting, shares. Equities is a term often used for stocks and shares.

eurobond An interest-bearing security issued across national borders, usually in a currency other than that of the issuer's home country, most commonly dollars.

ex-dividend When appended to the share price as xd, it means that investors who buy the shares will not receive the already declared dividend. Conversely investors will receive the dividend when they sell them xd, even though they no longer hold the shares at the actual time of payment.

execution only Execution-only orders are fulfilled by stockbrokers who offer low commission rates but no advice.

Fed Common name for the United States Federal Reserve Board, America's central bank.

fiscal policy The use of taxation measures to influence a company.

flotation The occasion on which a company's shares are offered on the market for the first time.

Footsie The popular name for the FTSE 100 Share Index, the British stock market's main benchmark index, which measures the daily share price performance of Britain's top hundred public listed companies.

FSA Financial Services Authority, the agency appointed by the Government under the Financial Services Act to oversee the regulation of the financial services industry.

FTSE Index Three indices comprise the FTSE All Share index: the FTSE 100, FTSE 250 and the FTSE Small Caps.

fund General term for any investment vehicle which pools together the money of many small individual investors and invests it according to a defined set of investment aims and objectives. These include such investments as unit trusts, investment trusts and pension plans.

fundamental analysis A method of researching the investment potential of a company.

fundamentals Usually refers to the underlying economic factors affecting a particular market, country or sector and includes such aspects as industrial output, wages and raw materials costs, currency strengths or weaknesses and trade balance.

fund manager A professional manager of investments in a pension fund, insurance company or unit trust, or other individual fund. He or she makes the day-to-day decisions on what investments to buy or sell on behalf of the fund's investors.

futures A futures contract enables an investor to buy or sell securities or other goods at a future date at a predetermined price. The price is established between buyer and seller on the floor of an exchange, such as the London International Financial Futures Exchange (LIFFE), using an 'open outcry' system. The contracts themselves may be traded with third parties.

gearing Company borrowing as a proportion of funds. A highly geared company is usually seen as a riskier investment.

gilt-edged securities See **bonds**.

goodwill Intangible assets such as reputation or brand names.

growth companies Those companies that are expected to have continual growth, year on year, in their earnings per share.

hedging A strategy used to offset investment risk. Usually makes use of futures or options.

index-linked Indicates that an investment is tied to the rate of price inflation.

inflation The amount in percentage terms by which prices rise or fall year on year. In Britain the primary measure of inflation is the Retail Price Index (RPI).

initial public offering (IPO) The offering of shares in the equity of a company to the public for the first time.

insider dealing The purchase or sale of shares by someone who possesses inside information on a company's performance that has not yet been made available to the market, and which might affect the share price. In Britain, as in most western countries, such deals are a criminal offence.

intangible assets The company assets that are usually non-monetary in nature and without physical form, but which represent an expected future benefit. Examples of intangible assets include brands, patents, intellectual property and goodwill on acquisition (the value placed on the acquired company's reputation and market presence).

interest cover Earnings before interest and tax divided by the cost of interest.

interims The company's results for the first six months of its reporting period, which is usually its financial year.

investment club A group of like-minded individuals, friends or colleagues who gather together for the purpose of investing in the stock market.

investment trust A closed-end investment fund that is a company listed on the Stock Exchange, the purpose of which is to invest in other shares. Investment trusts often specialise in specific types of companies, in a geographic area or in a single industrial sector.

ISA Individual Savings Accounts. The Government introduced ISAs in April 1999. ISAs are tax-efficient vehicles. There is no tax on dividends held within them and capital gains taxes are not levied if the ISA remains in place for five years or more.

issue price Price at which shares are first offered to investors when a company floats on the stock market.

LIFFE London International Financial Futures and Options Exchange.

limit order An order submitted to an electronic order book with a specified size and price. The order is either held on the order book or executed, either in part or in full, against any eligible order, with any remaining unexecuted portion being added to the order book.

liquidity The portion of an investment portfolio that is not fully invested but is represented by cash holdings. Also, the level of continual buy-and-sell activity making up the market demand for shares and indicating the ease with which securities can be traded on the market.

listed company A company whose securities have been admitted to the London Stock Exchange and which has had to comply with the Exchange's listing regulations.

market capitalisation The value of a company as measured by the total stock market price of its issued and outstanding shares. In other words, the number of shares in issue multiplied by the current share price. Market capitalisation is widely used as a definition of company size and value.

market maker A Stock Exchange member firm that is obliged to make a continuous two-way price in the shares it follows. It is also used to describe a broker's employee who sets a price at which he is prepared to buy or sell shares on behalf of his firm.

merger The agreed integration of two companies, usually in the same industry, to create a new, combined entity with control still reflected in the ownership shares of the original companies.

mid price The median (mid point) of the buying and selling spread quoted by the market makers. The price shown in the share price pages and market reports within the financial media, but not the price at which investors could necessarily expect to conclude a deal to buy or sell.

minority interest That part of a subsidiary company that the investing company does not itself hold or control. For instance, if a company has an interest in 87 per cent of the share capital of another company, then that other company is a subsidiary, and 87 per cent of its profits and assets will be featured in the consolidated accounts of the share-owning company. The 13 per cent not directly owned will be featured in the consolidated accounts as a minority interest.

monetary policy Influencing the direction of an economy through control of the money supply, usually by changing interest rates.

net asset value The net assets of a company divided by the number of shares it has issued.

net income Net income is pre-tax profits less taxation and other special charges. This is the amount that can be reinvested in the company or paid out in dividends or, usually, both. Those liable to lower rate or basic rate income tax will have no further liability to tax. Higher rate taxpayers will have to pay more when their tax return is due.

nominee A person or company holding securities on behalf of others. Those who use online or telephone brokerages almost always hold their shares through nominee accounts.

OFEX Off exchange. An unregulated alternative to the official stock market, organised by J.P. Jenkins Ltd and targeted at smaller companies that have a potentially higher risk and thus prospects of higher rewards.

offer for sale A method of bringing a company to the market.

option You pay a published amount to have the option to buy or sell at a specific date in the future. Call options give their holder the right to buy a nominated number of shares at a specified price before a specified date. Put options allow the holder to do the opposite: sell at a set price before the nominated date. However, most people trade their options before they expire.

P and L Profit-and-loss account. The statement that details income, costs, profits and losses of a company.

par value The face, or nominal, value attributed to each of a company's shares, which form part of the security's title. Par value has no relationship whatever to either the value of the company at any given time, or the quoted price of its shares.

PE Price/earnings ratio. This is another important Bell weather, calculated by dividing the market price of a company's ordinary shares by its earnings per share figure. This number, published for each share in the prices section of the *Financial Times*, provides a good insight into the market's expectations for the company's profits. It is used also to assess a company's performance against that of its peers. For example, in the food retail sector you will find major supermarkets have PEs that are different. If Tesco is on a lower PE than Sainsbury's, and you believe will outperform it, then you may conclude that Tesco's share price is too low, or Sainsbury's too high.

penny share A term applied to companies whose shares have a very low price, usually less than 50 pence a share. Many investors find penny shares attractive. A few pence gained can mean a good profit, but this argument applies conversely also.

PEP Personal Equity Plan. Introduced in 1987, PEPs are tax-efficient personal investment vehicles, which carry no income tax or capital gains tax on their investment returns. They were abolished and replaced by ISAs in 1999, but existing PEPs can continue, with profits reinvested on a tax-efficient basis. PEPs are slightly handicapped by high management charges.

plc Public limited company.

preference shares Shares in a company that usually pay a fixed rate of dividend. Though not as secure as bonds, they rank ahead of ordinary shares and are a way of creating unsecured debt. Generally frowned upon by stock exchanges, which prefer all shares to be equal.

preliminary statement An announcement made by a company prior to the publication of its annual results.

premium The potential profit on a share from its issue price; hence the expression 'trading at a premium'.

pre-tax profit The key figure reported by a company at half-year or year-end; the best measure of performance.

price-sensitive information Information that may impact on a company's share price and must be reported to a stock exchange.

private company A company that cannot offer its shares to the general public and is not listed on a stock exchange. Some companies that have once been public companies de-list, for various reasons, a recent example being the Virgin Group.

privatisation Conversion of a state-owned operation or enterprise into a publicly listed company, usually, but not always, as a result of the sale of its shares to the public.

Proshare An independent, not-for-profit organisation set up to encourage and support individual investment in the stock market by private individuals.

prospectus A formal document issued by a company when it first seeks entry to the Stock Exchange. The prospectus describes the company's business plan, financial background and details achievements and objectives. It also often includes an official forecast of future performance.

registrar An organisation contracted to maintain a company's share register.

rights issue This takes place when a company asks its shareholders for more money by offering them additional shares at a substantially discounted price. The money may be needed for expansion, or to reduce debt, as in BT's 2001 rights issue. Rights issues usually lead to a fall in share prices. For example, a two for five rights issue at 145 pence would allow existing shareholders to get two shares for every five they own at that price. Investment bankers normally underwrite rights issues, meaning that they take on the obligation of buying any newly issued shares not taken up by existing shareholders.

ROCE Return on capital employed. This is a key statistic often used in determining bonuses. It is the rate of return achieved by a company on the assets deployed in the business.

scrip issue Also known as a bonus issue, this occurs when a company issues additional shares to existing shareholders at no cost to them. Scrip issues usually result in a fall in price to reflect the additional number of shares in the market, but they can sometimes be effective in attracting additional shareholders, who buy in on the lower price.

SEAQ The London Stock Exchange's automated quotation system.

SEATS Plus This combines trading on the basis of orders (see **SETS**) and market making. It is used on the Alternative Investment Market, and on the main market where there are fewer than two market makers making a market in a given share.

securities Another name for shares and bonds, and other instruments with a money value.

SETS Stock Exchange Electronic Trading Service. Since October 1997, FTSE 100 shares have been traded through an electronic order book, rather than by market makers quoting bid and offer prices.

settlement Once shares have been traded, settlement is the process that transfers cash from buyer to seller and share certificates (or electronic registration) from seller to buyer.

shareholders' funds The total of shareholders' capital invested in a company. Mathematically it is the sum of the original issued capital plus reserves created since incorporation.

small caps Another name for smaller companies, as measured by their market capitalisation.

spread The difference between the buying (offer) and selling (bid) price.

stag A person who buys new issues or privatisation offers in the expectation of selling them quickly for a good profit.

stamp duty A polite description of a government tax on share purchases. It is not applied to sales, though capital gains taxes apply where there is a profit.

stockbroker A person or company that buys and sells securities on behalf of clients; see also **broker**.

suspension A halt in trading ordered by a stock exchange either at a company's request or of its own volition. Trading may be suspended, for example, when a company is announcing very bad news, or a takeover announcement is imminent.

switching Moving an investment from one fund to another.

technical analysis A way of studying the investment potential of a company using mathematics. Share price and underlying financials are examined and compared rather than looking at news and other developments.

tender Tender offers are used when securities are auctioned to the highest bidder. As with property auctions, a guide price is announced and then bidders offer their best price. Sometimes this is through an open option, more often through sealed bids.

tracker fund A professionally managed investment fund that uses a variety of techniques to emulate the investment performance of a specific stock market index.

turnover The volume of business, usually sales, of a company before cost deductions.

underwriter Not to be confused with an insurance underwriter, who assesses and takes on risk, an underwriter in the financial markets agrees to buy securities that are left unsold after a new issue, a rights issue or a privatisation. Underwriters get a fee for taking on this obligation.

unit trust A collective investment or fund which, unlike an investment trust, is not quoted on the Stock Exchange, but which invests in securities. Units can be redeemed on a daily basis at the price quoted by the fund manager, and the money withdrawn reduces the amount of money available to the fund manager.

USM Unlisted Securities Market. The predecessor of AIM, it closed in 1996.

warrant A security which can be traded on stock markets and which entitles the holder to buy specific shares at a set price at a future date.

working capital Cash and other liquid assets needed to finance the everyday running of a company.

yield Another important measurement tool, which reflects the annual income as a percentage of current market capitalisation. If share prices fall, reducing the value of a company, yields move up.

Index

rights issues 160–2, 179
risk, pooling of 21–2
Robinson, Gerry 73, 191
Russia, privatisation 172–3

Sainsbury's 216
Sakamaki, Hideo 126
salaries
  fund managers 12, 71
  independent directors 220
  inflation of 12, 33
  life assurance executives 216–17
  takeover advisors 189
Salomon Brothers 101, 135, 139
Sandler, Ron 52
Sandler report 52
save-as-you-earn schemes 82
savings for old age 86–9
savings industry, Sandler report 52
scandals 201–4, 206, 212–14, 218
Scardino, Marjorie 79, 145, 198
Schiff, Dorothy 39
school investment clubs 97–8
Schroder Investments Ltd 70
Schwab, Charles 12–14
SCM Corporation 195–6
Scott, W. R. 18
Scottish Power 176
Scottish Widows Unit Trusts
  Managers 70
SEAQ (Stock Exchange Automated
  Quotations System) 104–5
SEATS PLUS 166
Securities Administrators
  Association 210
Securities and Investments Board
  206
self-invested pension plans (SIPPs)
  88–9
SETS (Stock Exchange Electronic
  Trading System) 103
settlement 86, 109
S.G. Warburg and Co. 32, 70
share certificates 109–10

share ownership
  America 7, 66, 75, 77
  Great Britain 7, 65, 75, 78
  institutional investors 65–74
sharebrokers 140
Sharelink 13
shares
  causes of price fluctuations 36–9
  definition 3–5
  development of interest in 10–14
  effect of overproduction on 4
  electronic registration 109–10
  employee share ownership
    schemes 81–2, 179, 219
  freedom of ownership 5–6, 6–7
  growth shares 56
  income shares 56
  international ownership 6–7
  NAV 36
  origins of trade 16–18
  'partly paid' 20
  performance since 1979 9
  performance since WWI 8–10,
    8–9
  price fluctuations 35–9
  prices 4, 102, 156, 158, 224
  private investors 75–89
  privatisation issues 178
  purchase 99–110
  split capital trusts 55–6
  strike price 81, 157
  trading and new technologies
    12–14
  trendy 37–8
  value 4–5, 35–6
  value traded on New York Stock
    Exchange 111, 113
  volatility 10
  and warrants 49
  zero-dividend preference shares
    56
sharing, principle of 3–4
Shell 92, 212–13
short selling 60, 85–6